JUDAISM AND GLOBAL SURVIVAL

JUDAISM
AND
GLOBAL SURVIVAL

Richard H. Schwartz, Ph.D.

Lantern Books • New York
A Division of Booklight Inc.

2002
Lantern Books
One Union Square West, Suite 201
New York, NY 10003

Printed in the United States of America

Library of Congress Cataloging-in-Publication Data

Schwartz, Richard H.
    Judaism and global survival / Richard H. Schwartz.
        p. cm.
    Includes bibliographical references and indexes.
    ISBN 1-930051-87-5 (pbk.)
    1. Judaism and social problems. I. Title.

HN40.J5 S38 2001
296.3'8—dc21

2001038468

WHAT PEOPLE ARE SAYING ABOUT
JUDAISM AND GLOBAL SURVIVAL

This masterful volume provides a treasure of insights into the perspective of Judaism on many urgent social problems. People committed to the vital force of the Jewish heritage will discover in this work both richness of expression and creative application of old texts to new situations. This volume can make a significant contribution to the shaping of the social consciousness of our community.—**Rabbi Saul J. Berman**, Professor of Jewish Studies, Stern College of Yeshiva University; Founder and Executive Director, Edah (modern Orthodox community organization)

Everyone who believes in *Tikkun Olam* will be strengthened by this rich compendium of Jewish sources and ethical insights, which should stimulate many dialogues in the Jewish community about critical issues. Everyone who wants to apply Jewish values to the great concerns of our time will be nourished when they eat of this feast of Jewish values and treasures that is spread before us.
—**Rabbi Irving Greenberg**, President, Jewish Life Network; Founder, CLAL, National Jewish Center for Learning and Leadership

A superb task of research, compilation, and writing.... [This] book brings to bear scholarly insight in a way that is accessible to the interested layperson. The insights and the values of the Jewish tradition regarding crucial social issues of our time come alive in ... [this] presentation. Whether used as a textbook or as a personal guide for Jews who care about making Jewish values live in our world, this book makes a significant contribution to the modern understanding of Jewish social justice.—**Rabbi David Saperstein**, Director, Religious Action Center of Reform Judaism

Dr. Schwartz has written a significant book that will raise the ecological conscience of the reader, and he has supplied it with religious and secular erudition and global relevance. It speaks with the unmistakable diction of the prophetic moral sensibility.
—**Harold M. Schulweis**, Rabbi, Valley Beth Shalom, Encino, California

Dr. Schwartz's erudition and moral passion are admirable, as well as his ability to deal with so many subjects so readably and succinctly.—**Dr. Andre Ungar**, Rabbi, Temple Emanuel, Woodcliff Lake, New Jersey; Former chairperson of the Hebraic Studies Department, Rutgers University

Shows with eloquence and intelligence that Jewish tradition has much to teach us all about how to protect the earth and the human race from destruction—and how to nurture a decent world.
—**Rabbi Arthur Waskow**, Director of the Shalom Center; Author of *Godwrestling: Round 2* and many other books

My undergraduate years at Brandeis University were just beginning when the first edition of this book came out—and this one-stop collection of Judaic textual sources on issues of the day had a profound influence on me. It served me well through years of learning and activism, and was one of the few to accompany me on a cross-country walk for the environment ten years ago. In seminary at the Reconstructionist Rabbinical College, hardly a month went by without occasion to consult this important work. As a pulpit rabbi and Jewish-environmental educator, I still keep it handy. Not only is it time for me to replace my own dog-eared copy, but it's time for the newly-updated edition of this work to find a position of prominence on every Jewish bookshelf.—**Rabbi Fred Scherlinder Dobb**, Adat Shalom Reconstructionist Congregation, Bethesda, MD; Board of Trustees, Coalition on the Environment and Jewish Life

I urge every rabbi, Jewish teacher and concerned Jew to read *Judaism and Global Survival*. We face the future with a great need for ancient wisdom from our tradition dealing with justice and how to sustain our life on earth. Schwartz's visionary and wise book provides us with the spiritual tools to guide our way.—**Rabbi Warren Stone**, Environmental Chair, CCAR (Central Conference of American Rabbis)

An excellent sourcebook. Many of its ideas have found their way into my sermons.—**Rabbi Gerald Serotta**, Campus Hillel Rabbi, George Washington University; Associate Rabbi, Temple Shalom of Chevy Chase, MD

Among Judaism's most basic principles are God's affirmation of both the world and the moral potential of humankind. Therefore, to the Jewish mind, the proper concerns of religion are not only of a private, subjective nature, but necessarily extend to the spiritual and physical improvement of the world. Dr. Schwartz echoes the impassioned protest of the ancient prophets of Israel in his pointed consideration of contemporary social issues. In doing so, he also demonstrates that Judaism cannot be pigeonholed into the convenient ideological categories of "conservative," "liberal," etc., but must be encountered on its own terms.—**Rabbi Dovid Sears**, Author of *Compassion for Humanity in the Jewish Tradition*

A shofar calling the Jewish community to wake up to current crises and at the same time return to our roots. Through clear and compelling exploration, Schwartz calls us to pay attention to the destruction and injustice taking place around the world, realize how we are complicit in environmental degradation and human suffering, and take action rooted in basic Jewish values. Read this book, hear the shofar, and listen for the still, small voice inside that calls our Jewish souls to the work of healing and repairing our world.—**Mark X. Jacobs**, Executive Director, COEJL (Coalition on the Environment and Jewish Life)

A lovingly detailed synthesis of much of the best moral tradition of Judaism, relating it to modern problems of ecology, war, hunger, and other issues of world survival.—**Naomi Goodman**, Former President of the Jewish Peace Fellowship; co-author of *The Challenge of Shalom*

Richard Schwartz has written a profound and inspiring call to Jews to involve themselves in saving our planet from disaster. His book makes us proud of our Jewish heritage and eager to engage in environmental activism.—**Susannah Heschel**, Eli Black Professor of Jewish Studies, Dartmouth College

Richard Schwartz's book represents a generous, humane spirit. It is filled with examples of Judaism as a living guide to contemporary life. It says that Jews need only look into their own religious faith and history to discover that all people, not only Jews, are worthy of our concern—and, as Schwartz writes, "Each of us must be a Jonah, with a mission to warn the world that it must turn from greed, injustice, and idolatry to avoid global oblivion." *Judaism and Global Survival* is rich in the teachings of Judaism and reflective of the extraordinary ethical and moral way of life that has always made us distinctive. It is an important book.—**Murray Polner**, Former Editor, *Present Tense*; Chair of the Jewish Peace Fellowship, and editor of *Shalom: The Jewish Peace Letter*

This extremely eloquent, important, and timely book treats a subject of the utmost importance, one of vital concern to everyone —how we can save the earth and prevent the destruction of its life support systems and of humanity itself.—**Lewis G. Regenstein**, President, the Interfaith Council for the Protection of Animals and Nature; Author of *Replenish the Earth: The Teachings of the World's Religions on Protecting Animals and Nature*

"Richard Schwartz has crafted a magnificent contribution to Jewish ethical writing. He has insightfully raised important questions for concerned Jews and courageously taught a simple, yet profound Jewish message."—**Rabbi Hillel Norry**, Shaare Tzedeck Synagogue, Manhattan; Member of the Law and Standards Committee of the Rabbinical Assembly

"This book is not just for Jews. People of all faiths who want to know how the Hebrew Scriptures relate to the crucial issues of our times will find it invaluable. It can be common ground for those of us who want the kind of dialogue that will create the world that ought to be."—**Tony Campolo**, Professor Emeritus of Sociology, Eastern College

TABLE OF CONTENTS

FOREWORD

T HE TALMUD DECLARES THAT ONE WHO IS NOT COMPAS-
sionate cannot truly be of the seed of Abraham our father (*Bezah*
32b). In other words, to be authentically Jewish means to emulate
Abraham's compassionate conduct towards others. Underlying this statement is the view of Abraham in our Tradition, as the pioneer of ethical
monotheism. He not only recognized that there is one Creative Source of
the one Creation, but that this very unity conveys a moral imperative
concerning ethical behavior and conduct (Genesis 18:19). Accordingly,
based on the above statement, our sages declare: the more we are compassionate and engaged in relation to the world around us, the truer we are to
the moral essence of the Abrahamic faith affirmation.

Of course, there is also a very pragmatic dimension of enlightened self-
interest that demands such conduct of us. This is expressed in the Talmud
in the words of our sages, that Heaven grants compassion to those who
have compassion on others, but withdraws it from those who do not
(*Shabbat* 151b). In other words, compassion is the means by which we
secure our own future! Indeed, Judaism teaches that it is our responsibility
as human beings to be constructive co-workers in the Creation, ensuring
its sustainable development (Genesis 2:15; *Shabbat* 10a; *Ecclesiastes Rabbah*
7:28).

For thousands of years we have recited daily, evening and morning, the
"*kriyat shema,*" the second paragraph of which (Deuteronomy 11:13–21)
deals with the direct link between the observance of the Biblical
commandments and the condition of our ecosystem. Today, this connec-

tion between our ethical behavior or misbehavior and our environment is evident to us as it has never been before.

In this excellent book, Professor Richard Schwartz clarifies this connection most vividly, together with the dangers and injustices with which our planet has to contend. However, also in keeping with Biblical teaching, he makes it powerfully clear that we have the means to significantly address these challenges. Indeed, the degree to which we take up his call is the degree to which we demonstrate whether or not we are worthy and authentic children of Abraham our father.

Rabbi David Rosen
Former Chief Rabbi of Ireland
President for Israel of the International Jewish Vegetarian Society
International Director of Interreligious Affairs
    of the American Jewish Committee
President of the International Council of Christians and Jews
International President of the World Conference of Religions for Peace

*In loving memory of
my dear parents,
Rose and Joseph Schwartz,
for their constant devotion,
understanding, and encouragement*

PREFACE

I call heaven and earth to witness concerning you this day, that I have set before you life and death, the blessing and the curse; therefore choose life, that you may live, you and your descendants. (Deuteronomy 30:19)

THE TORAH EXHORTS US TO "CHOOSE LIFE," BUT IN MANY ways the world today is choosing death:

- Acts of terror, such as the horrific plane crashes into the World Trade Center and the Pentagon on September 11, 2001, kill and maim many people, cause many more to live in fear, and divert economic and human resources from basic human needs.
- While enough food is being produced to provide an adequate diet for all of the world's people, waste, greed, and inefficient or unjust systems of production and distribution result in millions of deaths annually due to hunger and malnutrition.
- While there is massive overconsumption and waste in wealthy countries, billions of the world's people lack adequate food, shelter, clean water, education, sanitary facilities, and employment.
- There are many signs of rapid climate change and its effects, including record heat waves, severe droughts and storms, flooding, spreading diseases, bleaching of coral reefs, melting glaciers and ice caps, and extensive forest fires.

- The world's primary ecosystems are threatened; many lakes and streams are polluted by acid rain, chemical fertilizer, manure, and other pollutants; the earth's forests are shrinking; fisheries are collapsing; water tables are falling; soils are eroding; concentrations of atmospheric carbon dioxide are increasing; and many of the world's people are threatened by pesticides and toxic wastes.
- Competition for scarce resources, such as oil and water, make conflicts and war more likely.
- The rates of destruction of plant and animal species are the most rapid in the world's history.

There is a need for major changes if the world is to avoid increasingly severe threats. In 1992, over 1,670 scientists, including 104 Nobel laureates—a majority of the living recipients of the Prizes in the sciences—signed a "World Scientists' Warning To Humanity."[1] Their introduction states:

Human beings and the natural world are on a collision course. Human activities inflict harsh and often irreversible damage on the environment and on critical resources. If not checked, many of our current practices put at serious risk the future that we wish for human society and the plant and animal kingdoms, and may so alter the living world that it will be unable to sustain life in the manner that we know. Fundamental changes are urgent if we are to avoid the collision our present course will bring about.

The scientists' analysis discussed threats to the atmosphere, rivers and streams, oceans, soil, living species, and forests. Their warning was blunt:

We the undersigned, senior members of the world's scientific community, hereby warn all humanity of what lies ahead. A great change in our stewardship of the earth and the life on it is required, if vast human misery is to be avoided and our global home on this planet is not to be irretrievably mutilated.

This book discusses challenges facing humanity and Jewish teachings that address these challenges, in order to further galvanize Jews to help repair the world, as required by Jewish law. It shows that we don't need to discover new values and approaches to address current global threats. What is needed is a rediscovery and application of basic Jewish teachings and mandates, such as to pursue peace and justice, to love our neighbors as ourselves, and to act as co-workers with God in protecting and preserving the world. We will consider how the application of Jewish values can help reduce global threats, such as climate change, pollution, atmospheric ozone depletion, hunger, poverty, energy and water shortages, and rapid human population growth.

Rabbi Abraham Joshua Heschel, a leading twentieth-century Jewish theologian, eloquently expressed the central role that Judaism must play in helping to solve current problems:

> Our civilization is in need of redemption. The evil, the falsehood, the vulgarity of our way of living cry to high heaven. There is a war to be waged against the vulgar, against the glorification of power, a war that is incessant, universal. There is much purification that needs to be done, ought to be done, and could be done through bringing to bear the radical wisdom, the sacrificial devotion, the uncompromising loyalty of our forefathers upon the issues of our daily living.[2]

Many Jews today are appropriately concerned about Jewish survival and the flourishing of Jewish culture and learning. As indicated in the "Guide to Activist Jewish Groups" in the Appendix, many Jewish groups are applying Jewish values to today's critical issues. However, many Jews have made peace with the powers that be. They often worship modern idols of materialism, state power, technology, fame, personal ambition, and overconsumption. There is little active involvement or protest against injustice, but much complacency and conformity. Unfortunately, there is far too little attention paid to the Judaism of the prophets and sages, with its passionate concern for justice, peace, and righteousness.

Many Jews have forgotten the mandate to strive to perfect the world. Today the synagogues and pronouncements of rabbis have frequently become irrelevant to the critical issues that face the world's people. God requires justice, compassion, involvement, and protests against evil, but our synagogues have too often focused solely on ritual and parochial concerns.

A person who takes Jewish values seriously would be alienated by much of what goes on and is sanctioned in Jewish life today. As Rabbi Heschel states, "One is embarrassed to be called religious in the face of religion's failure to keep alive the image of God in the face of man." Many idealistic Jews have turned away from Judaism because Judaism's teachings requiring involvement in today's crucial issues are not adequately disseminated and practiced.

For Jews, the acts of helping the needy and caring for the world are not voluntary options but responsibilities and Divine commandments. These are not only individual responsibilities, but also obligations for the whole society. Our tradition understands this principle as a covenant—an agreement that binds us to God. In this covenant, we assume the task of striving to perfect the world and, in return, receive the Divine promise that the world will be redeemed. The Jewish message is not only one of responsibility, but also one of hope.

It is a shame that some Jewish leaders and institutions have forgotten that the practical expression of justice, in our own community and toward all communities, has been and must continue to be a major emphasis of Jewish living. It is a tragedy that the Jewish community has generally failed to apply its rich theology to the preservation of the environment. Too often the Jewish establishment has been silent while our air is bombarded by poisons that threaten life, our rivers and streams are polluted by industrial wastes, our fertile soil is eroded and depleted, and the ecological balance is endangered by the destruction of rain forests and other essential habitats.

The Jewish community must become more actively involved. We must proclaim that it is a desecration of God's Name to pollute the air and water, to slash and burn forests, and to wantonly destroy the abundant resources that God has so generously provided. We cannot allow whatever other needs or fears we may have, however legitimate, to prevent us from applying fundamental Jewish values to the critical problems of today.

It is also unfortunate that many Jews are almost totally unaware of the rich legacy of the Jewish tradition and its focus on justice for both the individual and society. Indeed, Judaism provides a pragmatic path for implementing its progressive ideas. The Talmud and other rabbinical writings are filled with in-depth discussions, advice, and legal decisions on how to apply the principles of the prophets to everyday situations. Judaism also offers the richness and warmth of an ancient historical community, a meaningful inheritance for each Jew.

This book is not meant to be a complete analysis of all current social problems or of all Jewish positions on the issues discussed. It does not attempt to give all sides of every issue. What it does do is show that Judaism demands passionate concern and involvement in society's problems and requires protest against the current destructive forces that threaten humanity.

I hope this book will contribute to and help expand the ongoing dialogues about Jewish teachings concerning these critically important issues, and will play a part in turning our planet from its present perilous course and toward one that is more just, humane, and sustainable.

ACKNOWLEDGMENTS
TO THE SECOND EDITION

FIRST, I WISH TO EXPRESS MY THANKS TO GOD BY RECITING the traditional Jewish blessing pronounced when a person reaches a milestone in life: "Blessed are you, Lord our God, King of the universe, Who has kept us alive and sustained us and brought us to this season."

While it is essential that the issues discussed in this book be put on the Jewish agenda, I recognize my limitations in presenting this information. I have been very fortunate, however, to have input and suggestions from a wide variety of dedicated, extremely knowledgeable individuals.

The following (in alphabetical order) reviewed an entire draft of the manuscript and made valuable suggestions:

1. Rabbi Yonasson Gershom: Breslov Chassid; author of *Jewish Tales of Reincarnation* (Jason Aronson, 1999).

2. Ari Knoll, attorney, a longtime friend and advisor; Co-Chair of the Board of Beyond Shelter Coalition, the alliance of over thirty NYC synagogues and Jewish schools working for permanent housing for the homeless.

3. Mark Nagurka, Ph.D. (MIT): Associate Professor of Mechanical and Biomedical Engineering at Marquette University in Milwaukee, Wisconsin.

4. Charles Patterson, Ph.D: author of *Anti-Semitism: The Road to the Holocaust and Beyond* and eight other books. His most recent books are *From Buchenwald to Carnegie Hall* and *Eternal Treblinka: Our Treatment of Animals and the Holocaust*. His experience as a copy editor was very valuable in sharpening my writing.

5. Lewis Regenstein: author of *Replenish the Earth: The Teachings of the World's Religions on Protecting Animals and Nature, America the Poisoned,*

and *The Politics of Extinction*; President of the Interfaith Council for the Protection of Animals and Nature in Atlanta, an affiliate of the Humane Society of the United States.

6. Rabbi Dovid Sears: Breslov Chassid; author of many books, including *Compassion for Humanity in the Jewish Tradition: A Source Book* and *The Path of the Bal Shem Tov: Early Chassidic Teachings and Customs*. His latest writing project, *The Vision of Eden: Animal Welfare and Vegetarianism in Jewish Law and Mysticism*, provided valuable sources and concepts for the chapter on vegetarianism; he also reviewed the final two drafts.

7. Jonathan Wolf, who contributed to and reworked literally every page of this book (and compiled the Appendix of activist organizations and the Afterword). For almost three decades, Jonathan has been one of the leading promoters of a distinctively Jewish commitment to social change and community involvement. In the 1970s, he acted as liaison between Cesar Chavez's United Farm Workers and the organized Jewish community; served as Social Policy Director of the Synagogue Council of America (coordinating the rabbinic and congregational bodies of Conservative, Modern Orthodox, and Reform Judaism to take on critical issues); wrote the Social Action chapter of the Jewish Catalog; helped establish the Coalition for the Advancement of Jewish Education (CAJE); and was founder and president of the Jewish Vegetarians of North America. In the 1980s, he created and directed the Community Action Department of Lincoln Square Synagogue in NYC, the largest and broadest-ranging program of organized Jewish activism and volunteer service *hesed* in America; chaired the original conference and drafted the platform of New Jewish Agenda; was active in the Soviet and Ethiopian Jewry movements, visiting refusenik families in Moscow and Leningrad and, later, refugee compounds in Addis Ababa and Gondar; and widely lectured and taught, offering many adult classes at Lincoln Square Synagogue such as "Jewish Political Ethics," "Jews and Non-Jews in Jewish Tradition," "Pluralism and Tolerance as Jewish Values," and the class on "Judaism and Vegetarianism" at which this author first met him, inspiring my involvement. In the 1990s, Jonathan helped start and chaired L'OLAM, the NY-area environmental coalition of synagogues and Jewish organizations (which for years held annual regional conferences on Judaism and Ecology), as well as the Jewish

Environmental Network, the first such umbrella of national organizations; and also served as executive director and board chair of Beyond Shelter Coalition, New York's Jewish alliance of congregations and schools for housing the homeless. After twenty-six years in his famed Riverside Drive apartment, known as the West Side Center for Jewish Life, where he has hosted many hundreds of vegetarian events such as Tu B'Shvat Seders, Jewish celebrations for Thanksgiving, speakers series, and Shabbatons dedicated to Jewish political values, ecology, human rights, and oppressed Jewry, he is now leaving to direct the Institute for Jewish Activism (www.jewishactivism.net).

Also, Yosef Ben Shlomo Hakohen, a longtime friend, has been a constant source of wise advice and appreciated encouragement. He reviewed an early draft and suggested additional Judaic sources which have been incorporated. Yosef now lives in Israel; to receive his regular postings of Torah and insights on society, send an e-mail to chazon@netvision.net.

People who made major contributions to specific parts of the book include: Arnold Aronowitz, Aaron Gross, and Asher Waldman.

The excellent work done by Erica Weisberg in designing the cover is most appreciated. It is a worthy counterpart to the superb cover she designed for my *Judaism and Vegetarianism*. I am very grateful to Gene Rasmussen and Joseph Racombly for running off drafts of the manuscript, and to Lewis Carbonaro for his help in scanning material for use in this book.

I apologize to any contributors whom I have inadvertently omitted.

I wish to express deep appreciation to my wife, Loretta, our children, Susan (and David Kleid), David, and Deborah (and Ariel Gluch), and our grandchildren, Shalom Eliahu, Ayelet Breindel, Avital P'nina, and Michal Na'ama Kleid, and Eliyahu, Ilan Avraham, and Yosef Gluch, for their patience, understanding, and encouragement as I took time away from other responsibilities to gather and write this material.

Although all of these people have been very helpful, the author takes full responsibility for the final selection of material and interpretations.

Finally, I wish to thank in advance all who read this volume and send me ideas and suggestions for improvements so this book can more effectively show how the application of Jewish values can help move the world to a more sustainable path. My e-mail address is rschw12345@aol.com.

1: INVOLVEMENT AND PROTEST

Whoever is able to protest against the transgressions of his own family and does not do so is punished [liable, held responsible] for the transgressions of his family. Whoever is able to protest against the transgressions of the people of his community and does not do so is punished for the transgressions of his community. Whoever is able to protest against the transgressions of the entire world and does not do so is punished for the transgressions of the entire world. (Babylonian Talmud: *Shabbat* 54b)

JUDAISM URGES ACTIVE INVOLVEMENT IN ISSUES FACING society. A Jew must not be concerned only about his or her own personal affairs when the community is in trouble:

If a person of learning participates in public affairs and serves as judge or arbiter, he gives stability to the land. But if he sits in his home and says to himself, "What have the affairs of society to do with me? ... Why should I trouble myself with the people's voices of protest? Let my soul dwell in peace!"—if he does this, he overthrows the world.[1]

Judaism teaches that people must struggle to create a better society. The Torah frequently admonishes: "And you shall eradicate the evil from your midst" (Deuteronomy 13:6, 17:7, 21:21, 24:7). Injustice cannot be passively accepted; it must be actively resisted and, ultimately, eliminated. The Talmudic sages teach that one reason Jerusalem was destroyed was that its citizens failed in their responsibility to constructively criticize one

1

another's improper behavior.[2] They indicate that "Love that does not contain the element of criticism is not really love."[3]

The essential elements of Jewish practice include devotion to Torah, study, prayer, performing good deeds and other *mitzvot* (commandments), and cultivating a life of piety. But, as indicated in the following Midrash (a rabbinic story or teaching based on Biblical events or concepts), in order to be considered pious, a person must protest against injustice. Even God is challenged to apply this standard in judging people:

R. Acha ben R. Chanina said: Never did a favorable decree go forth from the mouth of the Holy One which He withdrew and changed into an unfavorable judgment, except the following: "And the Lord said to His angel: 'Go through the city, through Jerusalem, and put a mark upon the foreheads of the men who sigh and groan over all the abominations that are committed there' " (Ezekiel 9:4). (Thus, they will be protected from the angels who are slaying the wicked.)

At that moment, the indignant prosecutor came forward in the Heavenly Court.

Prosecutor: Lord, wherein are these (marked ones) different from those (the rest)?

God: These are wholly righteous men, while those are wholly wicked.

Prosecutor: But Lord, they had the power to protest, but did not.

God: I knew that had they protested, they would not have been heeded.

Prosecutor: But Lord, if it was revealed to You, was it revealed to them? Accordingly, they should have protested and incurred scorn for thy holy Name, and have been ready to suffer blows ... as the prophets of Israel suffered.

God revoked his original order, and the righteous were found guilty, because of their failure to protest.[4]

Hence, it is not sufficient merely to do *mitzvot* while acquiescing in unjust conditions. The Maharal of Prague, a sixteenth-century sage, states

that individual piety pales in the face of the sin of not protesting against
an emerging communal evil, and a person will be held accountable for not
preventing wickedness when capable of doing so.[5] One of the most important dangers of silence in the face of evil is that it implies acceptance or
even support. According to Rabbeinu Yonah, a medieval sage, sinners may
think, "Since others are neither reproving nor contending against us, our
deeds are permissible."[6]

Rabbi Joachim Prinz, a refugee from pre-World War II Nazi Germany
and former president of the American Jewish Congress, spoke to the
250,000 people who took part in the "March on Washington" organized by
the Reverend Dr. Martin Luther King, Jr. and others in 1963 on behalf of
civil rights. He stated that under Hitler's rule, he had learned about the
problem of apathy toward fellow human beings: "Bigotry and hatred are
not the most urgent problem. The most urgent, the most disgraceful, the
most shameful and most tragic problem is silence."[7]

Rabbi Abraham Joshua Heschel, a leading twentieth-century theologian, believed that apathy toward injustice results in greater wickedness. He
wrote that "indifference to evil is more insidious than evil itself" and that
silent acquiescence leads to evil being accepted and becoming the rule.[8]

Jews are required to protest against injustice and to try to agitate for
change even when successful implementation appears very difficult. The
Talmudic sage Rabbi Zera states, "Even though people will not accept it,
you should rebuke them."[9] We can never be sure that our words and actions
will be ineffective. The only responsible approach, then, is to try our best.
In Rabbi Tarfon's famous formulation in the Mishnah:

> It is not your obligation to complete the task. But neither are you
> free to desist from it.[10]

Just as many drops of water can eventually carve a hole in a rock, many
small efforts can eventually have a major impact.

There are times when a person must continue to protest in order to
avoid being corrupted:

A man stood at the entrance of Sodom crying out against the injustice and evil in that city. Someone passed by and said to him, "For years you have been urging the people to repent, and yet no one has changed. Why do you continue?" He responded: "When I first came, I protested because I hoped to change the people of Sodom. Now I continue to cry out, because if I don't, they will have changed me."

In his article "The Rabbinic Ethics of Protest," Rabbi Reuven Kimelman observes that the means of protest must be consistent with responsibility to the community. He states that protest must involve both love and truth, where love implies the willingness to suffer, and truth the willingness to resist. Together, he concludes, they encompass an approach of nonviolent resistance, toward the ends of justice and peace.[11]

The Talmud teaches that controversy and protest must be "for the sake of Heaven."[12] The protest of Korach against the rule of Moses in the wilderness (Numbers 16:1–35) is considered negatively by the Jewish tradition because it was based on jealousy and personal motives.

Involvement and Protest in Jewish History

From its beginning, Judaism has often protested against greed, injustice, and the misuse of power. Abraham, the first Jew, smashed the idols of his father although his action challenged the common belief of the time. He established the precedent that a Jew should not conform to society's values when they are evil. Later, he even challenged God, exclaiming, "Shall not the Judge of all the earth do justly?" (Genesis 18:25) In contrast, Noah, though personally righteous, was later rebuked by the Talmudic sages because he failed to criticize the immorality of the society around him.

At the beginning of the book of Exodus, the Torah relates three incidents in Moses' life before God chose him to deliver the Israelites from Egypt. They teach that Jews must be involved in helping to resolve disputes—whether between two Jews, a Jew and a non-Jew, or two non-Jews. On the first day that Moses goes out to his people from the palace of Pharaoh in which he was raised, he rushes to defend a Hebrew against an Egyptian aggressor (Exodus 2:11, 12). When Moses next goes out, he defends a Hebrew who is being beaten by another Jew (Exodus 2:13). Later, after being forced to flee from Egypt and arriving at a well in Midian, Moses comes to the aid of the shepherd daughters of Jethro who were being harassed by other shepherds (Exodus 2:15–17).

Balaam, the biblical pagan prophet, intends to curse Israel but ends up blessing it. He describes the role of the Jewish people: "Lo, it is a people dwelling alone, and not reckoning itself among the nations" (Numbers 23:9). To the Israelites, the keynote of their existence is: "I am the Lord thy God, who has separated you from the nations that you should be Mine" (Leviticus 20:26). Throughout their history, Jews have often been nonconformists who refused to acquiesce in the false values of the surrounding community.

When the Jews were in Persia, Mordechai refused to defer to an evil ruler. As the book of Esther states: "And all the king's servants ... bowed down and prostrated themselves before Haman....But Mordechai would not bow down nor prostrate himself before him" (Esther 3:2). Mordechai believes that bowing down to a human being is inconsistent with his obligation to worship only God. Later Mordechai condemns inaction in urging Esther to take risks to save the Jewish people (Esther 4:13, 14).

The greatest champions of protest against unjust conditions were the Hebrew prophets. Rabbi Abraham Heschel summarizes the attributes of these spokespeople for God: They had the ability to hold God and people in one thought at the same time; they could not be tranquil in an unjust world; they were supremely impatient with evil, due to their intense sensitivity to God's concern for right and wrong; they were advocates for those too weak to plead their own cause (the widow, the orphan, and the oppressed); their major activity was interference, remonstrating against wrongs inflicted on other people.[13]

In sharp contrast, although Jews are supposed to be *b'nei nevi'im* (descendants of the Biblical prophets), our communities often respond placidly to immoral acts and conditions. We try to maintain a balanced tone while victims of oppression are in extreme agony. But not so the prophets:

Cry aloud, spare not, lift up your voice like a trumpet, and declare
unto My people their transgression....Is this not the fast that I have
chosen: To loose the chains of wickedness, to undo the bonds of
oppression, to let the crushed go free, and to break every yoke of
tyranny? (Isaiah 58:1, 6)

The prophet Amos berates those content amidst destruction and injustice:

Woe to those who are at ease in Zion,
And to those who feel secure on the mountains of Samaria....
Woe to those who lie upon beds of ivory,
And stretch themselves upon their couches,
And eat lambs from the flock,
And calves from the midst of the stall;
Who sing idle songs to the sound of the harp....
Who drink wine in bowls,
And anoint themselves in the finest oils,
But are not grieved on the ruin of Joseph! (Amos 6:1, 4–6)

In order to carry out their role, to be a kingdom of priests and a light
unto the nations, Jews throughout history were compelled to live in the
world, but apart from it—in effect, on the other side. This, the sages
comment, is implied in the very name "Hebrew" (*ivri*), from *ever*, the other
side: "The whole world is on one side [idolaters] and he [Abraham, the
Hebrew] is on the other side."[14] Jacques Maritain, a French Catholic
philosopher, wrote in 1939 that the Jewish people were

found at the very heart of the world's structure, stimulating it,
exasperating it, moving it....It [the Jewish people] gives the world
no peace, it bars slumber, it teaches the world to be discontented
and restless as long as the world has not accepted God.[15]

Several distinguished Orthodox rabbis of the past two centuries,
including Rabbis Samson Raphael Hirsch, Jonathan Sacks, and Joseph B.

Soloveitchik, as well as Lord Immanuel Jakobovitz, stress that Judaism has a message for their surrounding cultures and that Jews should convey it to their host societies.[16] Rabbi Soloveitchik (the Rav), one of the foremost Torah leaders of the twentieth century, believed that Jews have a responsibility to work with others to promote the welfare of civilization. He felt that Jews must aid the needy and protect human rights, because such obligations are "implicit in human existence." He states: "We stand shoulder to shoulder with the rest of civilized society over against an order that defies us all."[17] Rabbi Sacks, the current Chief Rabbi of England, believes that working for *tikkun olam* (healing and improving the planet) can be a powerful counterforce to the dominance of secularism as well as an antidote to religious isolationism. He notes:

> One of the most powerful assumptions of the twentieth century is that faith ... belongs [only] to private life. Religion and society, many believe, are two independent entities, so we can edit God out of the language and leave our social world unchanged.[18]

Based on Jewish tradition and values, Jews have been active in many protest movements. Some of these movements have fought on behalf of Jewish needs, such as the effort to rescue European Jews from the Holocaust, the battle to support Jewish independence and survival in Israel, and the struggles for Soviet Jewry and later for Syrian and Ethiopian Jewry. But Jews also have been actively involved in struggles for a more peaceful world, human rights, and a cleaner environment. A group of rabbis, acting in accordance with the Jewish ethic of protest, explain why they came to St. Augustine, Florida, in 1964 to demonstrate against segregation in that community:

> We came because we could not stand silently by our brother's blood. We had done that too many times before. We have been vocal in our exhortation of others but the idleness of our hands too often revealed an inner silence....We came as Jews who remember the millions of faceless people who stood quietly, watching the smoke rise from Hitler's crematoria. We came because we know

that second only to silence, the greatest danger to man is loss of faith in man's capacity to act.[19]

The Current Lack of Involvement and Protest[20]

Religious practitioners frequently mischaracterize God's demands. Instead of crying out against immorality, injustice, deceit, cruelty, and violence, they too often condone these evils, concentrating instead on ceremonies and ritual. To many Jews today, Judaism involves occasional visits to the Synagogue or Temple, prayers recited with little feeling, rituals performed with little meaning, and socializing. But to the prophets, worship accompanied by indifference to evil is an absurdity, an abomination to God.[21] Judaism is mocked when Jews indulge in or condone empty rituals side by side with immoral deeds.

While ritual is extremely important, God's great concern for justice is powerfully expressed by the prophet Amos:

> Even though you offer Me your burnt offerings and cereal offerings, I will not accept them. And the peace offerings of your fatted beasts I will not look upon. Take away from Me the noise of your songs; to the melody of your harps I will not listen. But let justice well up as waters, and righteousness as a mighty stream. (Amos 5:22–24)

The prophet Hosea similarly states God's preference for moral and spiritual dedication rather than mere outward ritual:

> For I desire kindness and not sacrifice, attachment to God rather than burnt offerings. (Hosea 6:6)

Yet all too often, today's Jews have failed to speak out against an unjust, immoral society. While claiming to follow the ethical teachings of the prophets, many Jews have equivocated and rationalized inaction. Rabbi Heschel blames religion's failure to speak out and be involved in critical current issues for its losses:

Religion declined not because it was refuted but because it became irrelevant, dull, oppressive, insipid. When faith is completely replaced by habit, when the crisis of today is ignored because of the splendor of the past, when faith becomes an heirloom rather than a living fountain, when religion speaks only in the name of authority rather than with the voice of compassion, its message becomes meaningless.[22]

Many Jews are turned off to Judaism by the lack of moral commitment and involvement in struggles for a better world within some Jewish religious institutions. Rabbi Abraham Karp, who taught at Dartmouth College, felt that students would only be attracted to a "church or synagogue which dares, which challenges, which disturbs, which acts as a critic, which leads in causes which are moral."[23] Reinhold Niebuhr, the prominent Christian theologian, attributes religion's failure to attract idealistic people to its failure to protest injustice. He states that the chief reason many people turn from religion is that the "social impotence of religion outrages their conscience."[24]

Many Jews today justify their lack of involvement with the world's problems by stating that Jews have enough troubles of their own and that we can leave it to others to involve themselves in "non-Jewish" issues. Certainly, Jews must be actively involved in battling anti-Semitism, working for a secure and just Israel, and addressing many other Jewish issues. But can we divorce ourselves from active involvement with more general problems? Are they really "non-Jewish" issues? Don't Jews also suffer from polluted air and water, resource shortages, the effects of global climate change, and other societal threats? Can we ignore issues critical to our nation's future?

Perhaps the situation is, in mathematical terms, one of conditional probability. If conditions in the world are good, it is still possible that Jews will suffer. But if these conditions are bad, it is almost certain that Jews will be negatively affected. Hence, even considering self-interest alone, Jews must be involved in working for a just and harmonious world.

It is essential that Jews (and others) actively apply Jewish values to current critical problems. We must be God's loyal opposition to injustice, greed, and immorality, rousing the conscience of humanity. We must shout "NO!" when others are whispering "yes" to injustice. We must restore Judaism to the task of "comforting the afflicted and afflicting the comfortable." We must act as befits "descendants of the prophets,"[25] reminding the world that there exists a God of justice, compassion, and kindness. Nothing less than global survival is at stake.

As later chapters will show, the world is moving on a perilous path determined by its failure to take seriously religious values that have a direct impact on society at large, such as justice, kindness, compassion, peaceful relations, and concern for the environment. We must act to inform and influence Jews (and others) to become involved and to protest to help move the world to a more sustainable path before it is too late.

2: HUMAN RIGHTS AND OBLIGATIONS

One person (Adam) was created as the common ancestor of all people, for the sake of the peace of the human race, so that one should not be able to say to a neighbor, "My ancestor was better than yours."

One person was created to teach us the sanctity and importance of every life, for one who destroys a single life is considered by scripture to have destroyed an entire world, and one who saves a single life is considered by scripture to have saved an entire world.

One person was created to teach us the importance of the actions of every individual, for we should treat the world as half good and half bad, so that if we do one good deed, it will tip the whole world to the side of goodness.(Mishnah Sanhedrin 4:5)

A FUNDAMENTAL JEWISH PRINCIPLE IS THE EQUALITY and unity of humanity. We all have one Creator; one God is the Divine Project of every person. Judaism is a universal religion that condemns discrimination based on race, color, or nationality. God endows each person with basic human dignity.

The following teaching of the sages reinforces the lesson of universality inherent in the creation of one common ancestor: "God formed Adam out of dust from all over the world: yellow clay, white sand, black loam, and red soil. Therefore, no one can declare to any people that they do not belong here since this soil is not their home."[1] Hence Adam, our common ancestor, represents every person.

Ben Azzai, a disciple of Rabbi Akiva, also reinforces this concept in the Talmud. He states that a fundamental teaching of the Torah is the verse "This is the book of the generations of *humanity* (*Adam*)" (Genesis 5:1).[2] The statement does not talk about black or white, or Jew or Gentile, but *humanity*. Since all human beings share a common ancestor, they must necessarily be brothers and sisters. Hence these words proclaim the essential message that there is a unity to the human race.

Imitation of God's Ways

One of the most important ideas about the creation of humanity is that "God created people in God's own image; in the image of God He created him; male and female He created them" (Genesis 1:27). According to Rabbi Akiva, a Talmudic sage, "Beloved are human beings who were created in the image of God, and it is an even greater act of love [by God] that it was made known to people that they were created in the Divine image."[3]

Because human beings are created in God's image, we are to imitate God's attributes of holiness, kindness, and compassion: "And the Lord spoke unto Moses, saying: 'Speak unto all the congregation of the children of Israel, and say unto them: You shall be holy, as I, the Lord Your God, am holy' " (Leviticus 19:1, 2). The fact that the above mandate was delivered to the entire congregation means that it applies to every Jew, not just to a small, elite group of spiritual or moral specialists.

In the following verses, the Torah mandates that we walk in God's ways:

> And now, Israel, what does the Lord your God ask of you, but to revere the Lord your God, to walk in all his ways and to love Him, and to serve the Lord your God with all your heart and with all your soul. (Deuteronomy 10:12)

> For if you shall diligently keep this entire commandment which I command you to do it, to love the Lord your God, to walk in all His ways, and to cleave to Him.... (Deuteronomy 11:22)

The Midrash interprets the expression "walking in God's ways" to mean "Just as God is called 'merciful,' you should be merciful, just as God is called 'compassionate,' you should be compassionate."[4] The third-century sage Hama ben Hanina expands on the duty of imitating God:

> What is the meaning of the verse "You shall walk after the Lord your God" (Deuteronomy 13:5)? Is it possible for a human being to walk after the *Shechinah* (God's presence), for has it not been said, "For the Lord your God is a devouring fire" (Deuteronomy 4:24)? But the verse means to walk after the *attributes* of the Holy One, Blessed is He. As God clothes the naked, for it is written, "And the Lord God made for Adam and his wife coats of skin and clothed them" (Genesis 3:21), so should you clothe the naked. The Holy One, Blessed is He, visits the sick, for it is written, "And the Lord appeared to him (Abraham, while he was recovering from circumcision), by the oaks of Mamre" (Genesis 18:1), so should you also visit the sick. The Holy One, Blessed is He, comforts mourners, for it is written, "And it came to pass after the death of Abraham, that God blessed Isaac, his son" (Genesis 25:11), so should you comfort mourners. The Holy One, Blessed is He, buries the dead, for it is written, "And He buried Moses in the valley" (Deuteronomy 34:6), so should you also bury the dead.[5]

Maimonides finds a powerful statement about the importance of imitating God in these words from the prophet Jeremiah:

> Thus says the Lord:
> Let not the wise person take pride in his wisdom;
> Neither let the mighty person take pride in his might;
> Let not the rich person take pride in his riches;
> But let him that takes pride, take pride in this:
> That he understands and knows Me,
> That I am the Lord who exercises mercy, justice, and righteous-
>   ness, on the earth;
> For in these things I delight, says the Lord.
> (Jeremiah 9:22–23)

Maimonides interprets this statement to mean that a person should find fulfillment in the imitation of God, in being "like God in one's actions."[6] According to Heschel, Maimonides originally considered the highest goal to be contemplation of God's essence, but later came to believe that one's ultimate purpose is to emulate God's traits of kindness, justice, and righteousness. He renounced his former practice of seclusion and ministered to the sick each day, as a physician.[7]

While Judaism has many beautiful symbols, such as the *mezuzah*, *menorah*, and *sukkah*, there is only one symbol that represents God, and that is each person. As Rabbi Abraham Joshua Heschel taught, more important than to have a symbol is to *be* a symbol. And every person can consider himself or herself a symbol of God. This is our challenge: to live in a way compatible with being a symbol of God, to walk in God's ways, to remember who we are and Whom we represent, and to remember our role as partners of God in working to redeem the world.

Love of Neighbor

A central commandment in Judaism is "You shall love your neighbor as yourself" (Leviticus 19:18). According to Rabbi Akiva, this is a (or perhaps *the*) great principle of the Torah.[8] Rabbi Levi Yitzhak of Berditchev taught: "Whether a person really loves God can be determined by the love he or she bears toward other human beings."[9]

Many Torah authorities write that this should be applied not only to Jews but to all humanity. Rabbi J. H. Hertz, former Chief Rabbi of England, states that the translation of the Hebrew word *rea* (neighbor) does not mean "fellow Israelite." He cites several examples in the Torah where that word means "neighbor of whatever race or creed."[10] His view reflects that of Rabbi Pinchas Eliyahu of Vilna, author of the classic *Sefer HaBrit*, who states, "Love of one's neighbor means that we should love all people, no matter to which nation they belong or what language they speak….For all [people] are created in the Divine image, and all engage in improving civilization…."[11] Rabbi Pinchas states that "all of the commandments between man and man are included in this precept of loving one's neighbor,"[12] and he provides a scriptural proof text in which a non-Jew is also called "neighbor."[13]

The commandment "Love your neighbor as yourself" logically follows from the Jewish principle that each person has been created in God's image. Hence, since my neighbor is like myself, I should love him as myself. In fact, the proper translation of the commandment may be "Love your neighbor; he is like yourself." In the same chapter of Leviticus in which "Love your neighbor as yourself" appears, the Torah outlines some specific ways that this mandate can be put into practice:

> You shall not steal; nor shall you deal falsely nor lie to one another....You shall not oppress your neighbor, nor rob him....You shall not curse the deaf, and you shall not put a stumbling block before the blind....You shall do no injustice in judgment; be not partial to the poor, and favor not the mighty; in righteousness shall you judge your neighbor. You shall not go up and down as a tale-bearer among your people; neither shall you stand idly by the blood of your neighbor: I am the Lord. (Leviticus 19:11, 14–16)

The Talmudic sages spell out how one should practice love for human beings:

> One should practice loving-kindness (*gemilut chasadim*), not only by giving of one's possessions, but by personal effort on behalf of one's fellowman, such as extending a free loan, visiting the sick, offering comfort to mourners and attending weddings. For alms giving (*tzedakah*) there is the minimum of the tithe (one-tenth) and the maximum of one-fifth of one's income. But there is no fixed measure of personal service.[14]

Rabbi Moshe Leib of Sassov tells how to love our neighbor as ourselves by relating an experience in his life:

> How to love people is something I learned from a peasant. He was sitting in an inn along with the other peasants, drinking....[H]e asked one of the men seated beside him: "Tell me, do you love me or don't you love me?" The other replied, "I love you very much."

The first peasant nodded his head, was silent for a while, then remarked: "You say that you love me, but you do not know what I need. If you really loved me, you should know." The other had not a word to say to this, and the peasant who put the question fell again silent. But I understood. To know the needs of men and to bear the burden of their sorrow—that is the true love of man.[15]

Aaron, the brother of Moses, also teaches how we can love our neighbors. When two people were quarreling, he would go to each separately and tell him how the other deeply regretted their argument and wished reconciliation. When the two would next meet, they would often embrace and reestablish friendly relations. Because of such acts of love and kindness by Aaron, the great Talmudic master Hillel exhorts people to "Be of the disciples of Aaron, loving peace and pursuing peace, loving humanity, and drawing them closer to the Torah."[16]

When a pagan confronted Hillel and demanded that the sage explain all of the Torah while he, the potential convert, stood on one leg, Hillel's response was: "What is hateful to you, do not do unto others,—that is the entire Torah; everything else is commentary. Go and learn."[17]

Kindness to Strangers

To further emphasize that "love of neighbor" applies to every human being, the Torah frequently commands that we show love and consideration for the stranger, "for you know the heart of the stranger, seeing that you were strangers in the land of Egypt" (Exodus 23:9). The stranger was one who came from distant parts of the Land of Israel or, like the immigrants of our own day, from a foreign country. The Torah stresses the importance of treating them with respect and empathy.

The importance placed on the commandment not to mistreat the stranger in our midst is indicated by its appearance thirty-six times in the Torah, far more than any other *mitzvah*.[18] It is placed on the same level as the duty of kindness to and protection of the widow and the orphan.[19] (According to rabbinic tradition, most of these references to the "stranger" refer to one who converts to Judaism [ger tzedek] or to non-Jews living in the Land of Israel who accept Jewish sovereignty, observe basic laws of morality, and repudiate idolatry [ger toshav]. But since we were neither converts nor formally accepted fellow-travelers in Egypt, there must be additional meaning in our obligation to the "stranger.")

The German Jewish philosopher Hermann Cohen (1842–1918) stated that true religion involves shielding the alien from all wrong:

> The alien was to be protected, although he was not a member of one's family, clan, religious community, or people; simply because he was a human being. In the alien, therefore, man discovered the idea of humanity.[20]

In our world, with its great clannishness and nationalism, with its often harsh treatment of people who don't share the local religion, nationality, or culture, the Torah's teachings about the stranger are remarkable:

> And a stranger shall you not wrong, neither shall you oppress him; for you were strangers in the land of Egypt. (Exodus 22:20; Leviticus 19:33)

> Love you therefore the stranger; for you were strangers in the land of Egypt. (Deuteronomy 10:19; Leviticus 19:34)

> And you shall rejoice in all the good which the Lord, your God has given you ... along with the stranger that is in the midst of you. (Deuteronomy 26:11)

The stranger is guaranteed the same protection in the law court and in payment of wages as the native:

> Judge righteously between a man and his brother and the stranger that is with him. (Deuteronomy 1:16)

> You shall not oppress a hired servant who is poor and needy, whether he be of your brethren, or of the strangers that are in your

land within your gates. In the same day you shall pay him.
(Deuteronomy 24:14,15)

When it comes to Divine forgiveness, the stranger stands on an equal
footing with the native:

> And all the congregation of the children of Israel shall be forgiven,
> and the stranger that sojourns among them. (Numbers 15:26)

Like any other needy person, the stranger had free access to the grain
that was to be left unharvested in the corners of the field and to the gleanings of the harvest, as well as to fallen grapes or odd clusters of grapes
remaining on the vine after picking (Leviticus 19:9, 10; 23:22;
Deuteronomy 24:21). The stranger, like the widowed and the fatherless,
was welcome to the forgotten sheaves in the fields (Deuteronomy 24:19)
and to the olives clinging to the beaten trees (Deuteronomy 24:20). He
also partook of the tithe (the tenth part of the produce) every third year of
the Sabbatical cycle (Deuteronomy 14:28, 29; 26:12).[21]

Treatment of Non-Jews

Since God is the Creator and Divine Parent of every person, each human
being is entitled to proper treatment. A person's actions, and not his or her
faith or creed, are most important, as indicated in the following Talmudic
teachings:

> I bring heaven and earth to witness that the Holy Spirit dwells
> upon a non-Jew as well as upon a Jew, upon a woman as well as
> upon a man, upon maidservant as well as manservant. All depends
> on the deeds of the particular individual![22]

> In all nations, there are righteous individuals who will have a
> share in the world to come.[23]

The Talmud contains many statutes that require us to assist and care for
non-Jews along with Jews.

We support the poor of the non-Jew along with the poor of Israel and visit the sick of the non-Jew along with the sick of Israel and bury the dead of the non-Jew along with the dead of Israel, for the sake of peace (*mipnei darchei shalom*)....[24]

In a city where there are both Jews and Gentiles, the collectors of alms collect from both; they feed the poor of both, visit the sick of both, bury both, comfort the mourners whether they be Jews or Gentiles, and restore the lost goods of both, *mipnei darchei shalom*: to promote peace and cooperation.[25]

The essential spirit of Judaism toward other people was expressed by Maimonides in his *Mishneh Torah* (18:1):

Jew and non-Jew are to be treated alike. If a (Jewish) vendor knows that his merchandise is defective, he must inform the purchaser (whatever his or her religion).

Influenced by this statement by Maimonides, Rabbi Menahem Meiri of Provence HaMeiri ruled in the fourteenth century that a Jew *should* desecrate the Sabbath if it might help to save the life of a Gentile.[26] HaMeiri states that any previous ruling to the contrary had been intended only for ancient times, for those non-Jews who were pagans and morally deficient.[27] The late Israeli Chief Rabbi Chaim Unterman, in a responsum in which he vigorously denied a charge raised by Dr. Israel Shahak that Jewish law forbids violating the Sabbath to save a Gentile's life, quotes this decision.[28]

Rabbi Ezekiel Landau, eighteenth-century author of *Noda B'Yehuda*, ruled:

I emphatically declare that in all laws contained in the Jewish writings concerning theft, fraud, etc., no distinction is made between Jew and Gentile; that the (Talmudic) legal categories *goy*, *akum* (idolater), etc., in no way apply to the people among whom we live.

The following Midrash dramatically shows that Jews are to treat every person, not just fellow Jews, justly:

> Shimon ben Shetach worked hard preparing flax. His disciples said to him, "Rabbi, desist. We will buy you an ass, and you will not have to work so hard." They went and bought an ass from an Arab, and a pearl was found on it, whereupon they came to Rabbi Shimon and said, "From now on you need not work any more." "Why?" he asked. They said, "We bought you an ass from an Arab, and a pearl was found on it [hidden in the saddle]." He said to them, "Does its owner know of that?" They answered, "No." He said to them, "Go and give the pearl back to him." To their argument that he need not return the pearl because the Arab was a heathen, he responded, "Do you think that Shimon ben Shetach is a barbarian? He would prefer to hear the Arab say, 'Blessed be the God of the Jews,' than possess all the riches of the world....It is written, 'You shall not oppress your neighbor.' Now your neighbor is as your brother, and your brother is as your neighbor. Hence you learn that to rob a Gentile is robbery."[29]

According to Rabbi Ahron Soloveichik, the rabbinic leader, scholar, and Professor of Talmud at Yeshiva University, Shimon Ben Shetach in the above story gives a remarkable definition of a barbarian: "Anyone who fails to apply a uniform standard of *mishpat* (justice) and *tzedek* (righteousness) to all human beings, regardless of origin, color, or creed, is deemed barbaric."[30]

Slavery in the Biblical Period

From today's perspective, the widespread and legalized practice of slavery in biblical times seems to contradict Jewish values with regard to treatment of human beings. However, we must look at slavery as an evolving process; it was a common practice in ancient times and was thought to be an economic necessity. Therefore, the Torah does not outlaw it immediately, but, through its teachings and laws, the Torah paved the way toward the eventual elimination of slavery.

Slavery in Israel's early history had many humane features in comparison with practices in other countries. Slaves' rights were guarded and regulated with humanitarian legislation. They were recognized as having certain inalienable rights based on their humanity. For example, slaves had to be allowed to rest on the Sabbath Day, just like their masters.

The Talmud proclaimed legislation in order to mitigate slavery's harshness, especially with regard to a Hebrew slave:

> He [the slave] should be with you in food and with you in drink, lest you eat clean bread and he moldy bread, or lest you drink old wine and he new wine, or lest you sleep on soft feathers and he on straw. So it was said, "Whoever buys a Hebrew slave, it is as if he purchased a master for himself."[31]

It is significant that, unlike the law of the United States before the Civil War, the Biblical fugitive-slave law protected the runaway slave:

> You shall not deliver to his master a bondsman that is escaped from his master unto you. He shall dwell with you in the midst of you, in the place which he shall choose within one of your gates, where he likes it best; you shall not wrong him. (Deuteronomy 23:16, 17)

Violations of Human Rights

One test of the decency of a community is in its attitude toward strangers. A just society teaches its members to welcome outsiders and to be kind to those who are disadvantaged.

Unfortunately, the history of the world is largely a history of exploitation and the violation of human rights. Today in many countries there is widespread discrimination based on race, religion, nationality, and economic status. As will be discussed in Chapter Eight, half the world's people lack adequate food, shelter, employment, education, health care, clean water, and other basic necessities—often as a result of injustice and oppression.

Perhaps no people has historically suffered more from prejudice than the Jews. The Crusades, the Inquisition, and the Holocaust are just three of the most horrible examples in Jewish and human history. Many times Jews have been killed, expelled from countries where they had lived and contributed for many generations, subjected to pogroms, or converted at swordpoint, solely because they were Jewish. Whenever conditions were bad, the economy suffered, or there was a plague, Jews were a convenient scapegoat.

Anti-Semitism continues today. Nazi-type groups and the Ku Klux Klan use the Internet and other means to spread their hateful messages. There are several groups that preach that the Holocaust never occurred. Jewish organizations such as the Anti-Defamation League are working to reduce anti-Semitism, but much more needs to be done to eliminate this ancient but still ever-present and virulent disease.

It is essential to educate all people about the evils of anti-Semitism and other forms of discrimination. In addition to openly confronting and opposing anti-Semitism and racism, it is also necessary to work to reduce or eliminate injustice, poverty, slums, hunger, illiteracy, unemployment, homelessness, and other social ills. Just, democratic societies will be far safer for everyone, including Jews.

Jewish Views on Racism

Rabbi Ahron Soloveichik indicates how strong Jewish views against racism are:

> From the standpoint of the Torah there can be no distinction between one human being and another on the basis of race or color. Any discrimination shown to another human being on account of the color of his or her skin constitutes loathsome barbarity.[32]

He points out that Judaism *does* recognize distinctions between Jews and non-Jews, but this does not derive from any concept of inferiority, but "is based on the unique and special burdens that are placed upon Jews."[33] The prophet Amos challenges the state of mind that looks down on darker-skinned people, in a ringing declaration on the equality of all races and nations. He compares the Jewish people to blacks and indicates that God is even concerned with Israel's enemies, such as the Philistines and Syrians.

> Are you not as the children of the Ethiopians unto me,
> O children of Israel? says the Lord.
> Have I not brought up Israel out of the land of Egypt?
> And the Philistines from Caphtor,
> And the Syrians from Kir? (Amos 9:7)

Judaism teaches the sacredness of every person, but this is not what has always been practiced in our society. And, as with many other moral issues, religion has too seldom spoken out in protest. Rabbi Abraham Joshua Heschel points out the tremendous threat that racism poses to humanity:

> Racism is worse than idolatry; *Racism is Satanism*, unmitigated evil. Few of us seem to realize how insidious, how radical, how universal an evil racism is. Few of us realize that racism is man's gravest threat to man, the maximum of hatred for a minimum of reason, the maximum of cruelty for a minimum of thinking.[34]

He points out that bigotry is inconsistent with a proper relationship with God:

> Prayer and prejudice cannot dwell in the same heart. Worship without compassion is worse than self-deception; it is an abomination.[35]

Rabbi Heschel asserts that "what is lacking is a sense of the monstrosity of inequality."[36] Consistent with the Jewish view that every person is created in God's image, he boldly states: "God is every man's pedigree. He is either the Father of all men or of no men. The image of God is either in every man or in no man."[37]

It is an embarrassing fact that most of America's religious institutions did not originally take the lead in proclaiming the evil of segregation; they had to be prodded into action by the decision of the Supreme Court of the United States in the case of *Brown* v. *Board of Education* in 1954.

Based on Jewish values of compassion and justice, many Jews were active in the struggle for civil rights. Two Jewish college students, Andrew Goodman and Michael Schwerner, along with a black student, James Chaney, were brutally murdered while working for civil rights in Mississippi in 1964. After the Six-Day War, the Black Power movement, and the rise of ethnic pride in the late 1960s, some fissures developed in the decades-long alliance of Jews and African-Americans for progress in America. But while some on both sides would emphasize points of disharmony, Jews and African-Americans have many common interests and goals and have much to gain by working together for a more just, compassionate, peaceful, and harmonious society, as is modeled by the continuing close cooperation between the Congressional Black Caucus and Jewish members of Congress on many issues.

Jewish identification with disadvantaged people is rooted in Jewish historical experience: we were slaves in Egypt and have often lived as oppressed second-class citizens (or worse) in ghettos, deprived of freedom and rights. Hence, we should understand the frustrations of other minorities, here and elsewhere, and their impatient yearning for equality and human dignity.

It is significant that the government of Israel has for some time had a policy of preferential treatment for immigrants who need help adjusting to their new home. Special programs have been devised for the children of Mizrachi (Middle Eastern) and Ethiopian Jews who come from homes where there is low literacy. Compensatory measures include free nurseries, longer school days and school years, special tutoring and curricula, additional funds for equipment and supplies, extra counseling services, and preferential acceptance to academic secondary schools. Unfortunately, there is also some discriminatory treatment and segregation: Israel is not yet ideal in its treatment of some newcomers and minorities.

In summary, Jewish values stress the equality of every person, love of neighbor, proper treatment of strangers, and the imitation of God's attributes of justice, compassion, and kindness. Hence, it is essential that Jews work for the establishment of societies that will protect the rights of every person, each of whom is entitled, as a child of God, to a life of equitable opportunities for education, employment, and human dignity.

3 : SOCIAL JUSTICE

Justice, justice shall you pursue. (Deuteronomy 16:20)

THE PURSUIT OF A JUST SOCIETY IS ONE OF THE MOST fundamental concepts of Judaism. The prevalence of injustice in today's world makes this pursuit all the more urgent.

Note two things about the Torah verse above, which is a keynote of Jewish social values:

1. Words are seldom repeated in the Torah. When they are, it is generally to teach us something new. In this case, it is to stress the supreme importance of applying even-handed justice to all. Rabbenu Bachya ben Asher, a thirteenth-century Torah commentator, stresses, "justice whether to your profit or loss, whether in word or action, whether to Jew or non-Jew."[1]

2. We are told to *pursue* justice. Hence we are not to wait for the right opportunity to come along, the right time and place, but instead we are to actively seek opportunities to practice justice.

Many other statements in the Jewish tradition emphasize the great importance placed on working for justice:

The book of Proverbs asserts: "To do righteousness and justice is preferred by God above sacrifice" (Proverbs 21:3). The psalmist exhorts: "Give justice to the weak and the fatherless; maintain the right of the afflicted and the destitute" (Psalms 82:3). The prophets constantly stress the importance of applying justice:

Learn to do well—seek justice, relieve the oppressed, judge the fatherless, plead for the widow....Zion shall be redeemed with justice, and they who return to her, with righteousness. (Isaiah 1:17, 27)

The Lord of Hosts shall be exalted in justice,
The Holy God shows Himself holy in righteousness. (Isaiah 5:16)

To practice justice is considered among the highest demands of prophetic religion:

It has been told you, O human being, what is good
And what the Lord requires of you:
Only to do justly, love *chesed* (mercy, kindness)
And walk humbly with your God. (Micah 6:8)

The prophet Amos warns the people that without the practice of justice, God is repelled by their worship:

Take away from Me the noise of your songs
and let Me not hear the melody of your stringed instruments,
but let justice well up as waters,
and righteousness as a mighty stream. (Amos 5:23, 24)

The practice of justice is even part of the symbolic betrothal between the Jewish people and God:

And I will betroth you unto Me forever; And I will betroth you unto Me in righteousness, justice, loving kindness, and compassion. And I will betroth you unto Me in faithfulness. And you shall know the Lord. (Hosea 2:21–22)

The prophets of Israel were the greatest champions of social justice in world history. Jeremiah (5:28) rebukes the Jewish people when they fail to plead the cause of the orphan or help the needy. He castigates an entire generation, for "in your skirts is found the blood of the souls of the inno-cent poor" (2.34). Ezekiel rebukes the whole nation for "using oppression, robbing, defrauding the poor and the needy, and extorting from the stranger" (22.29). Isaiah (5:8) and Micah (2:2) criticize wealthy Jews who build up large holdings of property at the expense of their neighbors. The prophetic books are full of such moral reproof.

The patriarch Abraham even challenges God to practice justice: "That be far from You to do after this manner, to slay the righteous with the wicked ... shall the Judge of all the earth not do justly?" (Genesis 18:25) Rabbi Emanuel Rackman, former President of Bar Ilan University, points out that Judaism teaches a special kind of justice, an "empathic justice," which

> seeks to make people identify themselves with each other—with each other's needs, with each other's hopes and aspirations, with each other's defeats and frustrations. Because Jews have known the distress of slaves and the loneliness of strangers, we are to project ourselves into their souls and make their plight our own.[2]

This concept is reinforced by Rabbi Levi Yitzchak Horowitz, the Bostoner Rebbe:

> The fact that the Jewish people had to experience 400 years of Egyptian exile, including 210 years of actual slavery, was critical in molding our national personality into one of compassion and concern for our fellow man, informed by the realization that we have a vital role to play in the world....For this reason, God begins the Ten Commandments with a reminder that "I am the Lord, your God, who took you out of Egypt" (Exodus 20:2). We must constantly remember that we were slaves in order to always appre-ciate the ideal of freedom, not only for ourselves but also for others. We must do what we can to help others to live free of the bondage of the evil spirit, free of the bondage of cruelty, of abuse and lack of caring.[3]

Based on these teachings, Jews have regarded the practice of justice and the seeking of a just society as Divine imperatives. This has inspired many Jews throughout history to lead the struggle for better social conditions. The teachings of the Torah, prophets, and sages have been the most powerful inspiration for justice in the history of the world.

Giving Charity (*Tzedakah*)

Judaism places great stress on the giving of money to help the poor and hungry and to support communal purposes and institutions—as an act of righteousness (*tzedakah*). In the Jewish tradition, *tzedakah* is not an act of condescension from one person to another who is in need. It is the fulfillment of a *mitzvah*, a commandment, to a fellow human being, who has equal status before God. Although Jewish tradition recognizes that the sharing of our resources is also an act of love (as the Torah states, "Love your neighbor as yourself" [Leviticus 19:18]), it emphasizes that this act of sharing is an act of justice. This is to teach us that Jews are obligated to provide people who are in need with our love and concern. They are human beings created in the Divine image, who have a place and a purpose within God's creation.

In the Jewish tradition, failure to give charity is equivalent to idolatry.[4] Perhaps this is because a selfish person forgets the One Who created and provides for us all, and, in becoming preoccupied with personal material needs, makes himself or herself into an idol. The giving of charity by Jews is so widespread that Maimonides was able to say: "Never have I seen or heard of a Jewish community that did not have a charity fund."[5]

Charity even takes priority over the building of the Temple. King Solomon was prohibited from using the silver and gold that David, his father, had accumulated for the building of the Temple, because that wealth should have been used to feed the poor during the three years of famine in King David's reign (I Kings 7:51).

Judaism mandates lending to the needy, to help them become economically self-sufficient:

And if your brother becomes impoverished, and his means fail in your proximity; then you shall strengthen him....Take no interest

of him or increase....You shall not give him your money upon
interest. (Leviticus 25:35–37)

Every third year of the Sabbatical cycle, the needy are to receive the tithe
for the poor (one tenth of one's income) (Deuteronomy 14:28, 26:12).

The following Torah verse indicates the general Jewish view about
helping the poor:

> If there shall be among you a needy person, one of your brethren,
> within any of your gates, in your land which the Lord your God
> gives you, you shall not harden your heart, nor shut your hand
> from your needy brother; but you shall surely open your hand unto
> him, and shall surely lend him sufficient for his need in that which
> he wants. (Deuteronomy 15:7–8)

Jewish tradition views *tzedakah* not only as an act of love, but also as an act
of justice; in fact, the word *tzedakah* comes from the word *tzedek* (justice).
According to the Torah, the governing institutions of the Jewish community are responsible for helping needy people.

Maimonides writes in his code of Jewish law that the highest form of
tzedakah is to help a needy individual through "a gift or a loan, or by
forming a business partnership with him, or by providing him with a job,
until he is no longer dependent on the generosity of others."[6] This concept
is based on the following Talmudic teaching:

> It is better to lend to a poor person than to give him alms, and best
> of all is to provide him with capital for business.[7]

Hence Jews should provide immediate help for poor people while also
working for a just society in which there is no poverty. In Judaism, *tzedakah*
is intertwined with the pursuit of social justice.

An entire lengthy section of the Code of Jewish Law (*Shulhan Arukh*),
Yoreh De'ah 247–259, is devoted to the many aspects of giving charity.
Some of the more important concepts are given below:

247:1: It is a positive religious obligation for a person to give as much charity as he can afford. (A tithe of ten percent of one's income is incumbent upon every Jew.)

247:33: God has compassion on whoever has compassion on the poor. A person should think that, just as he asks of God all the time to sustain him and as he entreats God to hear his cry, so he should hear the cry of the poor.

248:1: Every person is obliged to give charity. Even a poor person who is supported by charity is obliged to give from that which he receives.

249:3: A man should give charity cheerfully and out of the goodness of his heart. He should anticipate the grief of the poor man and speak words of comfort to him. But if he gives in an angry and unwilling spirit, he loses any merit there is in giving.

250:1: How much should be given to a poor man? "Sufficient for his need in that which he requires" (Deuteronomy 15:8). This means that if he is hungry, he should be fed; if he has no clothes, he should be given clothes; if he has no furniture, furniture should be brought for him. (This is to be dispensed by the person in charge of community charity funds.)

According to the prophet Ezekiel, failure to help the needy led to the destruction of Sodom:

Behold this was the iniquity of thy sister Sodom; pride, fullness of bread, and careless ease ... neither did she strengthen the hand of the poor and needy ... therefore I removed them when I saw it.... (Ezekiel 16:49, 50)

A relationship between personal misfortune and a failure to help the poor is indicated in Proverbs 17:5, 21:13, and 28:27. For example, Proverbs 21:13 states: "The person who fails to hear the cry of the poor will later also cry, but will not be answered."

Acts of Loving Kindness

As important as *tzedakah* is, the Jewish tradition states that even greater is *gemilut chasadim* (acts of loving kindness):

> One who gives a coin to a poor man is rewarded with six blessings, but he who encourages him with kind words is rewarded with eleven blessings.[8]

Of course, providing both charity and kind words is best of all. The sages interpret "acts of loving kindness" to include many types of gracious action, such as hospitality to travelers, providing for poor brides, visiting the sick, welcoming guests, burying the dead, and comforting mourners.

Gemilut chasadim is deemed superior to acts of charity in several ways:

> No gift is needed for it but the giving of oneself; it may be done to the rich as well as to the poor; and it may be done not only to the living, but also to the dead (through burial).[9]

The purpose of the entire Torah is to teach *gemilut chasadim*. It starts and ends with an act of loving kindness.

> For in the third chapter of Genesis, the verse reads: "The Lord God made for Adam and his wife garments of skin and clothed them" (Genesis 3:21), and the last book of the Torah reports: "and He buried him (Moses) in the valley" (Deuteronomy 34:6).[10]

Jewish Views on Poverty

Judaism places emphasis on justice, charity, and kindness to the poor because of the great difficulties poor people face:

> If all afflictions in the world were assembled on one side of the scale and poverty on the other, poverty would outweigh them all.[11]

Judaism believes that poverty is destructive to the human personality and negatively shapes a person's life experiences: "The ruin of the poor is their poverty" (Proverbs 10:15). "Where there is no sustenance, there is no learning."[12] "The world is darkened for him who has to look to others for sustenance."[13] "The sufferings of poverty cause a person to disregard his own sense (of right) and that of his Maker."[14]

Judaism generally does not encourage an ascetic life. Insufficiency of basic necessities does not ease the path toward holiness, except perhaps for very spiritual individuals. In many cases the opposite is true; poverty can lead to the breaking of a person's spirit. This is one reason that holiness is linked to justice.

Many Torah laws are designed to aid the poor: the produce of corners of the field are to be left uncut for the poor to take (Leviticus 19:9); the gleanings of the wheat harvest and fallen fruit are to be left for the needy (Leviticus 19:10); during the Sabbatical year, the land is to be left fallow, and the poor (as well as animals) may eat of whatever grows freely (Leviticus 25:2–7).

Failure to treat the poor properly is a desecration of God: "The person who mocks the poor blasphemes his Maker" (Proverbs 17:5). Abraham, the founder of Judaism, always went out of his way to aid the poor. He set up inns that were open in all four directions on the highways so that the poor and the wayfarer would have access to food and drink when in need.[15]

The Jewish tradition sees God as siding with the poor and oppressed. He intervened in Egypt on behalf of poor, oppressed slaves. His prophets constantly castigated those who oppressed the needy. Two proverbs reinforce this message. A negative formulation is in Proverbs 14:31: "He who oppresses a poor man insults his Maker." Proverbs 19:17 puts it more positively: "He who is kind to the poor lends to the Lord." Hence helping a needy person is like providing a loan to the Creator of the universe.

Compassion

The Talmud teaches that "Jews are *rachmanim b'nei rachmanim* (compassionate children of compassionate parents), and one who shows no pity for fellow creatures is assuredly not of the seed of Abraham, our father."[16] The rabbis considered Jews to be distinguished by three characteristics: compassion, modesty, and benevolence.[17] As indicated previously, we are instructed to feel empathy for strangers, "for you were strangers in the land of Egypt" (Deuteronomy 10:19). The *birkat ha-mazon* (grace recited after meals) speaks of God compassionately feeding the whole world.

We are not only to have compassion for Jews, but for all who are in need.

Have we not all one Father?
Has not one God created us? (Malachi 2:10)

Rabbi Samson Raphael Hirsch writes very eloquently about the importance of compassion:

Do not suppress this compassion, this sympathy especially with the sufferings of your fellowman. It is the warning voice of duty, which points out to you your brother in every sufferer, and your own sufferings in his, and awakens the love which tells you that you belong to him and his sufferings with all the powers that you have. Do not suppress it!...See in it the admonition of God that you are to have no joy so long as a brother suffers by your side.[18]

Rabbi Samuel Dresner states that "Compassion is the way God enters our life in terms of man's relation to his fellow man."[19]

The Jewish stress on compassion finds expression in many groups and activities. Jewish communities generally have most, if not all, of the following: a *Bikur Cholim* Society to provide medical expenses for the sick, and to visit them and bring them comfort and cheer; a *Malbish Arumim* Society to provide clothing for the poor; a *Hachnasat Kalah* Society to provide for needy brides; a *Bet Yetomin* Society to aid orphans; a *Talmud Torah* Organization to support a free school for poor children; a *Gemilat Chesed* Society to lend money at no interest to those in need; an *Ozer Dalim* Society to dispense charity to the poor; a *Hachnasat Orchim* Society to provide shelter for homeless travelers; a *Chevrah Kaddishah* Society to attend to the proper burial of the dead; and *Essen Teg* Institutions to provide food and shelter for poor students who attend schools in the community.[20]

Judaism also stresses compassion for animals. There are many laws in the Torah which mandate kindness to animals. A farmer is commanded not to muzzle his ox when he threshes corn (Deuteronomy 25:4) and not to plow with an ox and an ass together (Deuteronomy 22:10), since the weaker animal would not be able to keep up with the stronger one. Animals must be allowed to rest on the Sabbath Day (Exodus 20:10, 23:12), a teaching so important that it is part of the Ten Commandments. A person is commanded to feed his animals before sitting down to his own meal.[21] These concepts are summarized in the Hebrew phrase *tsa'ar ba'alei chayim*—the mandate not to cause "pain to any living creature."

The Psalmist emphasizes God's concern for animals, for "His tender mercies are over all His creatures" (Psalm 145:9). He pictures God as "satisfying the desire of every living creature" (Psalm 145:16) and "providing food for the beasts and birds" (Psalm 147:9). Perhaps the Jewish attitude toward animals is epitomized by the statement in Proverbs: "The righteous person regards the life of his or her animal" (Proverb 12:10). In Judaism, one who does not treat animals with compassion cannot be considered a righteous individual.[22]

Rabbi Moshe Cordovero (1522–1570) indicates the importance Judaism places on the proper treatment of animals, as well as people:

[One should] respect all creatures, recognizing in them the greatness of the Creator who formed man with wisdom, and whose wisdom is contained in all creatures. He should realize that they greatly deserve to be honored, since the One Who Forms All Things, the Wise One Who is exalted above all, cared to create them. If one despises them, God forbid, it reflects on the honor of their Creator....It is evil in the sight of the Holy One, Blessed be He, if any of His creatures are despised.[23]

Consistent with this precept, the Jewish sages teach, "Whoever shows mercy to God's creatures is granted mercy from Heaven."[24]

Judaism and Business Ethics
The Torah provides instruction in honest business practices:

You shall do no wrong in judgment, in measures of length, of weight, or in quantity. Just balances, just weights, a just *ephah* [the standard dry measure] and a just *hin* [a measure for liquids], shall you have. I am the Lord your God, who brought you out of the land of Egypt (Leviticus 19:35, 36).

The rabbis of the Talmud give concrete expression to the many Torah and prophetic teachings regarding justice and righteousness. They indicate in detail what is proper when conducting business. Rabbinic literature translates prophetic ideals into the language of the marketplace in terms of fair prices, the avoidance of false weights and measures, proper business contracts, fair methods of competition, and awareness of the duties of employers to employees and of workers to their employers.

Rava, a fourth-century Babylonian teacher, taught the wealthy merchants of his town the importance of scrupulous honesty in business dealings. He stated that on Judgment Day the first question God asks a person is "Were you reliable in your business dealings?"[25] The rabbis stress that a person's word is a sacred bond that should not be broken. The Mishnah states that God will exact punishment for those who do not abide by their promises.[26] Cheating a Gentile is considered even worse than cheating a Jew, for "besides being a violation of the moral law, it brings Israel's religion into contempt, and desecrates the name of Israel's God."[27]

The sages are very critical of attempts to take away a person's livelihood by unfair competition.[28] Their overall view of business ethics can be summarized by the verses "And you shall do that which is right and good in the sight of the Lord" (Deuteronomy 6:18), and "better is a little with righteousness than great revenues with injustice" (Proverbs 16:8).

The very high ethical standards of the Talmudic sages are exemplified by the following story:

Reb Saphra had wine to sell. A certain customer came in to buy wine at a time when Reb Saphra was saying the *Sh'ma* prayer [which cannot be interrupted by speaking]. The customer said, "Will you sell me the wine for such an amount?" When Reb Saphra did not respond, the customer thought he was not satisfied with the price and raised his bid. When Reb Saphra had finished his prayer, he said, "I decided in my heart to sell the wine to you at the first price you mentioned; therefore I cannot accept your higher bid."[29]

It is essential that Jews work to establish systems and conditions consistent with the basic Jewish values of justice, compassion, kindness, the sacredness of every life, the imitation of God's attributes, love of neighbors, consideration of the stranger, compassion for animals, and the highest of business ethics.

4: ECOLOGY

In the hour when the Holy one, blessed be He, created the first human being (Adam), He took him and let him pass before all the trees of the Garden of Eden and said to him: "See my works, how fine and excellent they are! All that I have created, for you have I created them. Think upon this and do not corrupt and desolate My world, For if you corrupt it, there is no one to set it right after you."
(Midrash Ecclesiastes Rabbah 7:28)

WHEN GOD CREATED THE WORLD, HE WAS ABLE TO SAY, "It is very good" (Genesis 1:31). Everything was in harmony as God had planned, the waters were clean, and the air was pure. But what must God think about the world today?

What must God think when the rain He provided to nourish our crops is often acidic, due to the many chemicals emitted by industries and automobiles; when the ozone layer He provided to protect all life on earth from the sun's radiation is being depleted; when the abundance of species of plants and animals that He created are becoming extinct, before we have even been able to study and catalog many of them; when the fertile soil He provided is quickly being eroded; when the climatic conditions that He designed to meet our needs are threatened by global warming?

Consider the extreme differences between conditions at the time of creation and conditions today:

In the beginning God created the heavens and the earth. The earth was without form and void, and darkness was upon the face of the deep; and the Spirit of God hovered over the face of the waters. (Genesis 1:1–2)

In the beginning of the technological age, man recreated the heavens and the earth. To the earth he gave new form with dynamite and bulldozer, and the void of the heavens he filled with smog.

And God said, "Let there be a firmament in the midst of the waters....Let the waters under the heavens be gathered into one place, and let the dry land appear." (Genesis 1:6)

Then man took oil from beneath the ground and spread it over the waters, until it coated the beaches with slime. He washed the topsoil from the fertile prairies and sank it in the ocean depths. He took waste from his mines and filled in the valleys, while real estate developers leveled the hills. And man said, "Well, business is business."

Then God said, "Let the earth put forth vegetation, plants yielding seed and fruit trees bearing fruit in which is their seed, each according to its kind, upon the earth....Let the earth bring forth living creatures according to their kinds." And it was so. And God saw that it was good. (Genesis 1: 11, 24)

But man was not so sure. He found that mosquitoes annoyed him, so he killed them with DDT. And the robins died, too, and man said, "What a pity." Man defoliated forests in the name of modern warfare. He filled the streams with industrial waste, and his children read about fish ... in the history books.

So God created humans in His own image; in the image of God He created them. And God blessed them, and God said to them, "Be fruitful and multiply, and fill the earth and subdue it, and have dominion over ... every living thing." (Genesis 1:27–28)

So man multiplied and multiplied—and spread his works across the land until the last green blade was black with asphalt, until the skies were ashen and the waters reeked, until neither bird sang nor child ran laughing through cool grass. So man subdued the earth and made it over in his image, and in the name of progress he drained it of its life....Until the earth was without form and void, and darkness was once again upon the face of the deep, and man himself was but a painful memory in the mind of God. [1]

Today's environmental threats bring to mind the Biblical ten plagues that appear in the Torah portions which are read in synagogues in the weeks before the ecological holiday of Tu B'Shvat:

- When we consider the threats to our land, waters, and air due to pesticides and other chemical pollutants, resource scarcities, acid rain, threats to our climate, etc., we can easily enumerate ten modern "plagues."
- The Egyptians were subjected to one plague at a time, while the modern plagues threaten us all at once.
- The Jews in Goshen were spared most of the Biblical plagues, while every person on earth is imperiled by the modern plagues.
- Instead of an ancient Pharaoh's heart being hardened, our hearts today have been hardened by the greed, materialism, and waste that are at the root of current environmental threats.
- God provided the Biblical plagues to free the Israelites, while today we must apply God's teachings in order to save ourselves and our precious but endangered planet.

Jewish Teachings on Ecology

Many fundamental Torah principles express and make concrete the Biblical statement, "The earth is the Lord's and the fullness thereof" (Psalms 24:1):

1. People are to be co-workers with God in helping to preserve and improve the world.
The Talmudic sages assert that the assigned role of the Jewish people is to enhance the world as "partners of God in the work of creation."[2] The following Psalm reinforces this concept:

> When I look at Your heavens, the work of Your hands,
> The moon and work which You have established,
> What is man that You are mindful of him, and the son of man that You do care for him?
> Yet You have made him little less than God, and do crown him with glory and honor.
> You have given him dominion over the works of Your hands;
> You have put all things under his feet... (Psalms 8:4–7)

The Talmudic sages express great concern about preserving the environment and preventing pollution. They state: "It is forbidden to live in a town which has no garden or greenery."[3] Threshing floors must be placed far enough from a town so that it will not be dirtied by chaff carried by winds.[4] Tanneries must be kept at least fifty cubits (a cubit is about half a meter) from a town and may be placed only on the east side of a town, so that odors and pollution will be carried away from the town by the prevailing winds from the west.[5]

2. Everything belongs to God. We are to be stewards of the earth, to insure that its produce is available for all God's children.
There is an apparent contradiction between two verses in Psalms: "The earth is the Lord's" (Psalms 24:1) and "The heavens are the heavens of God, but the earth He has given to human beings" (Psalms 115:16). The apparent discrepancy is cleared up in the following way: Before a person says a *bracha* (a blessing), before he acknowledges God's ownership of the land and its products, then "the earth is the Lord's"; after a person has said a *bracha*, acknowledging God's ownership and that we are stewards to ensure that God's works are properly used and shared, then "the earth He has given to human beings."[6]

Property is a sacred trust given by God; it must be used to fulfill God's purposes. No person has absolute or exclusive control over his or her possessions. The concept that people have custodial care of the earth, as opposed to ownership, is illustrated by this ancient Jewish story:

> Two men were fighting over a piece of land. Each claimed owner-ship and bolstered his claim with apparent proof. To resolve their differences, they agreed to put the case before the rabbi. The rabbi listened but could come to no decision because both seemed to be right. Finally he said, "Since I cannot decide to whom this land belongs, let us ask the land." He put his ear to the ground and, after a moment, straightened up. "Gentlemen, the land says it belongs to neither of you but that you belong to it."[7]

As we have discussed, even the produce of the field does not belong solely to the person who farms the land. The poor are entitled to a portion:

> And when you reap the harvest of your land, you shall not wholly reap the corner of your field, neither shall you gather the gleaning of your harvest. And you shall not glean your vineyard, neither shall you gather the fallen fruit of your vineyard; you shall leave them for the poor and for the stranger; I am the Lord, your God. (Leviticus 19: 9–10)

These portions set aside for the poor were not voluntary contributions based on kindness. They were, in essence, a regular Divine assessment. Because God is the real owner of the land, He claims a share of the bounty which He has provided to be given to the poor.

As a reminder that "the earth is the Lord's," the land must be permitted to rest and lie fallow every seven years (the Sabbatical year):

> And six years you shall sow your land, and gather in the increase thereof, but the seventh year you shall let it rest and lie fallow, that the poor of your people may eat; and what they leave, the animals

of the field shall eat. In like manner you shall deal with your vine-
yard, and with your olive yard. (Exodus 23: 10, 11)

The Sabbatical year also has ecological benefits: the land was given a
chance to rest and renew its fertility.

Judaism asserts that there is one God who created the entire earth as a
unity, in ecological balance, and that everything is connected to everything else. This idea is perhaps best expressed by Psalm 104:

... You [God] are the One Who sends forth springs into
brooks, that they may run between mountains,
To give drink to every animal of the fields; the creatures
of the forest quench their thirst.
Beside them dwell the fowl of the heavens...
You water the mountains from Your upper chambers...
You cause the grass to spring up for the cattle,
and herb, for the service of humans, to bring forth
bread from the earth...
How manifold are your works, O Lord! In wisdom You have made
them all; the earth is full of Your property...

Some argue that people have been given a license to exploit the earth and
its creatures, because God gave humans "dominion over the fish of the sea,
and over the fowl of the air, and over every living thing that creeps upon
the earth" (Genesis 1:28).[8] However, the Talmudic sages interpret
dominion as meaning guardianship or stewardship, being co-workers with
God in taking care of and improving the world, not as a right to conquer
and exploit animals and the earth. The fact that people's dominion over
animals is limited is indicated by God's first (completely vegetarian)
dietary regime (Genesis 1:29).

Rabbi Abraham Isaac Ha-Kohen Kook, the first Ashkenazic Chief
Rabbi of pre-state Israel, states that dominion does not mean the arbitrary
power of a tyrannical ruler who cruelly governs in order to satisfy personal
desires.[9] He observes that such a repulsive form of servitude could not be
forever sealed in the world of God whose "tender mercies are over all His

work" (Psalm 145:9).[10] God indicates the intended human role when he tells Adam and Eve that they are to work the earth and protect it (Genesis 2:15).

3. We are not to waste or unnecessarily destroy anything of value.

This prohibition, called *bal tashchit* ("you shall not destroy") is based on the following Torah statement:

> When you shall besiege a city a long time, in making war against it to take it, you shall not destroy (*lo tashchit*) the trees thereof by wielding an ax against them. You may eat of them but you shall not cut them down; for is the tree of the field man, that it should be besieged by you? Only the trees of which you know that they are not trees for food, them you may destroy and cut down, that you may build bulwarks against the city that makes war with you, until it fall. (Deuteronomy 20:19, 20)

This Torah prohibition is very specific. Taken in its most literal sense, it prohibits only the destruction of fruit trees during wartime. During Talmudic times, the rabbis greatly expanded the objects, methods of destruction, and situations that are covered by *bal tashchit*:

> Whoever breaks vessels, or tears garments, or destroys a building, or clogs a well, or does away with food in a destructive manner violates the prohibition of *bal tashchit*.[11]

Early sages reasoned that if the principle applied even during a wartime situation, it must apply also at all other times. Similarly, they deduced that other means of destruction besides direct destruction with an ax (such as destroying trees by diverting a source of water) were also forbidden. Finally, they ruled by analogy that *bal tashchit* regulated not only trees, or even all natural objects, but everything of potential use, whether created by God or altered by people.[12] Talmudic rulings on *bal tashchit* also prohibit the unnecessary killing of animals[13] and the eating of extravagant foods when one can eat simpler ones.[14] In summary, *bal tashchit* prohibits the destruction, complete or incomplete, direct or indirect, of all objects of potential benefit to people.

The following Talmudic statements illustrate the seriousness with which the rabbis considered the violation of *bal tashchit*:

> The sage Rabbi Hanina attributed the early death of his son to the fact that the boy had chopped down a fig tree.[15]

> Jews should be taught when very young that it is a sin to waste even small amounts of food.[16]

> Rav Zutra taught: "One who covers an oil lamp or uncovers a naphtha lamp transgresses the prohibition of *bal tashchit*"[17] [Both actions mentioned would cause a faster (hence wasteful) consumption of the fuel.]

Maimonides makes explicit the Talmudic expansion:

> It is forbidden to cut down fruit-bearing trees outside a besieged city, nor may a water channel be deflected from them so that they wither....Not only one who cuts down trees, but also one who smashes household goods, tears clothes, demolishes a building, stops up a spring, or destroys articles of food with destructive intent transgresses the command "you must not destroy."[18]

The *Sefer Ha-Hinukh*, a thirteenth century text which explicates the 613 *mitzvot* in detail, indicates that the underlying purpose of *bal tashchit* is to help one to learn to act like the righteous, who oppose all waste and destruction:

> The purpose of this mitzvah [*bal tashchit*] is to teach us to love that which is good and worthwhile and to cling to it, so that good becomes a part of us and we avoid all that is evil and destructive. This is the way of the righteous and those who improve society, who love peace and rejoice in the good in people and bring them

close to Torah: that nothing, not even a grain of mustard, should be lost to the world, that they should regret any loss or destruction that they see, and if possible they will prevent any destruction that they can. Not so are the wicked, who are like demons, who rejoice in destruction of the world, and they destroy themselves.[19]

Rabbi Samson Raphael Hirsch, the leading Orthodox rabbi of nineteenth-century Germany, viewed *bal tashchit* as the most basic Jewish principle of all—acknowledging the sovereignty of God and the limitation of our own will and ego. When we preserve the world around us, we act with the understanding that God owns everything. However, when we destroy, we are, in effect, worshipping the idols of our own desires, living only for self-gratification without remembering God. By observing *bal tashchit*, we restore our harmony not only with the world around us, but also with God's will, which we place before our own:

"Do not destroy anything" is the first and most general call of God....If you should now raise your hand to play a childish game, to indulge in senseless rage, wishing to destroy that which you should only use, wishing to exterminate that which you should only gain advantage from, if you should regard the beings beneath you as objects without rights, not perceiving God Who created them, and therefore desire that they feel the might of your presumptuous mood, instead of using them only as the means of wise human activity—then God's call proclaims to you, "Do not destroy anything! Be a *mensch* [good human being]! Only if you use the things around you for wise human purposes, sanctified by the word of My teaching, only then are you a *mensch* and have the right over them which I have given you as a human. However, if you destroy, if you ruin, at that moment you are not a human ... and have no right to the things around you. I lent them to you for wise use only; never forget that I lent them to you. As soon as you use them unwisely, be it the greatest or the smallest, you commit treachery against My world, you commit murder and robbery against My property, you sin against Me!" This is what God calls unto you, and with this call does God represent the greatest and the smallest against you and grants the smallest as well as the greatest a right against your presumptuousness....In truth, there is no one nearer to idolatry than one who can disregard the fact that all things are the creatures and property of God, and who then presumes also to have the right, because he has the might, to destroy them according to a presumptuous act of will. Yes, that one is already serving the most powerful idols—anger, pride, and above all ego, which in its passion regards itself as the master of things.[20]

Rabbi Hirsch also teaches that "destruction" includes using more things (or things of greater value) than is necessary to obtain one's aim.[21] The following Midrash is related to this concept:

Two men entered a shop. One ate coarse bread and vegetables, while the other ate fine bread, fat meat, and drank old wine. The one who ate fine food suffered harm, while the one who had coarse food escaped harm. Observe how simply animals live and how healthy they are as a result.[22]

Ecology in Jewish History and Prayers
Much of early Jewish history is closely connected to the natural environment. The patriarchs and their descendants were shepherds. Since their work led them into many types of natural settings, including mountains, prairies, wilderness, and desert, they developed a love and appreciation of natural wonders and beauty. According to Charles W. Eliot, "no race has ever surpassed the Jewish descriptions of either the beauties or the terrors of the nature which environs man."[23]

Jews have often pictured God through His handiwork in nature. Abraham, the father of the Jewish people, when marveling at the heavenly bodies, intuits that there must be a Creator of these wonders. The prophet Isaiah exclaims:

Lift up your eyes on high,
And see: Who has created these?

He that brings out their host by numbers,
He calls them all by name;
By the greatness of His might, for He is strong in power,
Not one fails. (Isaiah 40:26)

The greatest prophet, Moses, during the years when he was a shepherd, learned many facts about nature, which were later useful in leading the Israelites in the desert. The Ten Commandments and the Torah were revealed to the Jews at Mount Sinai, in a natural setting. The forty years of wandering in the wilderness trained Israel in the appreciation of natural beauty.

Many Jewish prayers extol God for His wondrous creations. Before reciting the *Sh'ma* every morning, religious Jews say the following prayer to thank God for the new day:

Blessed are You, Oh Lord our God, King of the universe.
Who forms light and creates darkness,
Who makes peace and creates all things.
Who in mercy gives light to the earth
And to them who dwell thereon,
And in Your goodness renews the creation
Every day continually.
How manifold are Your works, O Lord!
In wisdom You have made them all;
The earth is full of Your possessions...
Be blessed, O Lord our God,
For the excellency of Your handiwork,
And for the bright luminaries
Which You have made:
They shall glorify You forever.

In the Sabbath morning service, the following prayer is recited: "The heavens declare the glory of God, and the firmament shows His handiwork" (Psalms 19:2).

However, Judaism does not only consider the "heavens above." It also deals with practical, down-to-earth issues. The following law, which commands disposal of sewage, even in wartime, illustrates the sensitivity of the Torah to environmental cleanliness, by mandating the burial of waste in the ground, not dumping it into rivers or littering the countryside!

> You shall have a place outside the military camp, when you shall go forth abroad. And you shall have a spade among your weapons; and it shall be when you sit down outside, you shall dig therewith, and shall turn back and cover that which comes from you. (Deuteronomy 23:13–15)

Traditionally, the preservation of the Land of Israel has been a central theme in Judaism. The three pilgrimage festivals (Pesach, Shavuot, and Sukkot) are agricultural as well as spiritual celebrations. Jews pray for dew and rain in their proper time so that there will be abundant harvests in Israel.

Current Ecological Threats
As mentioned in the Preface, in 1993 over 1,670 scientists, including 104 Nobel laureates in science, signed a "World Scientists' Warning to Humanity" which argues that human beings are inflicting "irreversible damage on the environment and on critical resources," and that "fundamental changes are urgent" if "vast human misery is to be avoided and our global home on this planet is not to be irretrievably mutilated."[24] While there has been some progress since that warning was issued, there has also been further deterioration in many areas:

- Scientists surveyed by the Museum of Natural History in New York City indicate that the Earth is experiencing the fastest rate of extinction of species in history.[25] Harvard biologist Edward O. Wilson writes:

> There is no question in my mind that the most harmful part of ongoing environmental despoilation is the loss of biodiversity. The reason is that the variety of organisms ... once lost, cannot be

regained. If diversity is sustained in wild ecosystems, the biosphere can be recovered and used by future generations to any degree desired and with benefits literally beyond measure. To the extent it is diminished, humanity will be diminished for all generations to come.[26]

- Industrial chemicals and pesticides are causing a depletion of the ozone layer. This increases the penetration of deadly ultraviolet radiation at the earth's surface, which causes cataracts, weakened immune systems, and skin cancers in humans and kills wildlife, crops, and vegetation. Every winter and spring, massive "holes" in the ozone layer appear over the North and South Poles. U.S. governmental agencies announced in October, 1998 that the hole in the ozone layer over Antarctica measured ten million square miles, an area larger than North America.[27]

- Inefficient use of depletable groundwater threatens food production and essential human systems. Due to heavy demand for water, there are serious shortages in about eighty countries (including Israel), which contain forty percent of the world's population.[28] According to a report released recently by Population Action International, over the next twenty-five years, the number of people facing chronic or severe water shortages could increase from 505 million to more than three billion. The report said water shortages would be worst in the Middle East and much of Africa.[29] Globally, two billion people live in areas with chronic water shortages.[30] The Ogalalla aquifer that provides water for one-fifth of all U.S. irrigated land is overdrawn by twelve billion cubic meters per year, a problem that has already caused more than two million acres of farmland to be taken out of irrigation. In California's Central Valley, which grows half of U.S. fruits and vegetables, groundwater withdrawal exceeds recharge by one billion cubic meters per year.[31] A combination of population growth, drought, desertification, waste of water, and global warming is causing a serious water shortage in China that experts say could induce environmental and political crises. Officials are blaming drought for a 9.3 percent drop in the summer grain yield, and water rationing has been imposed on residents and industries in nearly a hundred cities.[32]

- Pollution of lakes, rivers, and groundwater further limits supplies of usable water. In the past few decades, industrialization, population growth, and the heavy use of chemical fertilizers have doubled the amount of nitrogen in circulation, contributing to environmental problems worldwide and possibly to human health problems such as cancer and memory failure. Hardest hit are coastal bays and oceans— deadly algae blooms are cropping up from Finnish beaches to Hong Kong harbors, massive unexpected fish kills are occurring from Maryland's Chesapeake Bay to Russia's Black Sea, and coral reefs are in decline around the globe.[33]
- Acid rain and air pollution are causing widespread damage to humans, crops, and forests. Over 140 million Americans live in regions that fail air-quality tests for ozone pollution, according to an American Lung Association report.[34]
- About seventy percent of the world's 13.5 billion acres of agricultural dry lands—almost thirty percent of the Earth's total land area—is at risk of becoming desert.[35] Over a billion people in 135 countries depend on this land for food.[36]
- As global pesticide use increased from almost nothing in 1945 to 4.7 billion tons a year in 1995, at least six people are poisoned by pesticides each minute somewhere in the world and about 220,000 people die of its effects annually.[37]
- At current rates of destruction, the world's remaining rain forests will virtually disappear by about 2031.[38] According to a study published in the journal *Science*, as little as five percent of the Amazon rain forest in Brazil may remain as pristine forest by 2020. Researchers fear that roads, new homes, logging, and oil exploration will devastate the 1.3 million-square-mile Amazon forest, which makes up forty percent of the Earth's remaining tropical rain forest.[39]

The above examples, and many more, are not meant to imply that there has not been any good environmental news. Since 1970, when the first Earth Day was held to increase environmental awareness and promote action to reduce environmental threats, there has been much new legislation, including the Clean Air and Clean Water Acts in the U.S., that has led to improvements. For example, in 2000, for the second consecutive year, no first-stage ozone pollution alerts were reported in the greater Los Angeles area.[40] Many of the 16 million people who live in the region are now breathing air that meets all U.S. EPA health standards. Smog alerts have decreased seventy-five percent over the past fifteen years, despite sharp increases in the number of people and cars in the region. The improvements came about because tough air quality regulations led to the development of cleaner consumer products, cars, power plants, and factories. However, it may be difficult to maintain this progress, since 6.7 million more people are expected to live in the Los Angeles area by 2020.

Causes of Current Ecological Problems
The root cause of current ecological crises is that the realities of our economic and production systems are completely contrary to Torah values:

- While Judaism stresses that "the earth is the Lord's" and that we are to be partners in protecting the environment, many corporations consider the earth only in terms of how it can be used to maximize profits, with little concern about damaging environmental effects.

    Instead of starting with protection of the earth as a primary value and building production and economic systems consistent with this value, corporations and utility companies tend to operate with maximum profit as their overriding concern. Their shortsighted application of technology is a prime cause of current ecological crises.[41]
- While Judaism mandates *bal tashchit*, our economy is based on waste, on buying, using, and disposing. Advertisers aim to make people feel guilty if they don't have the newest gadgets and the latest styles. Every national holiday has become an orgy of consumption, with department store sales filling mall parking lots with cars.

    The United States has become a throwaway society. We're using increasing numbers of plastic containers, although they harm the environment more than glass or metal containers. For convenience, we are also using greater amounts of paper products each year. Many potentially valuable products that could be used for fertilizer are instead discarded; these include sewage sludge, garbage, agricultural and forest residues, and animal manure.

The world's richest countries, with twenty percent of the world's population, account for eighty-six percent of all private consumption expenditures. By contrast, the poorest twenty percent of the world's people spend only 1.3 percent.[42]

Due to waste, it has been estimated that the average American's impact on the earth's life support systems, in terms of pollution and resource consumption per person, is about fifty times that of a person in India or another less developed country.[43] Using this figure, the U.S. population has an impact equal to that of fourteen billion Third World people, well over twice the population of the world today.

As an example of our wastefulness, water consumption in the U.S. domestic sector (although small compared to agricultural and industrial consumption) is sizable; the average North American uses over 170 gallons per day, more than seven times the per capita average in the rest of the world and nearly triple Europe's level. By comparison, the World Health Organization says good health and cleanliness can be obtained with a total daily supply of about eight gallons of water per person.[44]

• While Judaism established a Sabbatical year in which the land is allowed to lie fallow and recover its fertility and farmers may rest, learn, and restore their spiritual values, today, under economic pressure to constantly produce more, farmers plant single crops (the same crops in the same land, with no crop rotation) and use excessive amounts of chemical pesticides and fertilizer, thereby reducing soil fertility and badly polluting air and water.

Jewish Values Can Help Solve the Environmental Crisis

Based on biblical values of "The earth is the Lord's" and *bal tashchit*, Jews and others who take religious values seriously must lead efforts to preserve the environment.[45] We must work to change the current system, which is based primarily on greed and maximization of profits and entices people to amass excessive material goods, thus causing great ecological damage. We must work for approaches that put primary emphasis on protection of our vital ecosystems.

To reduce potential threats to the U.S. and the world, we must change over to simpler, saner lifestyles. Religious institutions, schools, and private and governmental organizations must all play a role. We must reapply some of our industrial capacity toward recycling, solar energy, and mass transit. We must design products for long-term durability and ease of repair. We must revise our agricultural and industrial methods so they are less wasteful of resources and energy. Perhaps there should be a Presidential Commission appointed solely to consider how we can stop being such a wasteful society. Changing will not be easy, since our society and economy are based on consumption and convenience, using and discarding. But it is essential that we make supreme efforts. Nothing less than human survival is at stake.

The proper application of Sabbath values would help end environmental pollution. The Sabbath teaches that we should not be constantly involved in exploiting the world's resources and amassing more and more possessions. On that day each week we are to contemplate our dependence on God and our responsibility to treat the earth with care and respect. Rabbi Samson Raphael Hirsch powerfully expresses this:

> To really observe the Sabbath in our day and age! To cease for a whole day from all business, from all work, amidst the frenzied hurry-scurry of our age! [And Rabbi Hirsch was writing well over a century ago, when commerce and production were far less frenzied!] To close the stock exchanges, the stores, the factories—how would it be possible? The pulse of life would stop beating and the world perish! The world perish? On the contrary; it would be saved.[46]

The philosophy of the Sabbatical year provides yet another approach to environmental problems. There could be great benefits if land, on a rotating basis, could be left fallow, free from the chemicals and fertilizer that pollute air and water and reduce soil fertility. If people could spend a (Sabbatical) year from their usually harried lives, away from the numbing bustle of the marketplace, and from the constant pressure to produce and buy goods, they would have the opportunity to use their time for mental and spiritual development. Perhaps they might even have time to study methods of reducing pollution and other current problems.

As co-workers with God, charged with the task of being a light unto the nations and accomplishing *tikkun olam* (restoring and redeeming the earth), it is essential that Jews take an active role in struggles to end pollution and waste of natural resources. Based on the central Jewish mandate to work with God in preserving the earth, Jews must work with others for significant changes in our economic and production systems, our values, and our lifestyles.

5: ENVIRONMENTAL ISSUES IN ISRAEL

And I will bring back the captivity of My people Israel, and they shall build the wasted cities, and dwell therein; and they shall plant vineyards, and drink their wine; and they shall lay out gardens and eat their fruit. (Amos 9:14)

It took the Chosen People 2,000 years to end their exile and return to the Promised Land. It has taken them only 52 years to turn the land of milk and honey into a country of foaming rivers, carcinogenic water, and dying fish. (*Times* of London)[1]

JEWS ARE PROPERLY CONCERNED ABOUT THE WELL-BEING OF Israel and wish her to be secure and prosperous. But what about security, wealth, and comfort of another kind—the quality of Israel's air, water, and ecosystems? What about the physical condition of the eternal holy Land? While not discussed frequently enough, these and other environmental dangers and degradations have increasingly become serious issues that will affect Israel's future.

The State of Israel has accomplished amazing things in its few decades—in agriculture, education, law, social integration, technology, education, Torah study, human services, and academics. But simultaneous (and sometimes related) neglect and ruthless exploitation of its land, water, air, and resources have left Israel ecologically impoverished and endangered. Israel faces severe environmental problems. Among the contributing factors are some seemingly positive changes that most Israelis hope will continue: rapid population growth, widespread industrialization, and increased affluence, resulting in a sharp increase in the use of automobiles and other consumer goods. However, the environmental impact of these factors has been largely ignored for many years, mostly because of the need to make security the priority.

According to the Statistical Yearbook, 2000, released by the Israeli Central Bureau of Statistics, population density in Israel is among the highest in the world, with an average of 278 people per square kilometer in 1999.[2] The Tel Aviv area is the most crowded, with a density figure of 6,700 people per square kilometer.[3] Population is lowest in the South, where the population density is just sixteen people per square kilometer.[4] Jerusalem has the second highest density figures, with 1,130 people per square kilometer.[5] The Yearbook also measures growth rates among cities with populations of more than a hundred thousand. The fastest-growing city in this category is Ashdod, at 6.2 percent (annual increase), followed by Rishon Letzion at 4.6 percent.[6]

Water Shortages

Severe water shortages have become a very grave problem, potentially threatening Israel's very existence. Since the mid-1970s, demand for water has at times outstripped supply. Israel is a semi-arid country where no rain falls for at least six months of the year. While Israel was once known as a country that practiced water conservation and pioneered in the development of the drip irrigation method, the country now uses increasing amounts of water per person, often for non-essential uses. There has been a sharp increase in private pools, jacuzzis, water parks, and automatic car washes.

According to a report submitted to the Israeli Water Commission in December 2000, Israel's main water sources are expected to continue to decline, endangering drinking water quality and raising the specter of an insufficient supply.[7] According to the forecast, Israel will experience a water shortage of 90 million cubic meters in 2001, necessitating continued pumping of water from the mountain and coastal aquifers. The report indicated that the water in the two main aquifers already had reached dangerously low levels due to overpumping. The report concluded that none of the proposed methods for augmenting Israel's water supplies would solve its immediate needs.[8]

An advertisement by the Jewish National Fund (JNF) that appeared repeatedly in many publications, headlined "The day the water disappeared in Israel," states:

The day, the experts project, will come sometime in 2015. Some say it will be sooner.

On that day, there will be no more fresh water in [Israel's] cities to drink or to bathe in. No more recycled water for agriculture. Industry will cease. Wildlife will die. The wells will turn sour, the lakes will be empty, the rivers and streams gone.

And there will be no way to get them back again....

Today [Israel] is in the grip of its worst drought in recorded history. The devastating effects will be felt for years to come.[9]

A later JNF ad states that Israel's worst drought in a century has resulted in precariously low levels at Israel's main fresh water resources. One of these, Lake Kinneret (the Sea of Galilee), has reached its lowest levels in recorded history. This has led to water cuts of seventy percent for farmers and a major drop in tourism around the Kinneret, with prospects for painful future prohibitions on water use for individuals, cities, and businesses.

The JNF calls for the following "five-pronged attack": recycling water; water conservation; desalination; building a hundred new reservoirs; and drawing water from below the Negev Desert, "where there is a great deal of fossilized water."[10] Conservation efforts similar to some used in the United States could save ten to twenty percent of Israel's water.[11] A major problem is persuading the Israeli government to recognize the urgency of the situation. Getting a desalination plant built and running takes five to ten years—and the water crisis is already here.[12]

Amikim Nachmani, a Bar Ilan University Professor of political science who specializes in water issues, states, "What is happening now is a crime." When asked who is responsible, he responds, "Everybody. Those who haven't made the decisions. Those who made the wrong ones. Those who aren't willing to allocate the budgets. Those who didn't scream at the gates. Those who didn't listen."[13]

When asked to explain the situation, Meir Ben-Meir, Israel's Water Commissioner from 1977 to 1981 and again from 1996 until March, 2000 replies: "I don't know. How do you explain the fact that mass transportation has never been developed in this country, or that the public health system is collapsing, or that the traffic bottlenecks in Tel Aviv are not being dealt with? It's the same thing."[14]

Haim Gvirtzman, a Hebrew College hydrologist, gives a simple explanation: "No one cares. Everyone cares about politics, about peace, about making money. Who cares about things like health, the environment, or water?"[15] Unfortunately, the pattern of shortsightedness also applies to many of Israel's other severe environmental problems.

Water Pollution
Most of Israel's streams and rivers are seriously polluted, generally much more polluted than rivers in North America and Western Europe.[16] Only the rivers in the Golan Heights and Ein Gedi, where the number of people per unit area is still relatively small, can be considered clean.[17] Israel is ten to twenty years behind the United States in caring for its rivers.[18]

The horrible state of Israel's water is indicated by the fact that more than a dozen former commandos in an elite Israeli naval unit are filing suit against the government for endangering their health by requiring them to swim and dive in the horrendously polluted Kishon River as part of their training.[19] More than thirty of these naval commandos have been stricken with cancer and at least ten have died.[20]

Dr. Elihu Richter, an environmental health expert at Hebrew University's Hadassah School of Public Health in Jerusalem, says the warning signs about the Kishon's toxicity have been clear:

> The damage has been measured over the years in other [non-human] species. We've seen gross organ pathology ... and DNA breaks in the fish and mollusks of the river. DNA breaks are a sign of mutation and are indicative of cancer.[21]

The Kishon River has been especially hard hit because, for over forty years, Haifa Bay's chemical industry has discharged its raw industrial wastes directly into it. In 1994, tests of the river's waters by the Israeli Union for Environmental Defense (IUED, also known as *Adam, Teva, v'Din* [Humans, Nature, and Justice]) showed a startling mixture of pollutants, indicating massive non-compliance with pollution laws by major chemical factories. Recently IUED won two court cases against major polluters in Haifa. Hopefully, this will lead to a decrease in the dumping of industrial wastes.

Most of the rivers in Israel are now so badly polluted that fish can live in them for only a few minutes.[22] Already, admits Dalia Itzik, the country's Environmental Minister in 2000, forty percent of water piped to Israeli and Palestinian homes is "undrinkable."[23] Some scientists have already warned that carcinogens are turning up in tap water. "The situation is catastrophic," says Itzik. "We simply do not have enough water to meet the needs of the population."[24]

The Kishon's toxicity was demonstrated in a test performed by an Israeli TV station. A jar of the river's water was mixed with three liters of fresh water. Three varieties of fish were then put into the jar; every one of them died in less than three minutes.[25] According to Greenpeace and the University of Exeter, the Kishon River is a poisonous brew of heavy metals and other carcinogens.[26]

While the Kishon is probably the most polluted river in Israel, a fall into the Yarkon River, which runs through Tel Aviv, can also be fatal. In 1997, four Australian athletes, who were in Israel to participate in the Maccabiah games, died when a bridge over the Yarkon collapsed into the toxic soup that runs through what is known as "Israel's Central Park." Two died from their injuries, while two more perished after swallowing and inhaling the contaminated water.

According to a study by the Hydrologic Service of Israel's Water Commissioner's Office and the Institute of Soil, Water and Environmental Science, the pollution of ground water in the Tel Aviv-Givatayim-Ramat Gan area has reached alarming levels, damaging potable water and spreading into underground structures, such as parking lots.[27] Environment Ministry officials and other experts say that if urgent measures are not taken to contain it, the pollution may spread to the coastal aquifer, one of Israel's three main water sources.[28]

Air Pollution

Israel's major cities, Jerusalem, Tel Aviv, and Haifa, as well as industrial centers like Ashdod, face severe air pollution problems, primarily from industrial and automobile emissions. There were three hundred occasions of violations of air pollution standards in Tel Aviv alone in 1996. An epidemiological study has shown that children in some Tel Aviv neighborhoods have a greater probability of suffering from respiratory problems, including asthma, than their peers elsewhere.[29] Air pollution in Tel Aviv is so severe that planners are considering closing the city to traffic on days when climatic conditions make the pollution threat particularly severe.[30]

Professor Menachem Luria, Chair of Hebrew University's Environmental Science Department, has stated that if current trends continue, some aspects of the air quality in Jerusalem could be as bad as those in the much larger Mexico City by 2010.[31] A recent symposium sponsored by IUED was titled, "Don't Take a Breath—Urban Air Pollution."[32]

While many air pollutants have been increasing sharply, there has been a decrease in sulfur oxide emissions due to a shift to low-sulfur coal, and in lead emissions due to a reduction of the lead content of gasoline. However, the continued sharp increase in vehicle density constitutes an ever-growing threat to Israel's air quality.

Solid Waste

Israel faces a solid waste crisis due to increasing amounts of garbage and the country's meager land resources. Many garbage disposal sites are poorly designed and managed. Many are also at or near their full capacity. Yet over ninety percent of Israel's solid waste is still buried in landfills, left to rot in garbage dumps, or burned in open air pits throughout the country.[33] Less than five percent of the country's garbage is recycled. In 2000, then-Environmental Minister Dalia Itzik stated that she regarded garbage disposal as Israel's number one environmental problem.[34]

Even at the domestic level, there is little or no thought for the polluting effects of garbage disposal. Partly due to the lack of recycling programs and facilities, householders usually throw plastic, glass, aluminum, paper, and general waste into the same bin without a second thought. Paper recycling companies charge for collection, and insist on collecting white paper only.

There has been recent legislation requiring a major increase in recycling, but stricter enforcement is required. Also, many older, inefficient landfills are being closed and new, more environmentally sound landfills are being opened.

Open Space

Another serious environmental problem is the loss of open space and recreational areas. A recent nationwide demographic and developmental study prepared for the government concluded that some sixty percent of the Galilee would be under asphalt in less than twenty-five years, compared to only twelve percent today.[35] Municipal and industrial development has encroached on the borders of the Jerusalem Forest, the largest planted forest in Israel and one of the last green areas around Jerusalem.[36]

The loss of open space is not only an aesthetic issue. When open land is converted into concrete and asphalt, there is a loss of flood control plains, fertile agricultural land, natural habitats for other species, and areas for recreation and tourism. Also, because development causes a reduction in the amount of water that seeps back into the ground and recharges underground water sources, future water supplies are being sacrificed at a time when additional water is needed for a growing population.

Transportation

Israel's roads have become very congested due to the rapid increase in motor vehicles. There was a hundredfold increase in private cars from 1950 to 1995. At current rates, the number of cars will double every ten years.[37] Relative to the population, which has also been increasing sharply, the number of private cars grew from six per thousand inhabitants in 1951 to 198 per thousand in 1995, and this ratio doubles every twenty years.[38] This is occurring even though Israel has a very extensive bus system.

The very rapid increase in cars and other motor vehicles has resulted in major pollution and congestion problems and loss of open space. Because there has been inadequate planning of alternate forms of transportation, these problems are expected to worsen. Many studies have shown that building more roads is, at best, only a temporary solution, because traffic soon expands to again fill the roads. Only a comprehensive redesign of Israel's transportation system, with a far greater emphasis on public and non-motorized transportation, can help relieve current pollution and congestion problems.[39]

The Trans-Israel Highway

Many environmental problems in Israel today will be much exacerbated by the construction over the next few years of the Trans-Israel Highway, a six-lane major artery whose planned route traverses the country north to south, from the Lebanon border to the Negev desert. The initial section of the road, in the center of the country, is scheduled to be completed in 2002; additional sections are to open in 2004 or later. The highway's critics, reports the *Jerusalem Post*, "including environmentalists, public transport advocates, and traffic safety experts, view Israel's first super-highway as the most disastrous public works project ever conceived in the nation's history."[40] Among the reasons such groups as the Israel Union for Environmental Defense, the Society for the Protection of Nature in Israel, and the Committee for Public Transportation have been fighting against the highway are:

- It will make it more difficult to establish an integrated, balanced national transportation system: one which would place greater emphasis on rail and other forms of public transportation.
- Israel already has a very high number of private automobiles per square kilometer, and the highway will make this situation even worse by encouraging increased use of cars instead of other, more sustainable and less destructive means of transportation.
- It will significantly aggravate the already severe air pollution around major cities.
- The highway will permanently contaminate the Mountain Aquifer, which supplies water to one-third of the country, with oil, gas, and other carcinogenic runoffs.
- The death rate from automobile accidents, already very high, will be increased by the high speed limit on the highway, by the tendency of

drivers to exceed the speed limit on this wide-open road, and by the carryover of that habit of speeding onto other, narrower roads.

- Since the Israeli government budget and its taxpayers are legally committed to paying compensation to the consortium of corporations that is building the road for any shortfall in income from the planned tolls, citizens and the government could be on the hook for hundreds of millions of dollars each year.
- Israel's balance of payments deficit will worsen as increased reliance on automobiles leads to more outlays for buying cars (all of which are imported), spare parts, and fuel.
- There will be an increase in the suburbanization of the country, leading to urban deterioration in Jerusalem, Tel Aviv, and other cities. In the long run (as other countries have learned), the highway will draw more cars and end up producing greater traffic jams.
- Noise pollution and visual blight on the countryside will increase.
- The highway will aggravate social divisions in Israel: it will benefit mostly those who can afford autos and tolls, while geographically isolating the poor and dumping financial costs and increased pollution onto them. Also, since the planned route traverses Arab villages and cuts into their farmland, it will worsen the legitimate grievances of Israel's Arab citizens.
- Transportation Minister Ephraim Sneh, a highway supporter, acknowledges that it will "be a blight on Israel's few remaining open spaces."[41] In the central region of the country, where land reserves are few and the population density is high, the highway will pave over much of the remaining green space. This is especially true because the plan includes numerous access roads and interchanges, which will be flanked by strip malls and other construction. The anticipated profits from these businesses, and the vested interest of those who expect to reap them, are one of the reasons it has been so difficult to prevent this ecological disaster from happening.

Is it still possible to block this insane project? Perhaps some parts of it. At least fifty members of Knesset, from right to left, who want to preserve the Land for future generations, have called for a moratorium on construction until further study can be done. But the financial incentives for those who anticipate benefiting, as well as misguided ideas about progress and easier travel, may impose this legacy of pavement and pollution onto the face of Israel for many years to come.

In summary, Israel is on the edge of an environmental catastrophe that may not only destroy the livelihoods of thousands of its people, but also threaten the viability of the state.

Israeli Responses to the Environmental Crisis

There have been indications of greatly expanded Israeli concern about the environment. In December 1988, a breakthrough occurred when the Ministry of the Environment was established to replace the former Environmental Protection Service, and to assume many additional responsibilities. Since 1988, the scope of the ministry's jurisdiction has been expanded, and it has devoted energy and expertise to environmental management.

Israel has been taking steps to give greater priority to its environmental problems. There was a "Year of the Environment" in 5754 (September 1993–August 1994), with activities devoted to increasing the public's environmental awareness. Among the many nationwide projects were a bottle disposal campaign, the institution of eco-labeling on environmentally-friendly products, and various clean-up and recycling campaigns. The government also sponsored an information campaign involving all government ministries, every municipality, numerous public organizations, the private sector, and the entire educational system in a unique and unprecedented environmental partnership. The Israeli Ministry of Education adopted the environment as the central theme for the curriculum during that year.

Many new laws have been passed to reduce pollution and other environmental problems. However, a great deal more needs to be done, and existing laws must be enforced more strictly.

The IUED, Society for the Protection of Nature in Israel (SPNI), the Committee for Public Transportation, Green Trend, the A. J. Heschel Center, Neot Kedumim, and other Israeli environmental groups are increasing their efforts to raise the public's environmental awareness through hikes, lectures, and other educational activities. The IUED seeks to reduce pollution by promoting new legislation and taking polluters to court. (For further information about Israeli environmental groups and publications, see Appendix C and Appendix E.)

As discussed in the previous chapter, Jewish teachings carry a powerful ecological message. It is essential that these teachings be applied now to reduce the many threats to Israel's environment and, indeed, its survival.

6: HUNGER

Is not this the fast that I have chosen? To loose the chains of wickedness, to undo the bonds of oppression, and to let the crushed go free....Is it not to share your bread with the hungry? (Isaiah 58:6–7)

ON YOM KIPPUR, THE HOLIEST DAY OF THE JEWISH YEAR, Jews fast and pray for forgiveness, a favorable judgment, and a good year. On this same day, they are told, through the words of the prophet Isaiah, that fasting, confession of sins, and prayers are not sufficient; people must also work to end oppression and provide food for the needy.

Helping the hungry is fundamental in Judaism. The Talmud states, "Providing charity for poor and hungry people is as important as all the other commandments of the Torah combined."[1] The Midrash teaches:

> God says to Israel, "My children, whenever you give sustenance to the poor, I impute it to you as though you gave sustenance to Me...." Does then God eat and drink? No, but whenever you give food to the poor, God accounts it to you as if you gave food to Him.[2]

On Passover we are reminded not to forget the poor. Besides providing *ma'ot chittim* (funds for purchasing *matzah* and other holiday necessities) for the needy before Passover, we reach out to them during the *Seder* meal:

> This is the bread of affliction, which our ancestors ate in the land of Egypt. Let all who are hungry come and eat. Let all who are in need come and celebrate the Passover.[3]

We are even admonished to feed our enemies if they are in need:

> If your enemy is hungry, give him bread to eat.
> If your enemy is thirsty, give him water to drink. (Proverbs 25:21)

This is consistent with the rabbinic teaching that the greatest hero is a person who converts an enemy into a friend.[4]

World Hunger Today

The magnitude of world hunger is staggering: more than a billion people, over one out of six people in the world, are chronically hungry.[5] The Food and Agricultural Organization (FAO) estimates that twenty-one percent of India's population is chronically undernourished, but the situation may be far worse. Recent on-the-ground surveys indicate that forty-nine percent of adults and fifty-three percent of children in India are under-weight, which is a proxy measurement for hunger.[6] Hunger is found in the wealthier countries as well. The U.S. Department of Agriculture estimated that in 1998, some ten percent of U.S. households were hungry, on the edge of being hungry, or threatened by hunger.[7]

Children are particularly victimized by malnutrition. Throughout the world, over twelve million children under the age of five die every year –about 34,000 each day—from diseases brought on or complicated by malnutrition.[8] Each year, almost eight million children die before their first birthday, largely due to malnutrition.[9] Malnourishment also causes listlessness and reduced capacity for learning and work, thus perpetuating the legacy of poverty.

Jeremy Rifkin summarizes the anomaly of rich people dieting and poor people starving:

> While millions of Americans anguish over excess pounds, spending time, money, and emotional energy on slimming down, children in other lands are wasting away, their physical growth irreversibly stunted, their bodies racked by parasitic and opportunistic diseases, their brain growth diminished by lack of nutrients in their meager diets.[10]

Extensive hunger and malnutrition in so many parts of the world make rebellion and violence more likely. Professor Georg Borgstrom, international expert on food science, fears that "the rich world is on a direct collision course with the poor of the world....We cannot survive behind our Maginot line of missiles and bombs."[11] Unless the problem of global hunger is fully addressed soon, the outlook for global stability is very poor. Professor Robert Heilbroner, a noted economist, predicted that, in times of severe famine, countries like India would be sorely tempted to try nuclear blackmail.[12]

Prospects for reducing hunger are uncertain. In his book, *Tough Choices—Facing the Challenge of Food Scarcity*,[13] Lester R. Brown, former Director of the Worldwatch Institute, states that numerous factors, including rapidly increasing world population and affluence, environmental strains, climate changes, and significant decreases in clean water, arable land, fish catches, and land productivity, all threaten the world's food security. Worldwatch believes that providing enough food for the world's rapidly increasing population will be a critical issue for many decades.

Misconceptions About the Causes of World Hunger

There are many misconceptions about the causes of global hunger. Hunger is not caused primarily by overpopulation, bad weather, lack of technology, or the ignorance of people in poor countries.[14] These can all worsen the problem, but they do not cause it.

Population has been growing explosively in recent years. While it took until 1830 for the world's population to reach one billion people, in 1999 the population reached six billion and was projected to double in the next half century.[15] Yet population, while a very serious concern that must be addressed, is not a root cause of world hunger. Africa is relatively sparsely populated but still has much hunger. Japan and many European countries, such as Belgium and Holland, are very densely populated but have relatively few hungry people.

Rather than being a cause of hunger, rapid population growth is more often a result of hunger. When infant mortality is high, due to malnutrition and disease, couples will have many children so that some will survive. In societies where there are no unemployment insurance or pension programs, children, especially males, provide the only assurance that there will be help when the parents become disabled or too old to work. Rapid population growth and hunger are common in societies where land ownership, jobs, education, health care, and old age security are beyond the reach of most people.[16] In these very poor, hungry countries, the cost of raising a child is very low, but the economic value of the child providing financial assistance to the family, especially when the parents become too old to work, is great. Given these conditions, the answer to the population problem is not only better family planning techniques, but also an improvement of the people's economic and social conditions. Third World societies that have experienced rapid reductions of population growth rates—China, Sri Lanka, Colombia, Cuba and the Indian state of Kerala— clearly demonstrate that the lives of the poor, especially poor women, must improve before they will choose to have fewer children.[17]

Hunger is not due to insufficient food production. Research at the Institute for Food and Development in California has shown that the world produces enough grain alone to provide every person with 3,500 calories a day, enough to make most people gain weight.[18] (Over one-third of the world's grain is currently fed to animals destined for slaughter.) The 3,500-calorie estimate does not even include the fruits, vegetables, nuts, root crops, dairy products, and non-grain-fed meat that are produced around the world. If all foods are considered, the world provides an average of at least 4.3 pounds per person per day.[19] The problem is that many people lack the income to buy the available food. Even most "hungry countries" currently have sufficient food for all their people. Many are net exporters of food and other agricultural products.[20]

Hunger is also not primarily a result of bad weather. No matter how bad the weather, the wealthy in any country always manage to eat well. In a book published in 1928, it was reported that China had a famine in some provinces every year for over a thousand years.[21] Today China has an agricultural system that is much less vulnerable to weather changes. They have utilized their massive labor power to sink hundreds of wells, build reservoirs, and dam rivers to insure an adequate supply of water.

In the autumn of 1974, Bangladesh had one of the worse famines of modern times, with a hundred thousand lives lost. Though the government claimed that it was due to harvest-destroying floods, workers on the scene observed that there was adequate food, but that wealthy farmers were hoarding rice to maintain high prices.[22]

It is relatively easy to blame nature, but in fact food is readily available for people who can afford it—only the poorest face starvation during hard times. However, human-made forces are making people increasingly vulnerable to nature's vagaries.[23] Millions live on the brink of disaster in Africa, south Asia, and elsewhere, because they are inadequately paid for their labor, trapped in debt, or deprived of land by a powerful few. Natural events rarely explain deaths by starvation; they are generally the final push over the brink. Famine is primarily caused by social, political, and economic conditions, not nature.

What about lack of technology as a cause of global hunger? In many cases, new technology has made the situation worse, because it has not been combined with necessary social and economic changes.

New "miracle" seeds (the "Green Revolution") were proposed as an answer to inadequate food production. But these seeds require good land, proper irrigation, and heavy doses of fertilizer and pesticides. Only wealthy farmers with large farms can afford these. Also, increased production of grain lowers the price of food and drives many small farmers off the land when they can't compete.

Mechanization, so widely used on American farms, can also have negative effects. It forces many farm workers off the land and into increasingly crowded cities, seeking employment which often is not available.

The additional food produced by improved technology seldom goes to hungry people. It generally goes to wealthier people for luxury food products, animal feed, or as exports to more affluent countries.

Thanks to the technological advances of the Green Revolution, millions of tons of additional grain are being harvested annually. But focusing narrowly on increased production cannot reduce hunger, because it fails to alter the tightly concentrated distribution of economic power that determines who can buy the additional food. In several countries with the biggest Green Revolution successes—India, Mexico, and the Philippines— grain production and, in some cases, exports, have climbed, while hunger persists and the long-term productive capacity of the soil is degraded.[24]

The key question with regard to technology is: who stands to gain? If technology is used to benefit small local elites while driving many people off farms, it worsens the hunger situation. If it is used cooperatively, in conjunction with a country's vast labor power and local planning and initiative, so that individual peasants benefit directly from their added productivity, it can be of great value.

Is the ignorance of small farmers in poor countries a major cause of widespread hunger? On the contrary, small peasant farmers get much out of their land, working their very limited resources to the fullest, because it is all they have for survival. The problems of the poor are not due to backwardness. They just have very little to work with, since ownership of land and wealth is concentrated in very few hands.

Causes of World Hunger

What, then, are the root causes of global hunger? A significant part of the answer lies in a system of production and distribution that is rooted in inequality, injustice, and greed, and is at sharp variance with Torah values.[25] In a policy statement issued on October 11, 1975, the National Council of Churches (NCC) stated that the fundamental cause of world hunger was "the sinful behavior of humankind, including the denial of human solidarity; greed; and selfishness with which neighbor exploits neighbor." The NCC further noted: "Institutionalized injustice explains more than all other factors combined why half a billion persons [as of 2000, it is more than a billion people] suffer from chronic hunger in a world which could have enough food to go around."

There is great poverty and hunger in less developed countries because the social and economic inequalities prevalent in these countries prevent people from making an adequate living. Land and wealth are concentrated among a few, and with land and wealth goes power to control the destiny of the masses. Control of land, and of the things needed to make the land produce—seeds, tools, machinery, fertilizer, pesticides, and irrigation systems—are in relatively few hands.

According to *World Hunger: Twelve Myths* by Frances Moore Lappé and others (see Bibliography), powerful misconceptions block understanding of the true causes of hunger and thus prevent effective action.

"The true source of world hunger is not scarcity but policy; not inevitability but politics," according to Dr. Peter Rosset, Executive Director of Food First and co-author of *World Hunger*. "The real culprits are economies that fail to offer everyone opportunities and societies that place economic efficiency over compassion."[26]

Colonialism changed patterns of food production in many countries. The nineteenth-century English political economist John Stuart Mill stated that colonies should not be thought of as countries at all, but as "agricultural establishments" whose sole purpose was to supply the "large community to which they belong."[27] Using raw force and high taxes, Europeans changed the diversified agriculture of their colonies to single cash crops, often at the exclusion of staple foods. The best land was taken over to produce tea, coffee, bananas, and other crops that could be exported to enrich foreigners and local elites, at the expense of the native population. This process sowed the seeds of famine.

While the colonial period is over, its legacy remains in the form of neocolonialism. Less developed countries must still produce cash crops in order to meet their debts and to obtain badly needed money.[28] As a result, these countries are on a treadmill. They must work harder and harder just to maintain their inadequate economic conditions. They are prevented from developing their own resources for their own use, and conditions of trade are against them.

Another factor that greatly worsens the global food situation is the wastefulness of affluent countries, such as the United States. The American diet is extremely wasteful. As discussed in more detail in Chapter 12, we consume about five times as much grain per person (mostly by eating meat from grain-fed animals) as the average person in poorer countries. It takes up to sixteen pounds of grain to produce one pound of edible beef in a feedlot. Half of U.S. farm acreage is used to produce feed crops for livestock. Animal-centered diets require up to twenty-one times the land area per person that would be required for a vegan diet. Modern intensive livestock agriculture also requires tremendous amounts of chemical fertilizer and pesticides, irrigation water, and fuel, commodities which are becoming very scarce worldwide.

In view of these negative effects of animal-based agriculture, it is scandalous that U.S. meat conglomerates, aided by the World Bank and other international financial institutions, are promoting food policies and trade agreements that would double world production and consumption of meat and other animal food products in the next twenty years.[29] Most of this expansion would take place in less developed nations, through massive factory farming operations similar to these currently being used in the developed world. This would have very severe consequences for the poor countries and worldwide: more hunger, more poverty, more pollution, more animal suffering, less self-determination for the people in low-income nations, and less water for everyone. To help combat the expansion of western intensive animal-based agriculture into developing nations, the Farm Animal Reform Movement (FARM) has launched a "Global Hunger Alliance," which aims to convince the Food and Agricultural Organization (FAO) and the World Food Conference in Rome to promote plant-based diets as a solution to the scandal of widespread world hunger.[30] They are circulating a petition that they hope will help increase pressure on food-related groups and conference delegates.

In summary, millions of people are hungry today, not because of insufficient agricultural capacity, but because of unjust social systems and wasteful methods of food production, including the feeding of tremendous amounts of grain to animals to fatten them for slaughter and consumption by meat-eating societies.

Jewish Responses to Hunger

1. Involvement

Judaism teaches involvement and concern with the plight of fellow human beings. Every life is sacred, and we are obligated to do what we can to help others. The Torah states, "You shall not stand idly by the blood of your neighbor" (Leviticus 19:16).

Jews rightfully condemn the silence of the world when six million Jews and millions of other people were murdered by the Nazis. Can we be silent when millions die agonizing deaths because of lack of food? Can we acquiesce to the apathy of the world toward the fate of starving people?

Elie Wiesel has pointed out that there can be no analogies to the Holocaust, but that it can be used as a reference. In that context, we can consider the almost eight million infants who die each year due to malnutrition and the six million Jews who were slaughtered by the Nazis. True, victims of hunger are not being singled out because of their religion, race, or nationality, but, as did Holocaust victims, they die while the world goes about its business, grumbling about personal inconveniences, indifferent to the plight of the starving people. Since the Mishnah teaches that if one saves a single human life, it is as if one has saved an entire world (*Sanhedrin* 4:5), what then if one fails to save a single life? Or twenty million?

The Hebrew prophets berate those who are content and comfortable while others are in great distress:

Tremble you women, who are at ease,
Shudder you complacent ones;
Strip and make yourselves bare,
Gird sackcloth upon your loins. (Isaiah 32:11)

Woe to those who are at ease in Zion...
Woe to those who lie upon beds of ivory
And stretch themselves upon their couches...
Who drink wine from bowls
And anoint themselves with the finest oils
But are not grieved at the ruin of Joseph. (Amos 6:1,4,6)

Like other peoples, Jews have frequently experienced hunger. Because of famines, Abraham was forced to go to Egypt (Genesis 12:10), Isaac went to the land of Abimelech, king of the Philistines, in Gerar (Genesis 26:1), the children of Jacob went to Egypt to buy grain (Genesis 42:1–3), and Naomi and her family fled Israel and went to Moab (Ruth 1:1–2). There were also famines in the reigns of King David (2 Samuel 21:1) and King Ahab (1 Kings 18:1–2).

Jews know the agony of great hunger. The Prophet Jeremiah, referring to the time of the destruction of Jerusalem, proclaims "Happier were the victims of the sword than the victims of hunger, who pined away, stricken by want of the yield of the field" (Lamentations 4:9).

Based on Jewish values and Jewish history, we must empathize with the starving millions of the world. We must be involved by speaking out and working in support of more just, environmentally sustainable agricultural policies. Some traditional Jewish ways to help needy people are to pursue justice, practice charity, show compassion, share resources, and simplify lifestyles.

2. Sharing

Feeling compassion for the poor and hungry is not enough. A fundamental Jewish principle is that those who have much should share with others who are less fortunate. The Talmudic sage Hillel stresses that we must not be concerned only with our own welfare: "If I am not for myself, who will be for me? But if I am for myself alone, what am I?"[31] Indeed, the Haggadah read at Passover *Seders* exhorts us to welcome and share with all who are hungry and in need. The act of prolonging one's meal, on the chance that a poor person may come so that one may give him or her food, is so meritorious that the table of the person who does this is compared to the altar of the ancient Temple.[32]

Judaism's great emphasis on sharing is also illustrated in the following Chassidic tale:

> The story is told of a great rabbi who was given the privilege of seeing the realms of Heaven and Hell before his death. He was taken first to Hell, where he was confronted with a huge banquet room in the middle of which was a large elegant table covered with a magnificent tablecloth and the finest china, silver, and crystal. The table was covered from one end to the other with the most delicious foods that the eyes have ever seen or the mouth tasted. And all around the table, people were sitting looking at the food... and wailing.
>
> It was such a wail that the rabbi had never heard such a sad sound in his entire life and he asked, "With a luxurious table and the most delicious food, why do these people wail so bitterly?" As

he entered the room, he saw the reason for their distress. For although each was confronted with this incredible sight before him, no one was able to eat the food. Each person's arms were splinted so that the elbows could not bend. They could touch the food but could not eat it. The anguish this caused was the reason for the great wail and despair that the rabbi saw and heard.

He was next shown Heaven, and to his surprise he observed the identical scene witnessed in Hell: The large banquet room, elegant table, lavish settings, and sumptuous foods. And, in addition, once again everyone's arms were splinted so the elbows could not bend. Here, however, there was no wailing, but rather joy greater than he had ever experienced in his life. For whereas here too the people could not put the food into their own mouths, each picked up the food and fed it to another. They were thus able to enjoy not only the beautiful scene, the wonderful smells, and the delicious foods, but also the joy of sharing and helping one another.[33]

Rabbi Jay Marcus, former longtime spiritual leader of the Young Israel of Staten Island, comments on the fact that *karpas* (eating of greens) and *yahatz* (breaking of the middle *matzah* for later use as the dessert) are next to each other in the order of the Passover *Seder* service.[34] He suggests that those who can live on simple things like greens (vegetables, etc.) will more readily divide their possessions and share with others.

To help share God's abundant harvests with the poor, the Torah instructed farmers:

1) A corner of the field always had to be left unharvested; it was the property of the poor (*Pe'ah*). (Leviticus 19; 9–10)

2) If less than three ears of corn were dropped during the harvest, they were not to be gleaned, but were to be left for the poor (*Leket*). (Leviticus 19; 9–10)

3) A sheaf forgotten by the farmer could not be retrieved but had to be left for the poor (*Shik'khah*). (Deuteronomy 24: 19–21)

4) Every third year a part of the tithe of the harvest had to be set aside for the poor (*Ma'aser Ani*).

5) On the eve of every holy day, *mat'not yad*, a special gift to the poor, had to be put aside.

As discussed in Chapter 12, vegetarianism is consistent with this Jewish concept of sharing. As Jay Dinshah, late long-time President of the American Vegan Society, stated:

> After all, vegetarianism is, more than anything else, the very essence and the very expression of altruistic SHARING ... the sharing of the One Life ... the sharing of the natural resources of the Earth ... the sharing of love, kindness, compassion, and beauty in this life.[35]

The Los Angeles-based Jewish organization Mazon attempts to help Jews share their joyous events with hungry people. It urges people to contribute three percent of the money spent for weddings, bar mitzvahs, and other celebrations to the group, which funnels the money to organizations working to reduce hunger. For contact information, see Appendix C.

3. Simplifying Lifestyles

Because millions lack sufficient food, it is imperative that those of us who have so much simplify our lives so that we can share more with others. A group of major religious leaders, including representatives of several branches of Judaism in the United States and Israel, met in Bellagio, Italy, in May 1975 to consider "The Energy/Food Crisis: A Challenge to Peace, a Call to Faith." They agreed on a statement that included this assertion:

> The deepest and strongest expression of any religion is the "styles of life" that characterizes its believers. It is urgent that religious communities and individuals scrutinize their lifestyle and turn from habits of waste, overconsumption, and thoughtless acceptance of the standards propagated by advertisements and social pressures.

The cry from millions for food brought us together from many faiths. God—Reality itself—calls us to respond to the cry for food. And we hear it as a cry not only for aid but also for justice.[36]

Simpler lifestyles, including less wasteful diets, can be an important first step toward justice for the hungry of the world. Simpler diets do not mean a lack of joy or a lack of fellowship. As Proverbs 15:17 states, "Better a dinner of herbs where love is present than a stalled ox with hatred."

During the Middle Ages, local Jewish councils often established "sumptuary laws" for the community. People were forbidden to spend more than a specified amount of money for weddings and other occasions. These laws were designed so that the poor should not be embarrassed for being unable to match the expenditures of the wealthy and so that a financial strain was not placed on the community as a whole. Perhaps the spirit of such laws should be invoked today. Can we continue to consume flesh that requires so much grain to be fed to animals at a time when millions of people are starving? Is it not now time for officiating rabbis to specify guidelines to reduce waste and ostentation at weddings, bar mitzvahs, and other occasions? (Several Chassidic Rebbes have established limits on expenses and on the number of guests at weddings and other religious celebrations within their communities.)

It is a fundamental Jewish belief that God provides enough for every person's needs. In our daily prayers, it is said: "He opens His hand and provided sustenance to all living things" (Psalms 145:16). Jews are mandated to give thanks to God for providing enough food for everyone. In the *Birkat Hamazon* (Grace After Meals), we praise God "Who feeds the entire world with goodness, grace, loving kindness and compassion." The blessing is, of course, correct. God has provided enough for all. The bounties of nature, fairly distributed and properly consumed, would sustain all people.

The means are available for each person to have an adequate diet. Every nation could be self-sufficient in producing food. The conditions of inequality and injustice that are causing widespread hunger are outrageous and must be changed. As the Indian independence leader Mahatma Gandhi stated: "There is enough for the world's need, but not for its greed."

With so much hunger, poverty, and injustice in the world, explicit Jewish mandates to feed the hungry, help the poor, share resources, practice charity, show compassion, and pursue justice, along with the remembrance of the suffering and deprivation experienced throughout Jewish history, should provide the impetus for Jews to be in the forefront of efforts to create food production and distribution systems that will sharply reduce world hunger.

7 : PEACE

"Not by might, not by power, but by my spirit," says the Lord of Hosts.
(Zechariah 4:6)

JUDAISM DESCRIBES A SPECIAL OBLIGATION TO STRIVE FOR peace, and the tradition commands that people actively pursue peace. The Midrash states that there are many commandments that require a certain time and place for their performance, but with regard to the mandate to "seek peace and pursue it" (Psalms 34:15), we are to seek it in our own place and pursue it everywhere else.[1] The famous Talmudic sage Hillel states that we should "be of the disciples of Aaron, loving peace and pursuing peace."[2] Concerning the special duty of Jews to work for peace, the sages comment: "The Holy one, blessed be He, said: 'The whole Torah is peace. And to whom do I give it? To the nation which loves peace!' "[3]

The Midrash employs lavish words in praise of peace:

Great is peace, for God's name is peace....Great is peace, for it encompasses all blessings....Great is peace, for even in times of war, peace must be sought....Great is peace, for when the Messiah comes, he will commence with peace, as it is said, "How beautiful upon the mountains are the feet of the messenger of good tidings, who announces peace" (Isaiah. 52:7).[4]

Great is peace, for with peace the Holy One, Blessed be He, will announce the Redemption of Israel, and with peace He will console Jerusalem.[5]

See how beloved is peace; when the Holy One, Blessed be He, wished to bless Israel, He could not find a vessel great enough to contain their blessings, except for peace.[6]

The whole Torah was given for the sake of peace, and it is said, "all her paths are peace" (Proverbs 3:17).[7]

It is significant that many of the most important Jewish prayers conclude with a supplication for peace. These include the *Amidah* (silent prayer—also known as the *Shmoneh Esrei*—which is recited three times daily), the *Kaddish*, the Grace after Meals, and the Priestly Blessing.

In spite of Judaism's adamant opposition to idolatry, peace is so important that the rabbis taught:

Great is peace, for even if the Jews were to practice idolatry, and peace prevailed among them at the same time, God would say, "I cannot punish them because peace prevails among them."[8]

Judaism emphasizes the pursuit of justice and harmonious relations between nations to reduce violence and the prospects of war. The Prophet Isaiah proclaims:

And the work of righteousness shall be peace; And the effect of righteousness, quietness and confidence forever. (Isaiah 32:17)

Yet there are many sections in the Hebrew Scriptures which justify war under certain conditions and discuss rules for combat. War was universally accepted (and still is) as inevitable and therefore a legitimate foreign policy instrument. God commanded the Israelites to conquer the land of Canaan through warfare and to destroy or evict the inhabitants. After the Exodus from Egypt, God is joyfully praised as a "Man of War" (Exodus 15:3). The Israelites are told: "For the Lord, your God, is He Who goes with you. To fight against your enemies, to save you" (Deuteronomy 20:4). The books of Judges, Samuel, and Kings report many armed battles, some involving widespread destruction.

However, the general tone of Jewish tradition shudders at war and its instruments. God is often pictured as ultimately despising war and intending its elimination: "And I will break the bow and the sword and the battle out of the land, and will make them to lie down safely" (Hosea 2:20). "He [God] makes wars to cease unto the end of the earth; He breaks the bow, and cuts the spear in sunder; He burns the chariot in the fire" (Psalms 46:10).

The Talmudic sages forbade the use of instruments of war for ornamentation or anything connected with sacred services. Concerning the Sabbath laws, the Mishnah states:

> [On the Sabbath] a man may not go out with a sword, a bow, a shield, a club, or a spear; and if he goes out [with such as these] he is liable to a sin offering. Rabbi Eliezer says, "They are merely decorations." But the sages say, "They are nothing but shameful."[9]

The Talmud regards the sword as the opposite of the Torah: "If the sword is here, there cannot be the book; if the book is here, there cannot be the sword."[10] To the Talmud, the true hero is not the person with many conquests:

> One who conquers his impulses, it is as if he conquered a city of heroes....For the true heroes are the masters of Torah, as it is said, "mighty in power are those who obey God's Word."[11]

The Talmudic sages teach: "Who is mighty? One who controls his passions,"[12] and it is said: "Better is the long-suffering than the mighty..." (Proverbs 16:32).

The Torah forbids the use of metal tools in the construction of the Holy Altar. "And if you make Me an altar of stone, you shall not build it of hewn stones; for if you lift up your sword upon it, you have profaned it" (Exodus 20:22). Consistent with their abhorrence of war, the sages comment on this verse as follows:

Iron shortens life, while the altar prolongs it. The sword, or weapons of iron, is the symbol of strife, while the altar is the symbol of reconciliation and peace between God and man, and between man and his fellow.[13]

Because of his many violent battles, King David was denied the opportunity to build the Temple. He was told:

You have shed blood abundantly, and you have made great wars. You shall not build a house unto My name, because you have shed much blood upon the earth in My sight. Behold, a son shall be born to you who shall be a man of peace; and I will give him rest from all his enemies round about, for his name shall be Solomon (peaceful), and I shall give peace and quiet to Israel in his days. He shall build a house for My name.[14]

Despite the great yearning throughout the Jewish tradition for peace, Jews have had to fight wars throughout history, up to our own day. The prophets realized the horrible results of battle. The following words of Jeremiah, written over two thousand years ago concerning the conquest and despoiling of Jerusalem, could have been written about the aftermath of a modern war:

My innards, my innards! I writhe in pain!
The chambers of my heart!
My heart moans within me!
I cannot hold my peace!
Because you have heard, O my soul,
the sound of the horn,
The alarm of war.
Destruction follows upon destruction;
For the whole land is spoiled....

I beheld the earth,
And, lo, it was waste and void;

And the heavens, and they had no light.
I beheld the mountains, and lo, they trembled.
And all the hills moved to and fro.
I beheld, and, lo, there was no man,
And all birds of the heavens were fled.
I beheld, and, lo, the fruitful field was a wilderness,
And all the cities thereof were broken down
At the presence of the Lord,
And before His fierce anger....

For thus says the Lord:
"The whole land shall be desolate." (Jeremiah 4:19–27)

The Jewish tradition does not mandate pacifism, or peace at any price, although some Jews have become pacifists based on Jewish values. The Israelites frequently went forth to battle, and not always in defensive wars. But they always held to the ideal of universal peace and yearned for the day when there would be no more bloodshed or violence, and when the instruments of war would be converted into tools of production:

And they shall beat their swords into plowshares,
And their spears into pruning hooks;
Nation shall not lift up sword against nation,
Neither shall they learn war any more.
But they shall sit every man under his vine and
under his fig tree;
And none shall make them afraid;
For the mouth of the Lord of hosts has spoken.
(Isaiah 2:4; Micah 4:3–4)

However, throughout most of history, the world's people have too often beaten their plowshares into swords and their pruning hooks into spears.

Causes of War
Judaism teaches that violence and war result directly from injustice:

The sword comes into the world because of justice delayed, because of justice perverted, and because of those who render wrong decisions.[15]

The Hebrew word for war, *milchama*, is derived from the word *locham*, which means "to feed" as well as "to wage war." The Hebrew word for bread, *lechem*, comes from the same root. This has led the Sages to point out that lack of bread and the search for sufficient food make people more inclined to wage war.[16] Since the seeds of war are often found in the inability of a nation to provide adequate food for its people, failing to help reduce hunger across the world and feeding tremendous amounts of grains to animals destined for slaughter instead of feeding the grains directly to starving people can create conditions leading to war.

Former Senator Mark Hatfield of Oregon has stated:

Hunger and famine will do more to destabilize this world; it's more explosive than all atomic weaponry possessed by the big powers. Desperate people do desperate things....Nuclear fission is now in the hands of even the developing countries in many of which hunger and famine are most serious.[17]

Richard J. Barnet, a director of the Washington-based Institute for Policy Studies and author of *The Lean Years*, an analysis of resource scarcities, believes that the anger and despair of hungry people can lead to violence and spreading conflicts.[18] Just as scarcity of food can lead to war, so can scarcity of sources of energy. A prime current threat to peace is the perceived need for affluent countries to obtain sufficient oil to keep their economies running smoothly.

The Persian Gulf area, where much of the world's oil is produced, has been the site of much instability and competition, which resulted in the Gulf War in 1990.

Reducing Prospects for War

Judaism emphasizes that justice and harmonious relations among nations reduce violence and prospects for war. The prophet Isaiah states: "And the work of righteousness shall be peace; and the effect of righteousness, quietness and confidence forever" (Isaiah 32:17). The Psalmist observes: "When loving kindness and truth have met together, then righteousness and peace have kissed each other" (Psalms 85:11).

The Talmudic rabbis stress that justice is a precondition for peace: "The world rests on three things: on justice, on truth, and on peace. And all three are one, for where there is justice, there is also truth, and there is peace."[19]

According to the Jewish tradition, progress toward more just conditions, less waste, and more equitable sharing of resources will reduce the chances of war and violence. This means working to change economic and production systems that result in waste and exploitation and keep the majority of the world's people in poverty.

Judaism on Treatment of Enemies

Judaism offers very powerful statements about how one should regard and treat one's enemies:

> Rejoice not when your enemy falls,
> And let not your heart be glad when he stumbles.
> (Proverbs 24:17)

> If your enemy is hungry, give him bread to eat,
> And if he is thirsty, give him water to drink. (Proverbs 25:21)

God feels compassion even for the enemies of the Jewish people:

> In the hour when the Israelites crossed the Red Sea [while the waters drowned the Egyptians], the ministering angels wanted to sing a song of praise before God. But He said to them: "My handiwork is drowning in the sea, and you want to sing a song before Me!"[20]

On Passover, which commemorates the Exodus from Egypt, Jews temper their celebration of our freedom because Egyptians died during the Israelites' liberation. This is reflected in two Passover observances:

1.   At the Seder table, one drop of wine is spilled at the recitation of each of the ten plagues, to reduce our joy (since wine symbolizes joy).

2.   The complete Hallel, hymns of praise to God, is recited on only the first two days of Passover. On the rest of the holiday, only part of Hallel is said (because the crossing of the sea and drowning of the Egyptians took place on the last days). By contrast, on the harvest festival of Sukkot, the entire Hallel is recited during the entire week, because everyone, Jew and Gentile alike, can rejoice in the produce of the land.

Judaism does not believe that another person or nation need be considered a permanent enemy. Under the right conditions, positive changes can occur: "Who is the mightiest of heroes? He who makes his enemy into his friend."[21] Judaism believes that forbearance to adversaries can lead to understanding and eventually to reconciliation. Many statements in the Jewish tradition point to ways of eventually establishing reconciliation with enemies: "Say not, I will pay back evil" (Proverbs 20:22); and "When a man's ways please the Lord, he makes even his enemies to be at peace with him" (Proverbs 16:7).

The following story epitomizes the Jewish stress on converting an enemy into a friend. Samuel ibn Nagrela, a Spanish Jewish poet of the eleventh century, was vizier to the king of Granada. One day a certain man cursed Samuel in the presence of the king. The king commanded Samuel to punish the offender by cutting out his tongue. When Samuel treated his enemy kindly instead, the curses became blessings. When the king saw that Samuel had not carried out his command, he asked why not. Samuel replied, "I have indeed torn out his angry tongue and given him instead a kindly one."[22]

By treating an enemy as a human being created in God's image, entitled to respect and sometimes in need of help, we can often obtain a reconciliation. Based on a biblical verse, a Talmudic sage expounds the following lesson:

Rabbi Alexandri said: Two ass-drivers who hate each other are traveling on the road. The ass of one of them falls under its burden and his companion bypasses him. But then he says to himself, "It is written in the Torah: "If you see the ass of him that hates you lying under its burden, you shall forebear to pass by him; you shall surely release it with him" (Exodus 23:5). He immediately turns back and helps his fellow to reload. The other ass-driver then begins to meditate in his heart, saying, "This man is really my friend and I did not know it." Both then enter an inn, and eat and drink together.[23]

Philo, the great Jewish philosopher who lived in Alexandria, Egypt in the first century of the Common Era, comments on the same biblical passage. He indicates that, by fulfilling it,

> you will benefit yourself more than him: he gains help [with unloading his animal], you, the greatest and most precious treasure: true goodness. And this, as surely as the shadow follows the body, will be followed by a termination of the feud. He is drawn toward amity by the kindness that holds him in bondage. You, his helper, with a good action to assist your counsels, are predisposed to thoughts of reconciliation.[24]

The Talmud teaches: "If two people claim your help, and one is your enemy, help him first."[25] This is based on the importance of converting an enemy into a friend.

Significantly, history shows that even staunch foes often later establish positive relations. Germany and Japan, both bitter enemies of the United States during World War II, are now considered important trading and military allies of the U.S. While there was talk about a possible nuclear war with China not too long ago, that country has become a major trading partner. The "demonization of enemies" is incompatible with both Jewish values and the lessons of recent world history.

Jewish Teachings on Nonviolence

Although Jewish religious texts frequently deal with war, Judaism does not glorify war for its own sake. The underlying attitude of Jewish tradition is an abhorrence of violence and an affirmation of the obligation to work and make sacrifices for the ultimate goal of peace.

The prophets speak of the futility and limited benefit of unnecessary and inappropriate warfare:

> For thus says the Lord God, the Holy One of Israel:
> In sitting still and rest shall you be saved,
> In quietness and in confidence shall be your strength;
> And you would not.
> But you said: "No, for we will flee upon horses";
> Therefore shall you flee;
> And: "We will ride upon the swift";
> Therefore shall your pursuers be swift. (Isaiah 30:15, 16)

> Because you have trusted in your chariots
> And in the multitude of your warriors,
> Therefore the tumult of war shall arise among your people,
> And all your fortresses shall be destroyed. (Hosea 10:13, 14)

> His delight is not in the strength of the horse,
> Nor is his pleasure in the legs of a man.
> But the Lord takes pleasure in those who fear him,
> In those who hope in His steadfast love. (Psalms 147:10–11)

The prophets proclaim that Israel should not depend solely on military arms and alliances, but rather, "Zion shall be redeemed by justice, and her returnees by righteousness" (Isaiah 1:27).

In an extreme circumstance, Jeremiah even urged the leaders of Judah to submit to Babylonian invaders (who he believed had been sent to carry out God's punishment) without resisting, so that the Jewish people would live and continue to perform God's commandments:

> And I spoke to Zedekiah King of Judah according to all these words, saying: "Bring your necks under the yoke of the King of Babylon, and serve him and his people and live. Why should you die, you and your people, by the sword, by the famine, and by the pestilence, as the Lord has spoken concerning the nation that will

not serve the King of Babylon? And hearken not unto the words of the [false] prophets that speak unto you, saying: 'You shall not serve the King of Babylon,' for they prophesy a lie unto you....Hearken not unto them; serve the king of Babylon, and live; why should this city become desolate?" (Jeremiah 27:12–14, 17)

While Judaism recognizes the duty of each person to protect his own life and to defend others from violence, it specifically prohibits the shedding of *innocent* blood:

Murder may not be practiced to save one's life....A man came before Rabbi Yehuda HaNasi (Judah the Prince) and said to him, "The governor of my town has ordered me, 'Go and kill so and so; if not I will slay you.' " Rabba answered him, "Let him rather slay you than that you should commit murder; who knows whether your blood is redder? Perhaps his blood is redder."[26]

Even in a clear-cut case of self-defense, Judaism condemns the use of excessive violence. The Talmud stresses that if a person being pursued "could definitely save himself by maiming a limb of the pursuer, but instead kills him," the pursued is guilty of murder.[27]

Even when war is considered necessary, Judaism tries to minimize violence. When the Hebrews laid siege to a city in order to capture it, "it may not be surrounded on all four sides, but only on three in order to give an opportunity for escape to those who would flee for their lives."[28] Even when a war was for defensive purposes, each soldier had to make a sin offering, in recognition that any killing is an offense against God.

To emphasize the value of peaceful relations, the Talmudic teachers reinterpret Biblical texts to remove their violent aspects. The best example is the life of King David, the great hero of ancient Israel. The Bible describes David's character defects and misdeeds in his use of power. The Talmudic sages, however, stress his creative and contemplative abilities rather than his aggressive characteristics. They prefer to consider him a pious, humble man who spent his time in Torah study and writing psalms, rather than a military hero.

The Talmud similarly recasts the lives of the Jewish patriarchs. Whereas the Bible tells of Abraham leading forth 318 "trained men" to smite those who had captured Lot (Genesis 14:14), in the Talmud these men are considered scholars.[29] While Jacob refers to the portions he amassed "with my sword and my bow" (Genesis 48:22), the rabbis interpret Jacob's "sword" to be "prayer" and his "bow" to be "supplication."[30]

Even the character of festivals is modified by the rabbis in order to emphasize spiritual rather than military power. Originally, Hanukkah celebrated the guerilla military victory of the Maccabees over the tyranny of the Syrian Greeks. The Talmud de-emphasizes the military aspects of the victory and stresses the holiday's religious aspect. Not one word of rabbinic literature extols the Maccabean battles. For example, when the Talmud describes the "miracle which was wrought," it refers to "the oil in the cruse which burned eight days" rather than to the might of the Hasmoneans (Maccabean army).[31]

One of the Talmudic rabbis' favorite statements was: "Be of the persecuted rather than the persecutor."[32] The following statement summarizes their outlook:

> They who are reviled, but revile not others, they who hear themselves reproached but make no reply; they whose every act is one of love and who cheerfully bear their afflictions; these are the ones of whom scripture says: "They who love Him are as the sun going forth in his might."[33]

Nonviolence has often found support in Jewish history. Rabbi Yohanan ben Zakkai, a revered teacher of the first century CE, is the great hero of Jewish peaceful accommodation. When Rome was besieging Jerusalem, he saw the futility of further Jewish resistance to Roman power. He secretly left Jerusalem and met with the leader of the Roman army. When the Roman general saw his great wisdom, he stated that Rabbi Yohanan could have any wish that he desired. Rabbi Yohanan ben Zakkai chose to establish a school for the study of the Torah at Yavneh. Under his leadership and that of the many brilliant teachers who followed him, a national disaster that could have ended the Jewish people was converted into a new movement for perpetuating Judaism.

From the Roman destruction of the Temple in 70 CE until the establishment of modern Israel, with very few exceptions, the Jews as a people never waged war. Without a government, army, or geographical territory to defend, Jews and Judaism survived, not through armed might, but through keeping faithfully to the Jewish religion and way of life.

War is frequently not a solution, but rather brings on new and greater problems. The great military leader Napoleon once said to his Minister of Education, "Do you know, Fontanes, what astonishes me most in this world? The inability of force to create anything. In the long run, the sword is always beaten by the spirit."[34]

In a similar spirit, Chassidic master Rabbi Nachman of Breslov asserts:

Many foolish beliefs that people once held, such as forms of idol worship that demanded child sacrifice, etc., have disappeared. But, as of yet, the foolish belief in the pursuit of war has not disappeared....What great thinkers they [scientists who design certain weapons] must be, what ingenuity they must possess to invent amazing weapons that kill thousands of people at once! Is there any greater foolishness than this—to murder so many people for nothing?[35]

Another Jewish argument against the utility of warfare concerns today's tremendously powerful and destructive weaponry. A nuclear war would destroy not only soldiers, but civilians, either immediately or later (due to radiation). Modern nuclear weapons have the potential to put an end to humanity, as well as all other life on Earth. Judaism is very scrupulous about limiting destruction and not shedding innocent blood; shouldn't Jews be in the forefront of people striving for peace today?

Yet can a Jew responsibly reject all possibility of violence? Haven't we obligations to defend others as well as ourselves? Can we simply remain passive before terror, tyranny, and injustice? Shall we not defend human values when they are threatened? Can Israel, for example, fail to be militarily strong in the face of antagonism from many of its neighbors? Sometimes war is necessary, and a call must ring forth calling the people to their inescapable duty:

Proclaim this among the nations,
Prepare war;
Stir up the mighty men;
Let all the men of war draw near,
Let them come up.
Beat your plowshares into swords,
And your pruning hooks into spears;
Let the weak say, "I am strong."
Make haste and come, all you nations round about,
And gather yourselves together;
Cause Your mighty ones to come down, O Lord! (Joel 4:9–11)

A pragmatic position consistent with Jewish values today is what Rabbi Albert Axelrad, longtime Hillel Director at Brandeis University, has called the "pacifoid"[36] position. He defines this as one who is "like" or "resembling" or "near" pacifist—that is, a person who works like a pacifist in pursuing peace, but accepts the need to fight if there is no alternative. This would include Allied resistance to Hitler in World War II, defending Israel against attack by Arab countries today, and responding to acts of terror. It must be noted that the pacifoid position is not "passivism"—lack of involvement. Jews must act in nonviolent ways in attempting to change unjust conditions. There have been many such examples in Jewish history.

Perhaps the first recorded instance of civil disobedience is that of the midwives Shifra and Puah, who ignored Pharaoh's command to kill all male babies and saved the Israelite male children (Exodus: 1:15–21). The rabbis state that their action was praiseworthy because the law was genocidal and discriminatory (affecting only Jewish males), and therefore did not have to be obeyed.

The great medieval philosopher Maimonides held that Jewish law clearly allowed for civil disobedience under certain conditions.

One who disobeys a king's mandate, because he is engaged in the performance of one *mitzvah* or another, even an insignificant one, is relieved of guilt ... and one need not add that if the command itself involves the violation of one of God's mandates, it must not be obeyed![37]

May a Jew be a conscientious objector to particular military service, based on Torah values? The answer is yes. In 1970, the Synagogue Council of America, an umbrella group of Orthodox, Conservative, and Reform rabbis and congregational groups, stated in a letter to the director of the Selective Service System (U.S. military draft), that Jews may claim conscientious objection to war based on their understanding of the moral imperatives of the Jewish tradition:

> Jewish faith, while viewing war as a dehumanizing aberration and enjoining a relentless quest for peace, recognizes that war can become a tragic, unavoidable necessity. Judaism is therefore not a pacifist faith in the sense that this term is generally used.
>
> However, this fact does not preclude the possibility of individuals developing conscientious objection to war based on their understanding of and sensitivity to the moral imperatives of the Jewish tradition. In other words, Jewish faith can indeed embrace conscientious objection, and Jewish religious law makes specific provision for the exemption of such moral objectors. It is entirely proper for individuals claiming such conscientious objector's status to be questioned about the sincerity and consistency of their beliefs, provided they are not singled out to meet requirements not applicable to members of other faiths. It is entirely improper, however, to reject such applications on the false ground that Judaism cannot embrace conscientious objection.[38]

The Rabbinical Assembly (RA) (Conservative) made similar statements in 1934 (reaffirmed in 1941),[39] as did the Reform rabbis' Central Conference of American Rabbis (CCAR) in 1963.[40] In 1971, the multi-denominational Synagogue Council of America expanded on previous statements to assert that selective conscientious objection to war is consistent with Judaism:

Judaism considers each individual personally responsible before God for his actions. No man who violates the eternal will of the Creator can escape responsibility by pleading that he acted as an agent of another, whether that other is an individual or the state. It is therefore possible, under unusual circumstances, for an individual to find himself compelled by conscience to reject the demands of a human law which, to the individual in question, appears to conflict with the demand made on him by a higher law.[41]

What about people who are not pacifists but feel that a certain war is wrong? This became a profound ethical question when many Americans refused to fight in the Vietnam War because they felt that our involvement was illegal and immoral. Jewish tradition, which places great stress on the individual conscience, is consistent with selective conscientious objector status.

We must always question the basis and likely results of any potential resort to arms. Some questions that might be raised include: Is this really best for the people of this country? For the people of the world? Is there no other way to settle our disputes? Is this battle necessary to preserve our ideals and values, or is it to serve special interests? Are all the facts known, or have we only heard one side of the issue? Who stands to gain from this war? Could changing our lifestyles to become less wasteful and thus less dependent on imported resources reduce the need to go to war? Will this war really solve the problem? Has the possibility of fruitful negotiation been fully exhausted?

(A group that provides draft registration counseling based on Jewish values is the Jewish Peace Fellowship—see Appendix C.)

Peace is Judaism's greatest value. War is one of humanity's greatest threats. Hence it is essential that Jews be actively involved with others in trying to establish harmony between people and nations, and in working toward the time when "nations shall not learn war anymore" (Isaiah 2:4).

8:   INTERNATIONAL CONCERNS

I saw all the oppressions that are practiced under the sun. Behold, the tears of the oppressed, they had no one to comfort them! On the side of the oppressors there was power. (Ecclesiastes 4:1)

To SURVEY CONDITIONS FOR MOST OF THE WORLD'S people today is to see the extent to which Jewish teachings about justice, compassion, and sharing have been neglected. The tremendous injustice and inequality that prevail in the world today are well described by Lester Brown, former Director of the WorldWatch Institute:

> In effect, our world today is in reality two worlds, one rich, one poor; one literate, one largely illiterate; one industrial and urban, one agrarian and rural; one overfed and overweight, one hungry and malnourished; one affluent and consumption-oriented, one poverty stricken and survival-oriented. North of this line [separating the wealthy from the poor], life expectancy closely approaches the Biblical 'threescore and ten'; south of it, many do not survive infancy. In the North, economic opportunities are plentiful and social mobility is high. In the South, economic opportunities are scarce and societies are rigidly stratified.[1]

The vast social and economic gaps between countries can be demonstrated through many significant statistics comparing developed countries (U.S., Canada, Japan, England, France, etc.) and "developing" countries (Nigeria, India, Bangladesh, Nicaragua, Pakistan, etc.). The per capita

GNP of the United States is over seventy times that of Sierra Leone, even with an adjustment for "purchasing power parity."[2] A child born in Sweden can expect to live an average of forty-three years longer than a child born in Zambia.[3] Almost twenty percent of the babies born in Angola die before their first birthday, compared to less than one percent for France, Norway, Sweden, the Netherlands, Denmark, and many other European countries.[4] Only three percent of the population in all sixteen countries of Western Africa can expect to live to sixty-five, compared to eighty percent of the population in Italy.[5] A person's place of birth certainly makes a difference!

It is difficult for people in wealthy countries to realize the extent of the abject, chronic poverty experienced by so many of our brothers and sisters in the world:

- Poverty means malnutrition. One-third to one-half of the world's people are undernourished (not enough calories) or malnourished (not enough of certain nutrients). Over 450 million people are severely and chronically malnourished.[6]

- Poverty means illiteracy and lack of education. Only forty-six percent of women in Africa were literate in 1995.[7] In the less developed countries, only about half the children of secondary school age are in secondary schools, compared to almost a hundred percent enrollment in such schools in the more developed countries.[8]

- Poverty means sickness and inadequate health care.[9] One-third to one-half of the world's people have no access to health care. Few people infected with AIDS in poorer countries can afford the life-extending drugs used in wealthier countries.

- Poverty means high infant and child mortality. Almost nine percent of the children born in Africa in 2000 died before their first birthday.[10] Hunger and related preventable diseases kill about 34,000 children under the age of five daily—over twelve million per year.[11]

- Poverty means doing without basic necessities. Economist Robert Heilbroner has outlined what the lifestyle of a typical family living in an underdeveloped country is like: a minimum of furniture; a minimum of clothes; very crowded conditions; a paucity of food; no running water; no electricity, no newspapers, magazines, or books;

perhaps a radio; very few government services; no postal service or fire-fighters; perhaps a school three miles away consisting of two class-rooms; perhaps a clinic ten miles away, tended by a midwife; and barely any money.[12]

- Poverty means the anguish of impossible choices, the grief of watching the people you love die, the humiliation of not being able to provide for your family, the painful challenge of surviving day by day, and the powerlessness to change one's fortunes.

International movements have arisen to promote constructive responses to some of the worse elements of global poverty and exploita-tion. These include: groups who oppose sweatshop working conditions in developing countries (inspired in part by the labor organizers, many of them Jewish, who have rallied to fight sweatshops in America since before the Triangle Shirtwaist fire tragedy); the campaign for reducing the crushing and often undeserved debts of developing nations (which arises out of and is named after the biblical Jubilee, in which debts were cancelled); efforts to significantly increase aid to people in poorer regions; and many similar causes.[13]

Economic Globalization[14]
Poverty and other global issues cannot be fully discussed without consid-ering economic globalization, a process that is causing a fundamental redesign of the planet's economic, social, and political systems. It is producing a gigantic power shift, moving economic and political power away from local, state, and national governments and communities toward global banks, corporations, and the global bureaucracies these have created. Some of the aspects of globalization are:

- The expansion of trade, with much easier movement of goods and services across the world; between 1950 and 1998, export of goods between countries surged seventeen-fold—from $311 billion to $5.4 trillion—while the world economy only expanded sixfold.[15]
- The opening up of capital markets, which increases the movement of money across the world; capital flows to developing countries soared

from $21 billion in 1970 to $227 billion in 1998, an elevenfold increase.[16]

- Increased foreign investment, including building plants, buying stock in foreign countries, and contracting subsidiaries; global foreign direct investment increased from $44 billion to $644 billion from 1970 to 1998.[17]

- Improved access to communication, including the development of new technology like the Internet and greater availability of wireless and other telephones; the Internet grew by about fifty percent per year from 1995 to 1998, after more than doubling in size annually, on average, over the previous fifteen years;[18] the number of lines linking non-cellular phones to the global network jumped more than ninefold between 1960 and 1998, from eighty-nine million to 839 million.[19]

- A very rapid growth in transnational corporations; the number of TNCs worldwide soared from 7,000 in 1970 to 53,600 in 1998.[20]

To achieve such rapid growth, globalization requires unrestricted free trade, privatization of enterprise, and deregulation of corporate activity, which together remove the impediments that might stand in the way of expanded corporate activity. These impediments include: environmental, public health, and food safety laws; laws that guarantee workers' rights and opportunities; laws that permit nations to control investment in their countries; and laws that seek to retain national controls over local culture. These laws are viewed as obstacles to corporate free trade and are quickly being eliminated or scaled back by major new trade agreements. And while corporations are being deregulated and freed from constraints, nation-states and local governments are being harshly regulated and constrained, thus making it increasingly difficult to protect local tradition, identity, and jobs, as well as the environment and national sovereignty.

Economic globalization could be providing many more benefits than have so far been shown. However, it has resulted in many negative effects because of its values and objectives. These include:

- Giving primacy to economic—mainly corporate—values above all others. Through such institutions as the World Bank, the International Monetary Fund (IMF), the North American Free Trade Association (NAFTA), and the World Trade Organization (WTO), and treaties such as the General Agreement on Tariffs and Trade (GATT), corporations have gained extraordinary new powers. Corporate interests and profits are furthered by these unaccountable, undemocratic global bureaucracies, often at the expense of human needs and the web of life on earth. They are the true governing bodies in the global economy, usurping the powers that nations formerly had.

- Unifying and integrating all economic activity within a centralized "supersystem." Countries with very different cultures and economic traditions must all merge their economic activities within a single conceptual framework. The net result is what some economists call "global monoculture"—the global homogenization of culture, lifestyle, economic practice, and ideology with the corresponding sacrifice of local traditions, arts, values, and traditional small-scale economic practices. The result is that every place is starting to look very much like every other place, with the same malls and superstores, restaurant franchises, and chain hotels, the same clothes, the same cars, the same high-rise buildings, and increasingly the same music, art, and television programs.

- Undermining all considerations except economic ones. Economic globalization glorifies the free market and its principle actors—global corporations—as the engines and benefactors of the process. It places supreme importance on achieving increasingly rapid economic growth and thus constantly seeks new markets, new resources, and new and cheaper labor sources. The power of the largest corporations and of the wealthiest people is increasing. The collective worth of the world's 475 billionaires equals the combined incomes of the poorest fifty percent of humanity.[21] Fifty of the largest one hundred economies in the world are corporations. Mitsubishi is the twenty-second largest economy in the world, General Motors the twenty-sixth, and Ford the thirty-first. Each is larger than those of many countries, including Norway, Chile, Turkey, South Africa, Saudi Arabia, Malaysia, and New Zealand.[22]

It is questionable whether globalization can work even on its own terms. Can the limits of a finite planet be ignored? Are there sufficient resources—water, minerals, wood, fuel—to continue the desired rapid economic growth? Where will the effluents from this ambitious under-taking—the solids, the toxic wastes—be dumped? Can the ever-increasing consumption of commodities be ecologically sustained?

There is certainly great potential value for a closer, better-connected world. Today we can know much more quickly and fully about problems in every part of the globe, and therefore potentially respond faster and more effectively. Trade and communication can bring information and jobs to previously isolated groups of poor people. Activists and movements across the earth can more easily connect and work together. Oppressive govern-ments and terrorist organizations can be more closely scrutinized and exposed. Universal values such as human rights; the equality of women; vigilant protection of the environment; freedom of speech and religion; the rights of children; fighting disease and hunger; reducing or eliminating land mines, nuclear missiles, and chemical and biological weapons; and stopping torture and oppression can be widely advocated, publicized, and organized around. Everyone gains the opportunity to learn about, and can come to appreciate, cultures and sites and natural phenomena that are worlds away. When limited by stringent guarantees of fair conditions, hours, and compensation for workers and care for ecosystems, interna-tional trade can reach and empower impoverished and suppressed individ-uals and groups.

But many negative effects of globalization are already apparent:

- Working people in developed countries are losing jobs to corporate flight and to high-tech machines and have been placed in a downward wage competition with workers in poorer countries. Many people believe that big businesses employ more of the world's labor force than do smaller businesses. However, according to the Washington-based Institute for Policy Studies, while the two hundred largest corporations in the world account for approximately thirty percent of global economic activity, they employ less than 0.5 percent of the global work force.[23] The reason is *economies of scale*: as companies get larger, it becomes more efficient for them to replace thousands of workers with robots and other machines. And as large companies begin to dominate their industries, they drive out smaller competitors and reduce the workforce. Such economies of scale are intrinsic to globalization. Hence, consolidations and mergers result in *fewer* jobs, not more, in developed countries.

- In spite of the tremendous growth and spread of technology, with increasing numbers of people using computers, cellular phones, and other instruments of modern technology, poverty is still widespread and growing. In 2000, 1.3 billion of the world's six billion people lived on less than one dollar per day, and three billion people lived on less than two dollars a day.[24] From 1960 to 2000, the world's richest twenty percent increased their fraction of the world's wealth from seventy percent to 86 percent, while the poorest twenty percent of the world's population experienced a decrease from 2.3 percent to about one percent.[25] While some corporate profits were at record levels, with many top executives' annual salaries in the millions, the wages of most ordinary workers in developed countries were decreasing in real terms and good jobs were being replaced by temporary or part-time jobs.

- Diverse local farm production and local trades in poorer nations that encourage self-reliance are being replaced by huge corporate farms—monocultures—that no longer grow food for local people but instead grow flowers, beef, or coffee for export to the global economy. The result of this process is that millions of the world's formerly self-sufficient small farmers are becoming homeless, landless refugees.

- In India, Africa, and Latin America, millions of indigenous people and small farmers are displaced to make way for gigantic dams and other development projects. The result is that more people join the landless, jobless urban masses. Cities are now attempting to absorb millions of the newly landless refugees now roaming the globe in search of a home and the rare, poorly paid job.

- The gap between the wealthy and the poor within countries and among countries is rapidly increasing, and globalization accelerates the problem by separating people from their traditional livelihoods and creating a terrible downward pressure on wages everywhere—

including developing countries, where low wages represent the only so-called comparative advantage, meaning that if wages are not kept down, there might be no jobs at all.

A report from the Institute for Policy Studies in 1999 showed that American CEOs were paid, on average, 419 times more than assembly-line workers, the highest ratio in the world.[26] The report showed workers' median hourly wages (adjusted for inflation) down by ten percent in the past twenty-five years.[27] The U.S. Federal Reserve reports that the top twenty percent of the U.S. population owns 84.6 percent of the country's wealth.[28] That makes local self-reliance very difficult to achieve.

- For most developing countries, free trade has had negative effects. For example, in 1986, Haiti grew most of its rice, the main staple food of the country, and imported only 7,000 tons of rice. In the late 1980s, as Haiti lifted tariffs on rice imports in compliance with free trade policies insisted upon by international lending agencies, cheaper rice flowed in from the U.S., where the rice industry receives government subsidies. Haiti's peasant farmers could not compete, and by 1996, Haiti's rice production became negligible and the country was importing 196,000 tons of foreign rice at a cost of $100 million per year.[29] After the dependence on foreign rice was complete, and the Haitian people were dependent on grain imports, prices increased substantially, and a hungry nation became even hungrier.[30]

Because of such conditions, poor countries are on a treadmill and have to work harder and harder just to maintain their (inadequate) standard of living. These unfavorable trade relations produce what is known as the "spiral of debt." It happens because the developing countries are locked in by the economic, political, and military power of wealthy countries. They must export cheap items and import more expensive ones.

- The imperatives of global economic expansion, accelerated by free trade, the overuse of resources, and the worldwide promotion of the consumer lifestyle by advertising, are a major factor behind environmental problems such as global climate change, habitat destruction, ozone depletion, ocean pollution, and shortages of water and other resources. As environmental leader Paul Hawken says, "Given current corporate practices, not one wildlife reserve, wilderness, or indigenous culture will survive the global economy. We know that every natural system on the planet is disintegrating. The land, water, air, and sea have been functionally transformed from life-supporting systems into repositories for waste. There is no polite way to say that business is destroying the world."[31]

- Using the technologies of global computer networks, currency speculators can move vast amounts of money invisibly and instantaneously from one part of the world to another, destabilizing currencies and countries, and forcing nations to seek the harsh solution of an International Monetary Fund bailout. This practice has already destabilized many countries' economies and was a significant factor in the 1997–1998 Asian financial crisis.

- The central control of much of the world food and seed supply by giant corporations which effectively determine where food will be grown, by whom, and what price consumers will ultimately pay, contributes to widespread hunger. Food formerly eaten by the people who grew it is now exported—transported thousands of miles at major environmental cost—to be eaten by affluent people who are already well-fed, or fed in large amounts to farmed animals who are destined for slaughter. As indicated in Chapter 6, global agribusiness and international monetary organizations are trying to double the number of farmed animals by 2020, by encouraging the consumption of animal products in developing countries, despite the many negative effects of animal-based diets and agriculture.

- There have been recent outbreaks of deadly new diseases such as Ebola hemorrhagic fever, mad cow disease, E. coli infection, and the West Nile virus. Though it is generally not reported in the press, there is a connection between those outbreaks and the new mobility provided to disease vectors by global transport. Microbes and species that were once contained within geographic boundaries are now let loose by travel and trade. The industrialization of agriculture for mass export production to serve global economies plays a role in the outbreaks of E. coli, mad cow, and foot and mouth diseases.

- There have been assaults on the last indigenous tribes in the Amazon, Borneo, and the Philippines because the globalization process needs more water, forests, or genetic resources in areas where the Indians have lived for millennia, and because corporations wish to convert self-sufficient people into consumers. These forces are rapidly leading to the monoculturalization of peoples and lands, and the homogenization of cultural frameworks.
- The growing emphasis on export and import as part of the new global system requires vast new road-building and road-widening schemes and an expanded transport infrastructure with more high-speed traffic. As a result, the quality of rural life is rapidly worsening.
- Ed Ayres, editor of *WorldWatch*, summarizes the effects of globalization on local communities "where growing numbers of people find their sense of security being eroded by a phalanx of larger forces":

There is the "Wal-Mart" phenomenon, for example, in which a large chain store uses its marketing muscle to drive local stores out of business, while taking what used to be the local owners' revenues and sending them off to distant corporate coffers. There is the related "empty storefront" phenomenon, in which the increasing concentration of an industry into larger, more "efficient" outlets means fewer outlets remain in small communities (the numbers of independent car dealers, food stores, drug stores, book stores, and farms in the wealthy countries have all declined sharply in the past several decades). In the developing countries, there is the "structural adjustment" phenomenon, wherein international lending agencies have pushed governments to adopt policies favoring production for export at the expense of local self-sufficiency. And wherever urban areas are expanding around the world, whether into exploding suburbs or imploding shantytowns, there is the "don't know my neighbors" problem. Even as we humans become more numerous, we become more socially isolated and uneasy.[32]

In summary, many problems—overcrowded cities, unusual new weather patterns, the growth of global poverty, the spread of new diseases, the lowering of wages, the elimination of social services, the reduction of national soverignty and local democracy, the destruction of the environment, decaying communities, and the loss of indigenous culture—are all strongly linked to the same global processes. They are tied to the world's new economic arrangement, in the cause of an economic ideology that cannot serve social or ecological sustainability.

In the end it comes down to this: Who should make the rules we live by? Should it be democratic governments, influenced by local communities concerned about what is good for people and the environment? Or should it be the global community of transnational bankers, corporations, and speculators? The new rules of globalization are actively undermining people's ability to control their own fate.

Because of the many negative effects of economic globalization, there have been many recent protests against it. In November 1999, tens of thousands of people from all over the world took to the streets of Seattle in a massive protest against the policies of the WTO. The angry protesters comprised a very varied group, including farmers, immigration-rights activists, labor unionists, environmentalists, small-business owners, animal rights activists, religious practitioners, and many others.

The "battle of Seattle" marked a critical turning point. While only six or seven years ago the term "globalization" was virtually unknown, an outburst of anger against many aspects of it has erupted. Since Seattle, there have been major protests at meetings of international trade and monetary groups in Washington, D.C., in April 2000, in Chiang Mai, Thailand in May 2000, in Melbourne, Australia in early September 2000, in Prague in late September 2000, and in Genoa, Italy in July 2001. Resistance is growing, and the media are beginning to pay attention.

Many of these demonstrations have been marred by senseless violence, much of it initiated by relatively small groups of nihilistic conflict-seekers and faux "anarchists." The vast majority of protesters have been sincere and peaceful, and in fact the movement critical of the way globalization has developed in actual practice has created closeness and communication between such diverse groups as environmental campaigners, sweatshop opponents, trade unionists, advocates for the developing world, and critics of the bioengineering of foods.

A striking governmental confirmation of the extremely harmful impact of international monetary organizations came from a 1998 report of the International Financial Institution Advisory Committee. This committee was created by the U.S. Congress and its report is commonly known as the Meltzer Report, after its chairman Alan Meltzer, a conservative academic. Among its devastating conclusions are:[33]

- Rather than promoting economic growth, the IMF institutionalizes economic stagnation.
- The World Bank is irrelevant, not central, to the goal of eliminating global poverty.
- Both the World Bank and the IMF are driven primarily by the political and economic interests of the wealthy nations, rather than the needs of the poor.
- The IMF's mandate of ensuring a stable global financial order was often undermined by its encouragement of irresponsible investments, and by its prescribing of tight fiscal policies that worsened the situation rather than improved it in countries facing crises.

In September 2001, about 300 religious leaders signed a Statement and Call, "Global Arrogance or Planetary Community?—A Call to Communities of Faith" that was developed and distributed by the Shalom Center and several other organizations involved with global issues, including the Religious Working Group on the World Bank and IMF.[34] The introductory section of the Statement and Call indicated that the signers were covenanting together to oppose "unaccountable corporate globalization" and "to seek instead a planetary community of the earth and its peoples, workers and congregants, families and neighborhoods."[35]

The Statement called on signers to bring the Statement and Call and the teachings of their religious traditions about "globalization" to their home congregations and communities through a fast of contrition and commitment, and a gathering in Washington, D.C. for a religious service and a candlelight vigil.[36]

The Statement and Call asserted:

The global corporations have invented unaccountable, undemocratic institutions [including the World Bank and the International Monetary Fund] to shield them from the will of the people....[These institutions advance corporate interests by] insisting that loans and grants be conditioned on [cutbacks in desperately needed] social programs, public schools, public health, and water supplies ... [by imposing] privatization of the basic needs of life...[by encouraging] sweatshops and the smashing of labor unions ... by destroying the lives and hopes of children [and supporting child labor] ... by doing all this first to the poor in the poorest societies ... and then, through the threat of capital export and cut-throat competition, putting workers, consumers, and the earth itself in danger in even the more prosperous societies.

The call and statement ended by demanding that

The World Bank and IMF cancel the crushing debt of the nations that [those same international organizations] themselves have impoverished and forced into debt ... [condition all grants and loans on] workers' freedom to organize unions and everyone's freedom to [advocate protection of the environment] and ... that they open their own meetings and deliberation to public scrutiny and democratic control.[37]

As a follow-up to the Statement and Call, the Shalom Center is preparing study guides for synagogues and churches that will facilitate local congregational work on five major aspects of globalization—top-down control; damage to the earth; the oppression of workers; the pressure for overwhelming overwork that distorts families, neighborhoods, and spiritual life; and the destruction of public health and other public services—and to bring sacred texts and teachings to bear on those problems.[38]

Fortunately, there is an alternative to current economic globalization practices, an approach far better for the world's people as well as for global sustainability. This is the way of genuinely applying Jewish values: *bal tash-chit* (reducing waste), so that we are not dependent on repressive regimes for resources; treating every person as created in God's image, so that we will work to end violations of human rights wherever they occur; the pursuit of justice, to end the conditions whereby a minority of the world's people prosper while the majority lack food and other basic human needs; and the pursuit of peace, so that arms races that drain the world's labor, ingenuity, and resources can be reduced. Only these alternatives can result in global harmony and humane conditions for the world's people.

Judaism and International Concerns

Judaism encompasses universal as well as particular concerns. Particular aspects include observances of the Sabbath and holy days, rules of *kashrut* (kosher eating), and prayer obligations. Jews are taught to be especially concerned about their co-religionists: "All Israel is responsible, one for each other."[39] However, the message of Judaism is also universal, expressing concern for each person and every nation. We have already discussed many Jewish teachings related to humanity: every person is created in God's image; every life is sacred and is to be treated with dignity and respect; we should be kind to the stranger, for we were strangers in the land of Egypt; we should show compassion even to enemies. Additional Jewish universal teachings include:

- The first covenant God made was with Noah, on behalf of the entire human race as well as the animal kingdom (Genesis 9:11).
- Abraham challenged God on behalf of the pagan, evil-doing cities of Sodom and Gomorrah. In an attempt to save the righteous, he pleaded, "Shall not the Judge of all the earth do justly?" (Genesis 18:25)
- Some of the noblest characters in Scripture are not necessarily Jewish. Ruth, a Moabite who later became an Israelite, is presented as a model of an ideal human being, representing the values of kindness, self-sacrificing loyalty, and love. Job, the symbol of the righteous person

who maintains his faith in God in spite of unprecedented suffering, is not generally depicted as a Jew.

- Some of Israel's greatest leaders were descendants of proselytes. This includes King David, who is the ancestor of the Messiah. The Eighteen Benedictions of the Prayer Book include a special prayer for "righteous proselytes." Hillel, the foremost Talmudic sage of his day, received converts with special eagerness.

- Even of the traditional enemy of the Jewish people, the Edomites, it is said; "You shall not abhor an Edomite, for he is your brother" (Deuteronomy 23:8).

- The prophets stress that Jews have a universal mandate, a charge to improve conditions for all the world's people. Consider, for example, these words of Isaiah:

Thus says God, the Lord...
I the Lord have called you in righteousness,
And have taken hold of your hand,
And kept you, and set you for a covenant of the people,
For a light unto the nations;
To open the blind eyes,
To bring the prisoners from the dungeon,
And them that sit in darkness out of the prison house.
(Isaiah 42:6–7)

- Throughout their history, Jews have worked not for individual salvation, but for salvation for the entire world:

In that day, there shall be a highway from Egypt to Assyria. The Assyrians shall join with the Egyptians and Egyptians with Assyrians, and both countries shall serve the Lord. In that day, Israel shall be a third partner with Egypt and Assyria as a blessing on earth; for the Lord of Hosts will bless them, saying, "Blessed be My people, Egypt, My handiwork Assyria, and My very own Israel." (Isaiah 19:23–25)

- Hillel, in his famous formulation, teaches that we must be concerned with other people as well as ourselves:

  If I am not for myself, who will be for me? But if I am only for myself, what am I? And if not now, when?[40]

- The prophet Malachi powerfully expresses Jewish universal concerns:

  Have we not all one father?
  Has not one God created us?
  Why then do we deal treacherously with one another,
  profaning the covenant of our fathers? (Malachi 2:10)

- Amos proclaims God's concern for all nations:

  "Are you not like the Ethiopians to Me, O people of Israel?" says the Lord.
  "Did I not bring up Israel from the land of Egypt, and the Philistines from Caphtor; and the Syrians from Kir?" (Amos 9:7)

- Jeremiah was appointed as "a prophet to the nations" (Jeremiah 1:5). God tells him: .

  See, I have set you this day over nations and over kingdoms, to pluck up and to break down, to destroy and to overthrow, to build and to plant. (Jeremiah 1:10)

- The Book of Jonah shows God's concern for the Gentile inhabitants of the city of Nineveh, the very same people who destroyed the ancient state of Israel. Jonah, a Jew, is sent to teach the people of Nineveh to repent and serve God, and is taught, in turn, that God cares for all people, as well as animals.

- The Talmud states: "The pious of all nations shall have a place in the world to come."[41]

- During the festival of Sukkot in the days of the Temple of Jerusalem, seventy sacrifices were made for the "seventy nations" (a term that represented all sectors of humanity).

The *sukkah* (temporary harvest booth dwelt in by Jews during Sukkot) must possess enough of an opening through the top so that the person inside can see the stars and the universe beyond, perhaps to remind us that there are worlds and nations beyond our own, which always deserve consideration.

After a benediction is recited, the *lulav* (the palm branch that is held during Sukkot) is waved to the north, south, east, and west, and then up and down, to signify that God's sovereignty is universal in all directions. Hence, when we pray for salvation and help, we must have in mind these blessings not only for ourselves, but also for humanity.

Rabbi Hanina, a third-century sage, stated that salvation for the world would come only when the nations accepted the lesson of the *sukkah* and the *lulav*: that no nation can experience prosperity and happiness unless there is harmony among all nations.[42]

- The sages declare that any person can accept the Torah:

  The Torah was given in public, openly, in a free place. For had the Torah been given in the Land of Israel, the Israelites could have said to the nations of the world: "You have no share in it," but now that it has been given in the wilderness, publicly and openly, in a place that is free for all, everyone willing to accept it may come and accept it.[43]

- A Chassidic wisdom-story expresses the universal spirit of Judaism:

  "Why," a student asked, "is the stork called in Hebrew *Chassidah*, which means the loving one?"
  "Because," the rabbi answered, "he gives so much love to his wife and offspring."

"Then why," asked the student, "if he gives so much love to his mate and his young, is the stork considered *trayfe* (forbidden as food) rather than kosher?"

"He is considered *trayfe*," the rabbi answered, "because he gives love *only* to his own."[44]

• Rabbi Nachman of Breslov asserts:

[Our sages taught that] every person must say, "the whole world was created for my sake."[45] Therefore, since the whole world was created for my sake, I must always be concerned with improving the world, fulfilling the needs of humanity, and praying for its benefit.[46]

The concept of Jews as a "chosen people" has often been misinterpreted as a form of exclusivity. But the prophets remind the people that being chosen does not mean divine favoritism, nor does it guarantee immunity from punishment; on the contrary, it means being held to a higher standard and thus being more intensely exposed to God's judgment and chastisement:

Hear this word that the Lord has spoken against you, O people of Israel, against the whole family whom I brought up out of the land of Egypt. You only have I known of all the families of the earth. Therefore, I will punish you for all your iniquities. (Amos 3:1–2)

As Jewish history attests, "chosenness" certainly does not mean that Jews will always prosper and be free from troubles.

Judaism's international vision is one of peace and righteousness for all of humanity:

In the end of days it shall come to pass that the mountain of the Lord's house shall be established on the top of the mountains, and it shall be exalted above the hills. Peoples shall flow unto it, and many nations shall come and say, "Come, let us go up to the mountain of the Lord, To the house of the God of Jacob; So that He may teach us of His ways, and we will walk in His paths." For the Torah shall go forth from Zion, And the word of the Lord from Jerusalem. And He shall judge among many peoples, and rebuke strong nations afar off; they shall beat their swords into plowshares and their spears into pruning hooks; Nation shall not lift up sword against nation; neither shall they learn war anymore. They shall sit every man under his vine and under his fig tree; and none shall make them afraid; for the mouth of the Lord of hosts has spoken it. For all the peoples will walk every one in the name of his god; we will walk in the name of the Lord our God forever. (Micah 4:1–5)

For global harmony, "a law (Torah) must go forth from Zion." Such a "law" has been proclaimed, but the nations have refused to acknowledge it. It is a law that states that there is one Creator of the entire world, that every person, created in God's image, is of infinite worth and ought to be able to share in the bounties provided by God's earth, and that people and nations must seek peace, pursue justice, and love others, since they are like themselves. If people and nations took this law out of Zion seriously, there would be increased harmony and peace, and sufficient resources for all the world's people.

Micah's words provide a moral blueprint for the world, a covenant rooted in truth and justice that supports the structure of peace. This is explicitly spelled out by the Talmudic teaching mentioned in the previous chapter:

Upon three things the world rests, upon justice, upon truth, and upon peace. And the three are one, for when justice is practiced, truth prevails, and peace is established.[47]

While the prophets believed that different nations would continue to exist, they were true internationalists who urged and foresaw the creation of proper relations among nations, based on peace, justice, and truth. Their vision represented a farsighted view of national interests, in which love of one's country and loyalty to humanity represent two concentric circles.[48] The philosopher George Santayana stated, "A man's feet may be firmly planted in his own country, but his eyes serve the world." Rabbi Robert Gordis added: "The prophets went further; their hearts embraced the world."[49]

In ways consistent with Jewish tradition and values, Jews must be in the forefront of those working for greater international justice, so that the needs of all the world's people may be met, and nations will finally beat their swords into plowshares and their spears into pruning hooks, and each person will be able to sit unafraid, "under his vine and fig tree."

9: ENERGY

A generation goes and a generation comes but the earth endures forever.
And the sun rises and the sun sets—then to its place it rushes; there it
rises again. It goes toward the south and veers toward the north.
The wind goes round and round, and on its rounds the wind returns.
All the rivers flow into the sea, yet the sea is not full; to the place where
the rivers flow, there they flow once more. (Ecclesiastes 1:4–7)

IN 1973, A COMBINATION OF OIL SHORTAGES AND AN OPEC boycott produced an energy crisis in the United States. Six years later, the Iran-Iraq war shut off four million barrels of the world's daily oil supplies almost overnight, and energy prices more than doubled in one year. As a result, the 1970s was a time of energy shortages and a wave of inflation in all industrialized countries. This resulted in rationing and long lines of vehicles at service stations, and in drivers, homeowners, and industries having to pay very high prices for available fuel.

After these crises, energy supplies were relatively stable. However, in early 2001 a series of brownouts (rolling blackouts) in California and rapidly rising gasoline prices thrust the energy issue back into the foreground. Announcing the recommendations of his energy task force headed by Vice President Dick Cheney, President George W. Bush argued that if America failed to act now, "this great country could face a darker future, a future that is, unfortunately, being previewed in rising prices at the gas pump and rolling blackouts in the great state of California."[1] Bush stated that "America needs an energy plan that faces up to our energy challenges and meets them."[2] The White House task force's report cited a "fundamental imbalance between supply and demand" and depicted the potential for a very gloomy energy picture, including high gasoline and electricity prices across much of the country, soaring natural gas prices causing havoc with farmers, and the possibility of power blackouts in the West and Northeast.[3]

As long ago as the 1970s, energy expert Amory Lovins argued that there were two primary approaches to obtaining adequate energy: the "hard" path and the "soft" path.[4] The hard path assumes that we need to obtain energy from coal, oil, uranium, and synthetic sources to continue our historic increase in energy use and that, in fact, such increased energy consumption is necessary for our country to prosper. Advocates of the soft energy path assert that energy efficiency and conservation are the primary answers to current problems, and that renewable energy sources based on sun, wind, flowing water, and biomass should be used to provide much of our energy, without the dangers associated with hard energy fuels.[5]

While it has a few elements of conservation and renewable energy, the main thrust of the Bush task force is toward the hard energy path. Their plan calls for easing regulatory barriers to building nuclear power plants, expanding oil and gas development and the construction of fossil fuel power plants, building new refineries, and improving the nation's inadequate and sometimes precarious electricity grid. Among the report's most controversial recommendations is permitting drilling in the Arctic National Wildlife Refuge in Alaska.

Responses to the Bush task force energy recommendations were predictable, with Republicans and oil, gas, and nuclear interests strongly supporting it, and Democrats and environmentalists loudly opposing it. Republicans argued that the White House's call for expanded oil and gas exploration and the revival of the nuclear power industry was an important step toward ending the energy shortages that had led to the rolling blackouts in California and $2-a-gallon gasoline. Republican House and Senate leaders argued that the president's proposals were a balanced effort to develop new energy supplies while protecting the environment. Senator Frank H. Murkowski, the Alaska Republican who was chairman of the Senate Energy Committee stated, "Today we have an energy policy. Yesterday we didn't."[6]

He said Mr. Bush's plan "is the first national energy plan in a generation; it is comprehensive, it is balanced, and it delivers us to energy
stability and security."[7] Speaker of the House J. Dennis Hastert of Illinois
said the White House proposal "strikes the right balance by successfully
boosting conservation, implementing renewable fuels and 21st-century
technologies, and ensuring safe exploration."[8]

Congressional Democrats denounced the plan as a present to Mr.
Bush's old energy industry business colleagues and a severe environmental
threat. They said it failed to help consumers struggling to cope with fast-
rising prices for gasoline and electricity. Tom Daschle of South Dakota,
then Senate Minority Leader, now Majority Leader as of June 2001, vowed
to block any effort to legislate any parts of President Bush's plan, especially
its proposal for drilling in the Arctic refuge.[9] He stated that the president's
plan "is not a plan for America's future. It's a page from our past. It relies
almost exclusively on the old ways of doing things: drilling more oil wells,
burning more coal, and using more natural gas. That jeopardizes our environment."[10] Senate Democrats took the offensive, releasing an energy bill
that focuses on conserving energy and boosting renewable fuels. Senator
Daschle said the U.S. "cannot drill our way out of this problem" and
accused President Bush of using the country's energy problems to justify
"an all-out assault on the environment."[11] Like the GOP energy package
introduced earlier, the Democratic alternative would expand domestic
energy production. But it stresses tax incentives to promote energy efficiency and wind and solar power, and includes a provision that requires
light trucks and SUVs (sport utility vehicles) to achieve fuel efficiencies
by 2008 comparable to those required of (and achieved by) automobiles.[12]

In view of these sharply divergent opinions (which illustrate the vast
differences between advocates of the hard energy path and the soft energy
path), what criteria should be used to select a proper energy path? They
should include such Jewish values as *bal tashchit* (you shall not waste), "the
earth is the Lord's," the sanctity of human life, being mindful of the needs
and circumstances of future generations, the dignity of labor, and proper
use of the cycles of sun, water, and wind God has provided for our (respon-

sible) use and enjoyment. Let us consider future energy choices in light of each of these considerations.

Bal Tashchit

Consistent with the Biblical mandate not to waste or unnecessarily destroy anything of value (Deuteronomy 20:19, 20), supporters of the soft energy path advocate a strong reliance on conservation.

The U.S. is extremely wasteful of energy. With about 4.5 percent of the world's people, we are responsible for about twenty-four percent of its energy use (the highest per capita consumption in the world).[13] Europe and Japan use about half as much energy relative to Gross Domestic Product (GDP) as the United States. Yet European and Japanese people have comfortable standards of living.[14] Partly because of wasteful energy use, U.S. electrical energy demand doubled about every ten years during the twentieth century.

In spite of major improvements in the energy efficiency of appliances, lights, buildings, and industrial appliances, U.S. per capita energy consumption in 2000 was within two percent of its peak in 1973, before the first oil embargo.[15] This is primarily because (1) we buy bigger cars (minivans, SUVs, and pickup trucks account for more than half of all new vehicle sales—though it should be acknowledged that these vehicles sometimes meet legitimate needs, including work requirements and the challenges of severe winter weather); (2) we buy bigger homes (the average house size increased from 1,600 square feet in 1973 to 2,100 square feet in 2000, even though the average household shrank from 3.6 to 3 people); and (3) we use more electrical gadgets (since 1973, the average energy use by computers, VCRs, dishwashers, and other appliances has been increasing by five percent per year).[16]

Energy made available through conservation is cheaper, safer, more reliable, less polluting, and creates more jobs than energy obtained from any other source.[17] Conservation doesn't mean, as President Reagan once put it, being "too hot in the summer and too cold in the winter." It does mean more effective use of fuel: more efficient automobiles, better-insulated homes and offices, reuse of resources, design of equipment and machines for longer life, and the turning off of lights and equipment when they are not being used.

Several studies have shown that we can continue to grow economically and to maintain, even improve, our lifestyles while reducing our use of energy. According to a report released in September 2000 by the American Council for an Energy-Efficient Economy (ACEEE), the U.S. cut its energy intensity—or energy used per unit of gross domestic product (GDP)—by forty-two percent between 1970 and 1999, while also cutting its carbon emissions per unit of GDP by forty-seven percent.[18] Still, much more progress needs to be made. The ACEEE recommends creating incentives for the use of renewable power and efficient technologies, phasing out old coal-fired power plants, and taxing gas-guzzling light trucks and cars (using the revenue generated to give subsidies to buyers of fuel-efficient vehicles).[19]

Energy conservation saved California $34 billion between 1977 and 2000, roughly $1,000 for each resident, and has played a big role in helping the state's economy grow, according to a state-commissioned report.[20] (Conservation and efficiency also delayed the summer, 2001 crisis in California and made it shorter and easier to recover from; the feared disaster was averted.) The report came as the California legislature was considering bills to extend beyond 2000 a four-year-old charge on utility bills that helps fund energy conservation and costs most families a few dollars a month.[21] The report's lead author, Mark Bernstein, said the study's findings should "end the debate" about the wisdom of the charge because promoting energy conservation will likely lower utility payments for most families. The report indicates that simple changes, such as improving wall insulation and replacing old appliances, can cut as much as $400 from a household's annual utility bill.[22]

However, according to the late energy expert Donella Meadows, energy deregulation and restructuring not only contributed to the energy crisis in California in 2001, but reduced incentives for greater efficiency.[23] It is cheaper and far better for the environment to install more efficient devices. Before deregulation, it cost utilities less to subsidize more efficient bulbs than to build another huge power plant. In the deregulated system, however, utilities have only one incentive: to sell as much power as possible.

As a sign of the increasing interest in energy conservation, in September 2000 a coalition of thirty-eight businesses and environmental groups, ranging from the Whirlpool Corporation to the Natural Resources Defense Council, called on President Clinton to do more to promote energy efficiency.[24] The coalition urged Clinton to push for new tax incentives for buyers of energy-efficient products and increased government investment in renewable energy and clean technologies.[25] In a letter to the President, the coalition also called for $200 million in additional government funding to help low-income families weatherize their homes, and for more research and development on ways to reduce consumption of natural gas and oil.[26]

A valuable resource for religious congregations that wish to conserve energy is a 100-page guide, "Putting Energy into Stewardship," a publication of "ENERGY STAR for Congregations,"[27] a free technical support and information service of the U.S. Environmental Protection Agency. Energy Star helps with cost and savings calculations, responds to questions on facilities and equipment, and generally provides free technical support to prevent pollution through energy efficiency. The Web site also provides online "success stories," a national awards program for congregations' energy efficiency efforts, a directory of finance for energy upgrades, and an interactive map for locating energy efficiency products and services contractors and vendors.[28]

One indication that our society can do far more to conserve energy is found in a 2000 report by the U.S. Environmental Protection Agency, which indicates that the average gas mileage for year 2000 model passenger vehicles was only twenty-four miles per gallon, the lowest value since 1980.[29] The report indicates that the recent drop in fuel economy is due to a surge in sales of vans, pickup trucks, SUVs, and luxury cars, all inefficient users of gas. Faced with rising gasoline prices, some Americans are trading in their SUVs and gas-guzzling cars for more efficient vehicles. The trend, if it continues, is good news for the environment. According to a study by the James A. Baker III Institute for Public Policy at Rice University, the U.S. could decrease its crude-oil imports by 170,000 barrels a day—sixty-two million barrels a year—if consumers switched from SUVs to higher-mileage vehicles.[30] Michelle Robinson, Senior Advocate at the Union of Concerned Scientists' Clean Vehicles Program, states: "Curbing our oil appetite through more efficient SUVs and light trucks could save more oil within the next fifteen years than can be economically recovered from the [Alaskan] Arctic over the next fifty years."[31]

Affordable technologies to boost the fuel economy of SUVs and light trucks are readily available. Simple modifications, such as engine upgrades and more efficient transmissions, could make light trucks and SUVs fifty percent more efficient without sacrificing performance. Advanced technologies such as hybrid and fuel cell vehicles promise even greater gains. UCS's Michelle Robinson writes: "Technology has provided a way to reduce oil use. Now it's up to policymakers to supply the will. Nobody's saying we should go cold-turkey on fossil fuels. But it's time we wean ourselves off our oil addiction."[32]

However, even in the face of rising gas prices, White House spokesman Ari Fleischer said in May 2001 that President Bush would not urge Americans to conserve: "That [a focus on conservation] is a big no. The president believes that it [heavy energy use] is an American way of life, and that it should be the goal of policy-makers to protect the American way of life. The American way of life is a blessed one."[33] The administration's 2001 budget slashed funding for renewable energy research and development and for solar, wind, and geothermal energy programs by nearly fifty percent.[34] Alan Nogee, Clean Energy Program Director for UCS said: "The president's budget has nearly switched off funding for renewable power. Continued support would make these technologies even more competitive with fossil fuels."[35]

"The Earth is the Lord's and the Fullness Thereof" (Psalm 24:1)

Soft energy methods based on renewable resources and conservation have a relatively minor impact on the environment. The hard energy path, on the other hand, causes many threats to already fragile ecosystems:[36]

- Effluents from coal-burning power plants, such as sulfur dioxide and particulate matter (particles), pollute the air. Especially when acting together, these pollutants are extremely detrimental to human health.
- When high smokestacks are used, sulfur dioxide from coal-burning power plants combines with water vapor to form sulfuric acid. Later, this toxic chemical falls to the earth as acid rain, which has badly damaged crop areas and lakes in many regions, including eastern Canada and the Adirondack Mountains.
- Major oil spills severely damage marine life.
- Heated water ejected from power-plant cooling systems causes thermal pollution, which affects the delicate balance of ecological systems of lakes, rivers, and oceans.
- Surface strip mining for coal destroys land and results in acids running off and polluting nearby waters.

The Sanctity of Human Life
Soft energy methods involve minimal or no danger to human life. The hard energy path, in contrast, endangers life in several ways:

- In spite of numerous health and safety advances in the last ten years, underground coal mining is still the most dangerous job. On average, one worker dies in the coal industry every two working days; a coal miner is eight times more likely to die on the job than an average private sector worker.[37] Many miners suffer from the painful, debilitating "black lung" disease, which is caused by inhaling coal dust and often results in death.[38] Because of the high death rate and the recent sharp decline in jobs for coal miners, there are now more coal miners' widows in the U.S. than there are coal miners.[39]
- Air pollution from fossil-fuel power plants causes disease and death.
- Nuclear power plants can pose significant threats to life. Nuclear facilities expose workers and surrounding communities to cumulative doses of low-level radiation, which some scientists believe can result in various kinds of cancer, as well as genetic damage that may be passed on to future generations.

- Hundreds of uranium miners' deaths are linked to exposure to radiation.[40]

Consideration for Future Generations

Judaism teaches us to consider the effects of our actions on future generations. A Talmudic sage posed the question "Who is the wise person?" His response: "The person who foresees the future consequences of his or her actions."[41]

The Talmud tells a story of a very old man who was planting a carob tree, which would not bear fruit for many years after his death. The Talmudic figure Honi the circle-maker asked him why he was planting it, when he would not live to harvest its fruit. He explained that just as he had been able to partake of the fruits of trees which others had planted before he was born, he also would plant for his descendants and others to come after him.[42]

Soft energy methods do not endanger future generations. Conservation is actually an investment in the future, since saved energy and resources can help meet the needs of future generations. Use of renewable sources such as sun, wind, and water avoids future scarcities, which could result in inflation and war.

Once again, hard energy sources come out worse. Among potential negative effects on future generations are the following:

- Five decades after the U.S. atomic electric power industry began accumulating nuclear waste, as temporary repositories quickly fill up, there is no safe, practical method of storing radioactive waste material. Radioactive wastes are highly toxic and, once released into the environment, will contaminate land and water virtually "forever."
- A nuclear accident could release enough radiation to kill thousands of people and contaminate cities, land, and water for decades. Communities near nuclear power plants are finding it difficult to plan an adequate evacuation.
- Nations or terrorist groups may use nuclear waste products to make nuclear weapons.

- The many potential dangers related to nuclear power were summarized dramatically by Nobel Prize-winning physicist Hannes Alfven in the early 1970s:

Fission energy is safe only if a number of critical devices work as they should, if a number of people in key positions follow all of their instructions, if there is no sabotage, no hijacking of transports, if no reactor fuel processing plant or waste repository anywhere in the world is situated in a region of riots or guerrilla activity, and no revolution or war—even a "conventional" one—takes place in these regions....No acts of God can be permitted.[43]

After the horrific terrorist attacks that destroyed the twin towers of the World Trade Center, Tom Clements, head of the Nuclear Control Institute in Washington, D.C., stated that nuclear power plants are vulnerable to terrorists and that attacks on them could cause much more damage than was done when the World Trade Center was destroyed.[44] He said: "It's quite apparent that the facilities are very difficult to defend. I mean, [terrorists] can just go right in, over the fence, take out the guards, and get in."[45] In some simulated attacks, security systems proved completely inadequate at about half the U.S. reactors tested.[46]

- The guarding of nuclear facilities raises threats to civil liberties. In a document prepared for the Nuclear Regulatory Commission, a Stanford University law professor states that in light of potential nuclear-related theft and terrorism, there may be a need for "a nationwide guard force, greater surveillance of dissenting political groups, area searches in the event of loss of material, and creation of new barriers of secrecy."[47] He also anticipates possible wiretapping, detention, and harsh interrogation, perhaps even involving torture.
- The carbon dioxide buildup in the atmosphere due to fossil-fuel burning contributes to a "greenhouse effect," with all of the negative effects on the global climate discussed below in Chapter 10.

The Dignity of Labor

Unlike many ancient societies, such as those of Greece and Rome, where manual labor was done by slaves, Judaism recognizes the dignity of creative labor. Work is considered a character-developing process through which an individual earns self-respect and respect from others.

Many Jewish teachings express great esteem for labor:[48]

A man should love work, and no man should hate work. For even as the Sabbath was commanded to the Jews as a covenant at Sinai, so was labor enjoined in that covenant, as it is said, "Six days shall you labor and do all your work," (and only then it is written) "the seventh day is a Sabbath unto the Lord your God." (Exodus 20:9, 10)[49]

When a person eats of his own labors, his mind is at ease, but when a person eats of the labors of his father or mother or children, his mind is not at ease; how much more so when he has to eat of the labors of strangers.[50]

Many soft energy methods are labor-intensive. Such enterprises as weatherization of homes to make them more energy efficient, recycling of products, and construction of equipment for the production and distribution of renewable energy all create jobs. According to a study prepared for the Energy Subcommittee of the Congressional Joint Economic Committee, the U.S. can gain millions of jobs by adopting an energy policy based much more heavily on solar and other renewable energy sources and conservation.[51]

By contrast, hard energy paths are capital-intensive. They require sophisticated, expensive equipment, but relatively few workers. Some jobs result from construction of pipelines and power stations, but many of them are temporary. Long-term jobs in mining and drilling are often dangerous to those who do such work.

Proper Use of God's Cycles of Sun, Wind, and Water

A major cause of pollution and resource shortages in recent years is our inattention to God's cycles of sun, wind, and water. According to energy expert Denis Hayes, one of the founders of Earth Day, the U.S. could reduce carbon dioxide emissions by eighty percent in our lifetime by converting to the most efficient technologies currently available, and by switching as much as is practical to solar energy, wind power, biofuels, and other renewable sources of energy.[52] At present, solar energy and other forms of renewable energy are expensive, but increased research and greater use would significantly lower the cost of individual units. Hence, in partnership with good conservation practices, the second major element of the soft energy path is use of sun, wind, and water, as well as renewable fuels.

According to studies by the Union of Concerned Scientists and others, renewable energy could supply twenty percent of U.S. electricity needs by 2020.[53] Legislation sponsored by Senators James Jeffords (I-VT) and Joseph Lieberman (D-CT) in 2000 (but never adopted) attempted to ensure that renewable energy development met that target. In a report in 2000, five national laboratories found that renewable energy sources could supply at least 7.5 percent of U.S. electricity by 2010.[54] The study found that expanded use of renewable energy sources, along with improvements in energy efficiency, could substantially reduce energy costs for consumers.

There are many "hidden" benefits of renewable energy sources: they are generally pollution-free, undepletable, dependable, abundant, decentralized, safe, job-creating, and inflation-resistant. These factors contrast with the many "hidden costs" of hard energy sources: air and water pollution; negative health effects; contributions to global climate change; the distortion of foreign policy by our dependence on other countries for fuel; hazardous nuclear wastes that must be stored for thousands of years; balance of payment deficits; potential blackmail from terrorist groups producing or acquiring nuclear weapons; disenfranchisement of the poor, old, young, and disabled in societies based on automobiles; suburban sprawl, paving over farm land and fostering isolation instead of healthy community life; and deaths directly and indirectly caused by oil use (accidents, air and water pollution, and oil wars).

Some Jewish groups have become involved in campaigns for more effective energy policies. At its annual meeting in Baltimore, Maryland on February 28, 2000, the Jewish Council for Public Affairs (JCPA) adopted a resolution on National Energy Policy that calls for Congress and the Administration to move toward a clean and sustainable energy system.[55] Citing concerns about OPEC-induced increases in gasoline prices and growing awareness of the dangers of global warming and air pollution, the group called for swift action to reduce U.S. reliance on fossil fuels as part of a "Clean and Sustainable Energy System."[56] The JCPA is the forum through which 13 national and 122 local Jewish organizations and federations develop consensus positions on pressing public policy issues.

The JCPA resolution concluded:

We stand at the beginning of a new century. The vast majority of scientists and policy experts agree that if dramatic action is not taken soon, it is very likely that human well-being and global geopolitical stability in the 21st century will be gravely affected by global climate change. Aggressive development of environmentally friendly technologies and products will create U.S. jobs, enhance U.S. competitiveness in the global economy, and demonstrate U.S. leadership toward a sustainable energy future for the entire planet.

We have a solemn obligation to do whatever we can within reason both to prevent harm to current and future generations and to preserve the integrity of the creation with which we have been entrusted. Not to do so when we have the technological capacity—as we do in the case of non-fossil fuel energy and transportation technologies—is an unforgivable abdication of our responsibility.

Therefore, the Jewish Council for Public Affairs (JCPA) calls upon Congress and the Administration to move toward the creation of a clean and sustainable energy system for the U.S. that will diminish U.S. reliance on imported oil and significantly reduce greenhouse gas emissions, smog-forming compounds, and precursors to acid rain.[57]

In the summer of 2001, under the leadership of the Coalition on the Environment and Jewish Life (COEJL), over 600 U.S. rabbis representing all denominations, and other religious leaders, signed a statement ("Energy Conservation and God's Creation: An Open Letter to the President, the Congress, and the American People") recommending that religious values (such as the ones discussed in this book) should be considered in formulating energy and global warming-related policies.[58] Their pioneering statement included the following:

> As heads of major religious communities, we pray that all Americans will reflect carefully and speak clearly from their deepest moral and religious convictions about the President's recently announced energy plan.
>
> Far more than rolling blackouts and gasoline price increases are at stake: the future of God's creation on earth; the nature and durability of our economy; our public health and public lands; the environment and quality of life we bequeath our children and grandchildren. We are being called to consider national purpose, not just policy....
>
> Humankind has a fundamental choice of priorities for its future. By depleting energy sources, causing global warming, fouling the air with pollution, and poisoning the land with radioactive waste, a policy of increased reliance on fossil fuels and nuclear power jeopardizes health and well-being for life on Earth. On the other hand, by investing in clean technology, renewable energy, greater vehicle fuel efficiency and safer power plants we help assure sustainability for God's creation and God's justice. Energy conservation is intergenerational responsibility.
>
> We call on all Americans, and particularly our own leaders and congregants, to consider carefully these values, which should guide our individual energy choices and by which we should judge energy policy options. In securing human well-being by preserving creation and promoting justice, conservation is a personal and a public virtue—a comprehensive moral value—a standard for everything we do to assure energy for a wholesome way of life. We

pray that the wisdom, faith, and solidarity of the American people will bring us together—at this critical juncture—to redirect our national energy policy toward conservation, efficiency, justice, and maximum use of the perennial abundance of clean and renewable energy that our Creator brought into being by proclaiming, **"Let there be light"** (Gen 1:3).

In summary, our nation and the world can best be served by an energy policy based on Jewish values, embodied in the acronym CARE (Conservation and Renewable Energy).[59] Such a policy would involve turning away from sources of energy that have become environmentally destructive and extremely costly; adopting simpler technology instead of relying on inefficient central electrical generating plants; and decreasing dependence on large energy companies and foreign governments, which can cut off supplies or sharply raise prices. This could help create a simpler, healthier world, with more conservation of energy and resources; a safer world, with less competition for scarce fuels and other commodities; a more stable economy; less unemployment; and more money available for education, health, housing, transportation, nutrition, and social services. For all these profoundly Jewish reasons, the Jewish community must take a leading role in advocating energy policies that will help usher in this safer, saner future.

10: GLOBAL CLIMATE CHANGE

Where there is no vision, the people perish. (Proverbs 29:18)

GLOBAL CLIMATE CHANGE MAY BE THE MOST CRITICAL problem the world will face in the next few decades. There is a growing scientific consensus that we are already experiencing the effects of global warming, and that human actions are playing a significant role.[1] Global average temperatures have increased about one degree Fahrenheit since 1900. This doesn't sound like much, but it is causing major changes in our weather patterns. The warmest decade in recorded history was the 1990s. The ten warmest years on record have all occurred since 1983, with seven of them since 1990. The global temperature in 1998 was the warmest in recorded history.

Until recently, researchers were not fully certain whether human activities significantly contributed to this warming, or whether it simply reflected natural variations in the earth's climate. However, in the fall of 1995, scientists affiliated with the Intergovernmental Panel on Climate Change (IPCC), a U.N.-sponsored group of leading climate scientists from over a hundred nations, concluded that the observed global temperature increase during the last century "is unlikely to be entirely natural in origin" and that "the balance of evidence suggests that there is a discernible human influence on global climate."[2] These conclusions are in their Second Assessment Report, a document that received contributions and peer review from over 2,500 of the world's leading climate scientists, economists, and risk analysis experts.

In the year 2000, in its Third Assessment Report, the IPCC made two momentous revisions in its forecasts of global warming. It estimated that by 2100, the average world temperature could rise between 2.5 and 10.4 degrees Fahrenheit, a range significantly higher than the 1.8 to 6.3 degree rise predicted by the IPCC in 1995.[3] Also, the group became far more emphatic that it is human activities, rather than natural planetary cycles, that are "contributing substantially" to the increase, and they indicated that they expect these human contributions to continue to grow.[4] The IPCC report, which is over a thousand pages and was written by 123 lead authors from many countries who drew on 516 contributing experts, is one of the most comprehensive ever produced on global warming.[5] Hence, the conclusions of the report represent an unprecedented consensus among hundreds of climate scientists from all over the world. This makes their summary statement that "Projected climate changes during the 21st century have the potential to lead to future large-scale and possibly irreversible changes in Earth systems," with "continental and global consequences" especially ominous.[6]

The main cause of global warming is the increase in atmospheric concentrations of heat-trapping gases, including carbon dioxide, methane, nitrous oxides, and chlorofluorocarbons. These gases act as a "greenhouse," trapping heat radiated out from the earth. While a certain amount of these gases is natural and necessary to retain enough of the sun's energy to support life on earth, current excessive amounts will cause the earth's temperature to rise abnormally.

The human activities that climate scientists have linked to the increases of these heat-trapping gases in the atmosphere include the burning of fossil fuels (coal, oil, and natural gas), cattle ranching, deforestation, and rice farming. In 1999, seven environmental groups, including the Union of Concerned Scientists, produced a world map showing eighty-nine "Global Warming Early Warning Signs."[7] The groups conclude that "the earth is heating up." Their ten categories of "early warning signs" (along with some of their examples of each) are presented below to help illustrate the damage that global climate change has already done, and its potential for major future damage:[8]

1. Heat waves and periods of unusually warm weather (frequent and severe heat waves lead to increases in heat-related illness and death, especially among the ill, the poor, the elderly, and the young).

- A deadly heat wave in the summer of 1998 claimed over a hundred lives in Texas. Temperatures in Dallas were over 100 degrees Fahrenheit for fifteen consecutive days.
- In 1999, New York City had its driest and warmest July in recorded history. Temperatures were above 95 degrees Fahrenheit on eleven days—the most ever in the city in any single month.
- In 1998, Cairo, Egypt had its warmest August on record, with a temperature of 105.8 degrees Fahrenheit on August 6, 1998.

2. Spreading disease (warmer temperatures allow disease-transmitting mosquitoes to extend their ranges).

- There was a deadly malaria outbreak in the summer of 1997 in the Kenyan highlands, although the area had never previously been exposed to the disease.
- In the Andes mountains of Colombia, disease-carrying mosquitoes have appeared at 7,200 feet, although they previously never appeared above 3,300 feet.
- In Mexico, dengue fever has been found at 5,600 feet, far above its previous limit of 3,300 feet.

3. The earlier arrival of spring (this may disrupt animal migrations, alter competitive balances among species, and cause additional unforeseen problems).

- Mirror Lake, New Hampshire has thawed about half a day earlier each year for the past thirty years.
- In the United Kingdom, toads, frogs, and newts are spawning about ten days earlier than they were seventeen years ago, and in 1995 about one-third of sixty-five bird species studied had moved up the date of egg-laying by an average of 8.8 days compared to 1971.
- In southern England, the four earliest leafing days ever for oak trees occurred in the 1990s, in response to increasing temperatures from January to March over the past forty-one years.

4. Plant and animal range shifts and population declines (such shifts, caused by warmer temperatures, may hasten extinctions).

- In Europe, twenty-two of thirty-five butterfly species studied have shifted their range northwards by 22 to 150 miles, probably due to a 1.4 degree Fahrenheit warming in the past century.
- Adelie penguin populations have declined by thirty-three percent in Antarctica in the past twenty-five years, due to shrinking of their winter ice habitat caused by ice pack melting.
- In Monterey Bay, California, invertebrate species such as limpets, snails, and sea stars have been shifting northward, probably due to warmer air and ocean temperatures.

5. Sea level rise and coastal flooding (global sea level has risen four to ten inches in the past century and may rise an additional half a foot to three feet during the next century, causing major losses of coastal areas).

- In the Chesapeake Bay, the current rate of sea level rise is triple the historical rate and appears to be accelerating. About a third of the Blackwater National Wildlife Refuge marsh has been gradually submerged since 1938.
- In many areas of the world, rising sea levels are having negative effects, including saltwater inundation of coastal mangrove forests in Bermuda; loss of coastal land at Rufisque on the south coast of Senegal; considerable beach loss in Hawaii; and the receding of shoreline by an average of half a foot per year in Fiji and over a foot and a half per year in Western Samoa for at least ninety years.

6. Coral reef bleaching (reefs in or near thirty-two countries experienced major bleaching in 1997–98, and continued bleaching due to warmer sea temperatures and other factors could have a major negative impact on aquatic life).

Global warming is the most serious of the threats facing reefs, since rising water temperatures cause the coral to expel microscopic organisms that are crucial to their health, a phenomenon known as coral bleaching. Among the many areas where significant bleaching of coral reefs has occurred are American Samoa; Papua, New Guinea; the Persian Gulf; the

Florida Keys and Bahamas; Australia's Great Barrier Reef; and the Philippines.

7. Melting of glaciers (over the past 150 years, the majority of monitored mountain glaciers have been shrinking, with many at low altitudes disappearing; continued shrinkage could disrupt an important source of water).

- At current rates of glacial retreat, all the glaciers in Glacier National Park, Montana will be gone by 2070.
- Other examples of glacial retreat include a fifty percent reduction in Spain since 1980; a twenty-five percent reduction on China's Tien Shen Mountains over the past forty years; and, in the past century, a fifty percent reduction in the glaciers of the Caucasus Mountains of Russia and a ninety-two percent melting of Kenya's Lewis Glacier.

8. Arctic and Antarctic warming (as parts of Canada, Alaska, Siberia, and Antarctica have been experiencing warming well above the global average for the past few decades, melting permafrost requires the reconstruction of buildings, roads, and airports, and is increasing soil erosion and the frequency of landslides).

- The ground has subsided from sixteen to thirty-three feet in parts of interior Alaska due to permafrost thawing.
- Nearly 1,150 square miles of the Larson B and Wilkins ice shelves in Antarctica collapsed between March 1998 and March 1999, after four hundred years of relative stability.
- The area covered by sea ice has shrunk by about five percent in the Bering Sea over the past forty years and by six percent in the Arctic Ocean from 1978 to 1995.

9. Downpours, heavy snowfalls, and flooding (heavy rainfall and other types of storms have been occurring more frequently, substantially increasing damage from storms. U.S. insurance companies have become strong advocates of efforts to reduce global warming because of major insurance claims resulting from recent severe storms and flooding. At the international climate change summit in the Hague in 2000, Dr. Andrew Dlugolecki, Director of General Insurance Development of CGNU, the world's sixth largest insurance company, told delegates that the rate of damage caused by changing weather is increasing at about ten percent per year, and losses related to global climate change could exceed the world's wealth and bankrupt the global economy by 2065).[9]

- Korea experienced severe flooding during July and August 1998, with rainfall on some days exceeding ten inches.
- New England experienced double the normal amount of rain in June, 1998, with a 117-year-old record broken in Boston on June 13–14.
- New South Wales, Australia had its wettest August on record in 1998. A storm dumped twelve inches of rain on Sydney on August 15–17, while only four inches of rain normally falls there during the entire month.

10. Droughts and fires (as temperatures increase, droughts have become more frequent and severe in many areas).

- Mexico experienced its worse fire season ever in 1998, with 1.25 million acres burned during a severe drought. Smoke from the fires caused a statewide health alert in Texas.
- In 1999, several states in the Eastern U.S. had the driest growing season in 105 years, with fifteen states declared agriculture disaster areas. In West Virginia alone, losses exceeded $80 million.

These are just a small sampling of recent events with possible connections to global warming. While no single event offers conclusive proof that global warming is occurring, the sum total of so many cases, along with the overall global temperature increases, has led a vast majority of climate scientists to agree on the reality of global warming. And there are news reports of additional examples almost weekly. For example:

- A study appearing in the September 2000 journal *Science* concludes that twenty-six bodies of water in the Northern Hemisphere are freezing an average of 8.7 days later and thawing 9.8 days earlier than they did 150 years ago.
- According to scientists assembled in Indonesia at a major coral reef conference, more than twenty-five percent of the world's coral reefs

have been destroyed by global warming, pollution, and destructive fishing techniques. Most of the rest could be lost in the next twenty years if serious action isn't taken to address these problems.[10] Up to ninety percent of coral reefs have been killed around the Maldives and Seychelles Islands in the Indian Ocean.[11] Loss of the world's reefs would be a major blow not only to the environment and biodiversity, but also to the 500 million people around the world who depend on coral reef systems for part of their food or livelihood.

- Britain's Prime Minister, Tony Blair, suggested that global warming is contributing to the country's disastrous weather when heavy rains brought the most widespread flooding Britain has seen in fifty years in October and November of 2000.[12] Deputy Prime Minister John Prescott stated that the storms should serve as a "wake-up call for everyone" about the impact of global warming.[13] Meanwhile, the first comprehensive scientific assessment of the effects of climate change in Europe predicted more flooding in northern European countries such as Britain, and more heat and drought in southern European countries.[14]

Responses to Global Warming

How should the world respond to the threat of global climate change? In part by applying the Jewish teachings analyzed in previous chapters, including:

- *Bal tashchit* (you shall not waste): Conserving energy and increasing the efficiency of energy use would reduce the emission of greenhouse gases.
- "The earth is the Lord's": Judaism mandates a sacred obligation to protect the integrity of ecological systems so that their diverse constituent species, including humans, can thrive.
- The sanctity of every life: The agricultural, transportation, and energy approaches that minimize emission of greenhouse gases reduce the threats to human life discussed above, now and for future generations.
- Consideration of the lives and needs of future generations: Rapid climate change threatens the very existence of future generations.

Conservation and renewable energy thus help insure that human life will continue.

- "Justice, justice shall you pursue": Actions to address climate change should also protect those most vulnerable to climate change, including poor people, those living in coastal areas, and subsistence farmers. Along with reducing global warming by weaning ourselves off of depletable and polluting energy sources, it is important to aid the poor in acquiring heat and transportation and to assist dislocated energy workers and others affected by the changes.

- Proper use of God's cycles of sun, wind, and water: Use of solar, wind, and other renewal forms of energy reduces emission of greenhouse gases.

Several Jewish groups, including the Coalition on the Environment and Jewish Life (COEJL)[15] and its parent body, the Jewish Council for Public Affairs (JCPA), the national coordinating organization for the 13 national and 125 local Jewish community relations agencies, have been urging their members to contact elected officials to stress the harmful effects of global climate change, and to urge them to support effective remedies. These groups support the position that industrial nations' emissions should be decreased below 1990 levels by 2010. They also propose that the U.S. and other industrialized countries take the leadership role, as we are primarily responsible for the problem. However, they also recommend that developing nations—whose emissions, while still far below these of industrialized countries per capita, are sharply rising—should likewise be required by treaties to commit to emission reductions.

On October 27, 1997, the JCPA unanimously adopted a comprehensive statement based on Jewish values and teachings, "Confronting the Challenge of Climate Change".[16] It includes the following:

The Jewish Council for Public Affairs urges the Jewish community, and all other Americans, to conduct energy audits of, and institute energy efficiency technologies and practices into, private homes and communal facilities, including synagogues, schools, community centers, and commercial buildings....

Furthermore, we call on JCPA member agencies to initiate dialogues with Jewish businesspeople and the broader business community aimed at increasing responsible participation by business in addressing global climate change....

Together, the people of the world can, and must, use our God-given gifts to develop innovative strategies to meet the needs of all who currently dwell on this planet without compromising the ability of future generations to meet their own needs.

Consistent with Jewish teachings, the JCPA statement also urged the following policies:

- The U.S. government should negotiate, and the U.S. Senate should ratify, binding international agreements to minimize climate change by committing the world's nations to reducing their current and projected emissions in order to stabilize atmospheric carbon concentrations so that they will not result in widespread human and/or ecological harm.
- Congress should appropriate the funds necessary to fulfill our nation's responsibility to reduce global carbon emissions, as "an important down payment on what will be needed to achieve safe atmospheric carbon levels in the long run."
- The federal government should immediately adopt policies to reduce greenhouse gas emissions, particularly programs which employ economic incentives to lower demand for fossil fuels, in order to encourage the development of non-polluting energy sources and to raise revenue for public projects, such as mass transit, that would lower carbon emissions.
- The government should also adopt standards, such as power plant emissions standards and motor vehicle fuel efficiency (so-called CAFE) standards, that require the use of the best fuel-efficiency and emissions-reduction technologies available.

The important, comprehensive statement on energy signed by over six hundred U.S. rabbis and other religious leaders that was discussed in the last chapter also included a statement on global warming:

These concerns have entirely unprecedented moral urgency in the twenty-first century. In its reliance on fossil fuels, American energy policy is a cause of global climate change....We must join in binding international agreements, such as the Kyoto Protocol, which set energy conservation targets and timetables. Preventing climate change is a preeminent expression of faithfulness to our Creator, God. Energy conservation is global leadership and solidarity.[17]

Unfortunately, instead of responding to the global warming problem, in 2001 U.S. President George W. Bush chose not to act. First, he reversed his campaign promise to reduce carbon dioxide emissions from power plants, the biggest U.S. contributor to global warming. Defending his decision, Bush insisted that "an energy crisis" threatening the country's economic health had caused him to back away from his pledge. Next, the President decided to withdraw U.S. support from the Kyoto Protocol, an international global warming treaty, claiming that it placed an unfair burden on the United States, even though the U.S., with only about four percent of the world's population, is responsible for twenty-five percent of gases that contribute to global warming. IPCC Chair Robert Watson argues that the U.S. should be doing far more: "A country like China has done more, in my opinion, than a country like the United States to move forward in economic development while remaining environmentally sensitive."[18] According to the Commission for Environmental Cooperation, the Bush administration's energy plan, which calls for the creation of two thousand new electrical generating plants in the next six years, would increase the greenhouse gas emissions that spur global warming by fourteen to thirty-eight percent by 2007.[19]

Reduction of fossil fuel emissions would improve, not hinder, our economy, since such reductions could be based on strategies such as improving energy efficiency, changing to renewable energy sources, improving mass transit, preserving and planting forests, and encouraging people to shift to plant-based diets. These approaches have the added benefits of reducing air and water pollution, creating jobs, and reducing expenditures for energy. Contrary to a common perception that reducing global warming will have major negative economic effects, a properly financed, public-private global transition to high-efficiency and renewable energy technologies could produce an unprecedented worldwide economic boom involving the creation of millions of new jobs, a reversal of the widening economic gap between people living in the northern and southern hemispheres, the raising of living standards in developing nations (without compromising the economic achievements of industrial nations), and the establishment of the renewable energy industry as a central driving engine of growth of the global economy.[20] The technology and knowledge are already available; all that is needed is vision and dedicated efforts to promote the proper policies.

Jews should play a leading role in the efforts to reduce global climate change, in order to fulfill the mandate that we should be co-workers with God in preserving the world, and to illustrate how Jewish values can have a major impact on the solution of global problems.

11: POPULATION GROWTH

For the Jewish people, the problem [of the population bomb] does not exist. On the contrary, it would be more accurate to describe our situation as a "Population Bust"... which spells demographic disaster for Jewry. ("Jewish Population: Renascence or Oblivion"—a report of the N.Y. Jewish Federation)[1]

JEWS ARE RIGHTFULLY CONCERNED ABOUT THE SERIOUSness of the world population problem. However, there is also widespread concern in the Jewish community about the effects of reduced Jewish population and assimilation.[2]

Rapid Population Growth
Explosive population growth, a critical world issue, is largely the result of an increase in life expectancies, due to improved standards of living and advances in sanitation and medical technology.[3] There is now widespread concern about the world's ability to provide enough food, energy, housing, employment, education, and health care for the rapidly increasing global population while simultaneously protecting our environment, quality of life, and political freedom. While, as indicated in Chapter 6, rapid population growth is more a result of poverty and injustice than their cause, it is still a serious issue that needs to be addressed.

While it took until about 1830 for the world's population to reach one billion people, now the human population is growing by approximately one billion people every twelve years. According to the Population Reference Bureau's 2001 "World Population Data Sheet," world population in mid-2001 was 6.137 billion people. It is projected to reach 7.818 billion by 2025 and 9.036 billion by 2050.[4] These figures assume a slowing of present population growth rates; if current rates of population growth continued, the world population would double in only fifty-four years.[5] There is currently a world population increase of almost eighty million people each year.[6] At this rate, the world population increases more than the entire present population of the United States every four years![7] It increases as much every three days as it did in an entire century for most of the centuries that humans have been on Earth.[8]

Many poor countries, such as Somalia, Guatemala, and Nicaragua, have population-doubling periods of less than twenty-five years.[9] This means that in order to maintain present, generally inadequate conditions, these countries must more than double their supply of food, energy, clean water, housing, schools, and jobs each quarter century. Since this is extremely difficult, if not impossible, for many countries, the result will almost surely be increasing poverty, malnutrition, and civil unrest.

Additional population problems are created by the growing movement of people from rural areas to cities, searching for better jobs and social conditions. The very rapid increases in urban populations can be seen from the following: while the world's three largest cities in 1960 were New York (14.2 million), Tokyo (11.0 million), and London (9.1 million), by 2015, the three largest cities are expected to be Tokyo (28.9 million), Mumbai (formerly Bombay), India (26.2 million), and Lagos, Nigeria (24.6 million).[10] Many cities of the developing world have been unable to meet the needs of their rapidly growing populations. People living on the sprawling outskirts of many of these cities have inadequate housing, sanitation, employment, and education; hence there is vast human suffering and great potential for social unrest.

Rapid population growth is not only a problem for poorer countries. The U.S. population is projected to more than double from 281 million people in 2000 to 571 million in the next century, largely as a result of immigration.[11] Considering the very high average standard of living in the U.S. and the many environmental problems created by the present population, this projection has very severe implications for air and water pollution, climate change, deforestation, soil erosion, and the availability of sufficient oil, water, and other resources. There may be food shortages in the United States, and in countries dependent on food imports from the U.S., because arable land is expected to shrink from 400 million acres today to 290 million by 2050.[12]

Even without the expected continued sharp increase in population, an estimated twenty million people now die each year from hunger and its effects, and over seven million infants died in 2000 before their first birthday.[13] Meanwhile, environmental dangers and degradations increase everywhere.

The 1992 Union of Concerned Scientists' "World Scientists' Warning to Humanity" proclaims: "Pressures resulting from unrestrained population growth put demands on the natural world that can overwhelm any efforts to achieve a sustainable future. If we are to halt the destruction of our environment, we must accept limits to that growth."[14] While there has been some recent progress in slowing the rate of population increase, the following factors contribute to population growth momentum:

- While birth rates have actually dropped recently in most countries of the world, death rates have decreased even more sharply, due to better medical and sanitary conditions, and are likely to continue to decline.
- The largest population increases are occurring in poor countries, where children are desired for economic reasons.[15] Even while advances have reduced the level of poverty in developing societies, the absolute number of destitute people is increasing.
- Thirty-three percent of people in poorer countries are under fifteen years of age.[16] These young people will soon be moving into their reproductive years.

Many people believe that rapid population growth is the greatest problem currently facing the world. They emphasize correlations between population increases and hunger, resource depletion, pollution, and other problems. One group, "Zero Population Growth" (ZPG)[17], argues that only with a stabilized population will the world's people be able to have clean air and water, a decent place to live, a meaningful job, and a good education. They have been working to publicize problems caused by population growth and to advocate for reducing U.S. births and the rate of immigration to the U.S. They encourage couples to voluntarily limit their reproduction to a maximum of two children. Another group, "Negative Population Growth," argues that we have already passed the optimum U.S. population and must soon decrease our population.[18] They also advocate restrictions on immigration and reductions in birth rates.

Jewish Teachings Concerning Population

How should Jews respond to arguments of advocates of reduced family size? The first *mitzvah* of the Torah is the duty of procreation. On the sixth day of creation, God created human beings, male and female, and blessed them and commanded them:

> Be fruitful and multiply, and replenish the earth, and subdue it; and have dominion over the fish of the sea and over the fowl of the air, and over every living thing that moves upon the earth. (Genesis 1:28)

Later, after the Flood, this mandate was repeated to Noah: "Be fruitful and multiply, and replenish the earth" (Genesis 9:1).

The blessing of fertility was extended to Abraham and Sarah (Genesis 17:16). Through Isaac, Abraham was to be blessed with seed as numerous as the stars of heaven and as the sand on the seashore (Genesis 15:5). This blessing was repeated to Jacob, in the early years of his life (Genesis 28:14) and also later (Genesis 35:11). The principal blessing that Torah personalities conferred on their children and grandchildren was that of fertility. This was true of Isaac's blessing to Jacob (Genesis 28:3), Jacob's blessing to Manasseh and Ephraim (his grandchildren) (Genesis 48:16), and Jacob's blessing to Joseph (Genesis 49:25).

The following is one of many Talmudic passages that stress the importance of having children:

> Rabbi Eliezer stated: "He who does not engage in the propagation of the race is as though he sheds blood; for it is said, 'whoever sheds man's blood, by man shall his blood be shed,' and this is immedi-

ately followed by the text, 'And you, be you fruitful and multiply.' "
Rabbi Jacob said: "[One who does not propagate], it is as though
he has diminished the Divine image; since it is said, 'For in the
image of God He made man,' and this is immediately followed by,
'And you be fruitful.' " Ben Azzai said: "It is as though he sheds
blood *and* diminishes the Divine image, since it is said, 'And you,
be you fruitful and multiply.' "[19]

Every human life is sacred and every new life brings God's image anew into
the world. Hence Judaism has always regarded marriage and procreation as
sacred duties and divine imperatives. People are to populate the earth, for
the world that God created is "very good" and people should follow God's
commandment to be fruitful and multiply "with the intention of
preserving the human species."[20]

Judaism is never content with general formulations. It always provides
specific indications of how commandments are to be carried out. Hence
the Mishnah considered the question of how large a family one needs in
order to satisfy the injunction to have children:

> A married man shall not abstain from the performance of the duty
> of propagation of the race unless he already has children. As to the
> number, Beit Shammai (the school of Shammai) ruled: two males,
> and Beit Hillel ruled: a male and female, for it is stated in scripture,
> male and female He created them.[21]

According to the Talmud, for Beit Shammai, the model for the sufficiency
of two sons was Moses, since he had two sons.[22] The disciples of Hillel base
their opinion on the story of creation (Adam and Eve). The prevailing
halachic opinion agrees with Beit Hillel. Although the rabbis considered
it meritorious for Jews to have large families, they looked at birth control
more favorably after a couple had a son and a daughter.[23] However, rabbis
generally encouraged couples not to limit themselves to two children. This
is consistent with Maimonides' injunction:

Even if a person has fulfilled the commandment of "be fruitful and multiply," he is still enjoined not to refrain from fruitfulness and increase as long as he is able, for he who adds a life in Israel [is as he who created a world].[24]

The Jewish tradition teaches that those who have no biological children can give "birth" in other ways. For example, the Talmud states that if someone teaches Torah to his friend's child, "it is as if he gave birth to him,"[25] as it is written: "These are the offspring of Aaron and Moses..." (Numbers 3:1). The Talmud points out that the verses that follow only list the sons of Aaron, yet the Torah calls them the "offspring" of both Moses and Aaron! This is because Moses taught them Torah, and through his teaching, states the Talmud, he became their spiritual parent.

Another example is the following Talmudic statement: "Whoever teaches his friend's child Torah, it is as if he made him, as it is written (concerning the disciples of Abraham and Sarah): 'the souls they made in Haran' (Genesis 12:5)."[26] In Haran, Abraham and Sarah served as teachers and guides to the spiritually-searching men and women of their generation and brought them to God and the Abrahamic tradition. Rashi, in his commentary on the words, "the souls they made," says that they brought people "under the wings of the Shechinah—the Divine Presence." Their teachings gave new life to these searching souls, and from the perspective of the Torah, these are "the souls they made in Haran."

Current Jewish Population Issues

Probably the most detailed study of recent Jewish population statistics is "Prospecting the Jewish Future: Population Projections, 2000–2080,"[27] a study conducted for the American Jewish Committee. The report provides the following facts about current Jewish population and population trends:

- While Jewish population has grown in the past fifty-five years, it has not replaced the six million Jews who were murdered during the Holocaust.[28]

- Annual average population growth rates for world Jewry were 0.18 percent in the 1970s, 0.04 percent in the 1980s, and 0.22 percent in the 1990s—hence close to zero population growth.[29]
- An important demographic factor is the rapid increase of intermarriages between Jews and non-Jews in Diaspora communities, especially since the 1960s, and the failure of most of these couples' children to identify themselves as Jews.[30] While marriages across religious lines occur rarely in Israel, fifty percent of marriages in the United States involving Jews join Jews with a non-Jewish mate. In other Diaspora communities, it is about seventy percent in Russia and the Ukraine, fifty percent in France, forty percent in the United Kingdom, and above thirty percent in Canada and Australia.[31] A majority of Jews in the United States are indifferent to Judaism and/or lack knowledge of basic Jewish teachings.[32]
- The Diaspora Jewish community decreased from 10.4 million people in 1945 to 10.2 million in 1960, to an estimated 8.3 million in 2000.[33] Meanwhile, Israel's Jewish population increased from about half a million people in 1945 to almost 4.9 million in 2000.[34]
- Fertility rates (average number of children per woman during childbearing years) in Diaspora communities vary from 0.9 to 1.7 children, far below the replacement fertility level of 2.1 children that replaces the parents and thus keeps the population constant. By contrast, the Jewish fertility rate in Israel is 2.6, well above the replacement fertility level.[35]
- The world Jewish population is projected to increase from 13.1 million in 2000 to 13.8 million by 2020, 14 million by the beginning of the 2030s, and 15 million around the year 2080, producing about a seventeen percent increase for the entire period.[36] This increase masks very different trends in Israel and the Diaspora. In Israel, the Jewish population is projected to increase from 4.9 million in 2000 to over 10 million in 2080, more than doubling.[37] By contrast, the Diaspora Jewish community is projected to decrease from 8.3 million in 2000 to 5.2 million in 2080.[38] Because of these trends, it is projected that more Jews will live in Israel than in any other country by 2020, and an absolute majority of the Jewish population will live there by 2050.[39]

(The seventeen percent increase in the world's Jewish population mentioned above is far smaller than the population growth rate projected for the world, meaning that the percentage of the world's people who are Jews will continue to sharply decrease.)

Based on these facts, many Jews believe that one of the critical challenges today is the issue of Jewish survival in the Diaspora. They argue that the low Jewish birth rate, along with high rates of intermarriage and assimilation, poses a grave danger to the Jewish people.

This is the central thesis of a reference work: *Jewish Population: Renascence or Oblivion*, edited by Judith Zimmerman and Barbara Trainin, which is a record of the proceedings of a conference on Jewish population in 1978, sponsored by the Commission on Synagogue Relations of the Federation of Jewish Philanthropies of New York. In her introduction Judith Zimmerman, chairperson of the Federation's task force on Jewish population, outlines the twofold purpose of the conference (and of the report): (1) To sound an alarm and alert the Jewish community that the Jewish population is declining. We are practicing negative population growth, i.e., we are not even replacing our present numbers. This phenomenon, coupled with increased assimilation and mixed marriages, threatens Jewish survival. (2) To determine whether the Jewish community can, in the words of Dr. Steven M. Cohen (who presented a paper at the conference), "effectively intervene to minimize population losses."[40]

A *Time* magazine article, "The Disappearing Jews," reports that Orthodox Rabbi Norman Lamm—president of Yeshiva University—recommends that "each Jewish couple should have four or five children because Jews are a disappearing species." Rabbi Lamm calls for immediate "bold and courageous action" by Jewish educators and community leaders to reverse a situation that "borders on the catastrophic."[41] He suggests steps to increase the Jewish birth rate, such as local federations providing scholarship money for children from large Jewish families to attend Jewish schools, and instructing our children as young as nursery-school age in the concept that large families should be the norm.

In June 1977, the Reform Movement's Central Conference of American Rabbis, a group that generally adopts liberal stances, urged Jewish couples "to have at least two or three children."[42] Rabbi Sol Roth, former president of the New York Board of Rabbis, suggests that "Jewish families should have at least three children, and the goal of zero population growth should find no application in the Jewish community."[43]

Jews have responded to arguments by advocates of zero population growth in several ways:

- Since Jews constitute less than one-tenth of one percent of the world's population, the Jewish contribution to world population growth cannot matter significantly.
- Since six million Jews—one-third of the Jewish people—were killed in the Holocaust, Jews have a special obligation to bring children into the world to replace their numbers.
- Jews have made special contributions to the world, far beyond their very small proportion of the world's population, in areas such as science, the arts, education, business, and politics. Hence increasing the number of Jewish children might well increase the general level of accomplishment in the world. It is also important that Judaism survive because the world badly needs the Jewish messages of peace, justice, and righteousness.

Rabbi David M. Feldman argues that "Jews have the paradoxical right to work for the cause of population control while regarding themselves as an exception to the rule."[44]

Some advocates of maintaining or increasing the Jewish population have attacked the premises of the zero population growth movement. There is much merit in their argument, since, as discussed, rapid population growth, while a very serious concern, is not the prime cause of the world's problems. But these critics have often ignored the facts that millions are dying annually due to hunger and its effects, that half the world's people suffer from poverty, illiteracy, malnutrition, and disease, and that the world's ecosystems are being increasingly threatened. They also put great faith in technology as a solution to global problems, not taking into account that many of today's problems have been caused or worsened by the misuse of technology over many years.

It should be pointed out that there are many encouraging signs for future Jewish survival and security:[45]

- Some segments of Judaism, such as the fervently Orthodox and Chassidim, are growing in numbers; they tend to have high fertility rates, little or no intermarriage, and relatively little assimilation or defection from Judaism. The fact that these groups are often underrepresented in surveys throws some doubt on the estimates of Jewish population trends previously discussed. These groups may be replenishing Jewish population, matching losses among the rest of the Jewish population. This possibility is supported by the fact that in Israel, ten percent of the families produce forty percent of the children.[46]

- There has been a tremendous increase in the number of Jewish day schools in the United States. There was record enrollment in 2000, with 185,000 students enrolled in about 670 Jewish day schools.[47] Eighty percent of day school students are enrolled in Orthodox schools.[48] But non-Orthodox schools have been experiencing rapid growth as well, with an increase in registration of about twenty percent in the 1990s.[49]

- The many yeshivas for high school and college students make the U.S. a potential new center of Talmudic learning. There are currently more yeshivas and yeshiva students in Israel than in any time or place in Jewish history.

- There are many *ba'alei* and *ba'alot teshuvah* (returnees to traditional Jewish observance) in the U.S., Israel, and the rest of the world. These people generally bring a renewed dedication and involvement to Judaism.

- There has been evidence of renewed Jewish commitment among Reform Jews, a large number of whom assimilated in previous generations. New Reform prayerbooks contain more Hebrew and increasingly engage concepts such as *mitzvot*. In recent decades, the Reform movement has affirmed Jewish peoplehood, encouraged *aliyah* (moving to Israel), and asserted that Jews have a stake and responsibility in building the state of Israel.

- Jewish programs on college campuses have been developing rapidly. Many young Jews are having serious encounters with Judaism on college campuses.
- Thousands of scholars are researching *Yiddishkeit* (Jewish tradition). Hebrew literature and Jewish scholarship are flourishing in Israel.

Thus in many ways, as a counter to the assimilation of many Jews, there has been a marked improvement in the quality and intensity of Jewish life in the last generation.

It should be pointed out that there have been many false prophecies of Jewish disappearance in the past. The late Professor Simon Rawidowicz pointed out that Jews are "the ever-dying people," with each generation since early in Jewish history believing that it might be the last one.[50] It is interesting to note that each of the patriarchs Abraham and Isaac had two children with his matriarchal wife, and in each case one of them (Abraham's son Ishmael and Isaac's son Esau) left the faith. But in spite of Judaism's strong emphasis on procreation, there are justifications in Jewish sacred writings for some aspects of the zero population growth philosophy:

- While in Egypt, Joseph had two sons during the seven years of plenty, but no additional children during the seven years of famine. The renowned Biblical commentator Rashi interprets this to mean that when there is widespread hunger, one should not bring additional children into the world.[51]
- According to the Talmud, Noah was commanded to desist from procreation on the ark, since it contained only enough provisions for those who entered the ark.
- It can be argued that when Adam and later Noah were commanded to "Be fruitful and multiply," the earth was far emptier than it is today. Now that the earth is "overfilled," as indicated by the poverty, malnutrition, and squalor faced by so many of the world's people, perhaps Jewish tradition should come to a new understanding of this commandment.

There would thus seem to be some rationale for Jews to advocate some version of zero population growth. But we should look more deeply into the problem. Are current crises due primarily to too many people or are there other, more important causes?

Perhaps what the world needs today is not zero population growth (ZPG), but zero population-impact growth (ZPIG).[52] For it is not just the number of people that is important, but how much they produce, consume, and waste. The impact that affluent nations have on the environment is extremely disproportionate to their populations. The United States, with about 4.5 percent of the world's population, consumes thirty percent of the world's natural resource base, using twenty percent of the planet's metals, twenty-four percent of its energy (the highest per capita consumption in the world), and twenty-five percent of its fossil fuels.[53] It has been estimated that an average American has fifty times the impact of an average person in poorer countries, based on resources used and pollution caused. This means that the U.S. 2000 population of 281 million people[54] has an impact on ecosystems equal to over fourteen billion people in the developing world, or over twice the world's 2000 population of about six billion people.

Most people connect widespread hunger and resource scarcities to overpopulation. Yet numerous studies have concluded that there is enough food to feed all the world's people adequately: the problem lies in waste, injustice, and inequitable distribution.[55] For example, over seventy percent of U.S.-produced grain goes to feed the almost ten billion animals destined for slaughter in the U.S. each year, and two-thirds of U.S. grain exports are used for animal feed, while at least a billion of the world's people lack enough food.

Poverty, injustice, and inequality also contribute to continued population growth. The poorer countries do not provide unemployment benefits, sick leave, or retirement pensions. Hence, children become the only form of security in periods of unemployment, illness, and old age. They are also regarded as economic assets, since by the age of seven or eight, children are net contributors to their families—fetching water and firewood from distant places, looking after younger children, cooking and cleaning, thus freeing adults for other jobs. Furthermore, infant death rates are still relatively high in the underdeveloped world, so that parents desire many children in order to insure that some will survive to provide security in their old age.

Because of these conditions, family planning programs by themselves are ineffective in lowering birth rates. It is necessary to improve economic and social conditions so that people will not feel the need for more children to provide economic survival and old-age security. With an improved economic outlook, people start to limit the size of their families, as has occurred in the United States and in the more affluent countries of Europe. However, unless the world changes its present unjust and inequitable social, political, and economic conditions, population will continue to grow rapidly, along with global hunger, poverty, illiteracy, unemployment, and violence.

There need be no inconsistency between Jewish survival and global survival in the area of population growth. A Jew can have a large family and still help reduce famine and poverty in the world by working for conservation and justice. A family of five that has an impact (in terms of consumption and pollution) equal to that of five or ten families in India or another poor country does far less harm (in using resources and causing environmental damage) than a family of three with an impact equal to fifty Indians per person.

A Jew who has few or no children can work for Jewish survival by striving to increase Jewish commitment through example, teaching, and writing. Judaism teaches that our good deeds can be our "main offspring."[56] The Torah states: "These are the offspring of Noah: Noah was a righteous man..." (Genesis 6:9). The verse begins to introduce the offspring of Noah, and before it mentions the names of his children, it tells us that he was righteous. The classical biblical commentator Rashi states that this teaches us that Noah's most important offspring were his "good deeds," and he cites Midrash *Tanchuma*, which states: "The main offspring of righteous people are their good deeds."

The Jewish community should help provide support to those Jews who wish to have large families by:

- Providing Jewish day-care facilities (these can be also used to educate and provide a social and psychological support system for Jewish children);
- Providing child care during synagogue services, in Jewish centers, and during other Jewish organizational activities, to make it easier for young parents to be involved in Jewish and general community activities;
- Providing scholarship help for larger families in Jewish schools;
- Changing the dues structures of synagogues and Jewish centers so that they do not penalize large families.[57]

There are additional ways that the Jewish community can work for Jewish survival besides exhorting Jews to have large families:

- Providing programs to make Judaism more challenging and exciting. For example, involvement in some of the issues discussed in this book might entice alienated Jews to return to Judaism and thereby reduce assimilation and intermarriage.
- Improving Jewish education and lowering tuition rates at Jewish schools so that more children can attend.
- Applying "physical fitness for Jewish survival" by teaching Jews the benefits of nutritious meals, proper exercise, and avoidance of alcohol and drug abuse and tobacco.

Ways in which Jews can work for better global conditions that would eventually lead to reduced population growth rates are discussed in "Action Ideas" in the Appendix.

Jews can and should work for both Jewish and global survival and can play a major role in addressing current critical population issues. While reaffirming that every human life is sacred and that every birth brings God's image anew into the world, we should support family planning programs consistent with Jewish teachings and other cultures and religious beliefs. We should strive to make people aware that rapid population growth is more a *result* of global problems than their root cause.

While helping Jews who wish to have large families, the Jewish community should strive to create a more meaningful, dynamic, committed Jewish life, and also work for a global society that conserves resources, practices justice, seeks peace, and reduces hunger and poverty, thereby lessening people's need to have many children. Finally, as we battle for justice and a more equitable sharing of the earth's abundant resources, which are necessary to improve conditions for all the world's people, we should make others aware that this is also the most effective way to move the world to a more sustainable population path.

12: VEGETARIANISM—A GLOBAL IMPERATIVE?

And God said: "Behold, I have given you every herb yielding seed which is upon the face of all the earth, and every tree that has seed-yielding fruit—to you it shall be for food." (Genesis 1:29)

THIS CHAPTER ADDRESSES A WIDELY ACCEPTED ASPECT OF modern life that contradicts many Jewish teachings and harms people, communities, and the planet—the mass production and widespread consumption of meat. It will illustrate how high meat consumption and the ways in which meat is produced today conflict with Judaism in at least six important areas:

1. While Judaism mandates that people should take care to preserve their health and their lives, numerous scientific studies have linked animal-based diets directly to heart disease, stroke, many forms of cancer, and other chronic degenerative diseases.

2. While Judaism forbids *tsa'ar ba'alei chayim*, inflicting unnecessary pain on animals, most farm animals—including those raised for kosher consumers—are raised on "factory farms," where they live in cramped, confined spaces and are often drugged, mutilated, and denied fresh air, sunlight, exercise, and any enjoyment of life before they are slaughtered and eaten.

3. While Judaism teaches that "the earth is the Lord's" (Psalm 24:1) and that we are to be God's partners and co-workers in preserving the world, modern intensive livestock agriculture contributes substantially to soil erosion and depletion, air and water pollution, overuse of chemical

161

fertilizers and pesticides, the destruction of tropical rain forests and other habitats, global warming, and other environmental damage.

4. While Judaism mandates *bal tashchit*, that we are not to waste or unnecessarily destroy anything of value, and that we are not to use more than is needed to accomplish a purpose, animal agriculture requires the wasteful use of grain, land, water, energy, and other resources.

5. While Judaism stresses that we are to assist the poor and share our bread with hungry people, over seventy percent of the grain grown in the United States is fed to animals destined for slaughter, while an estimated twenty million people worldwide die of hunger and its effects each year.

6. While Judaism stresses that we must seek and pursue peace and that violence results from unjust conditions, animal-centered diets, by wasting valuable resources, help to perpetuate the widespread hunger and poverty that eventually lead to instability and war.

In view of these important Jewish mandates to preserve human health, attend to the welfare of animals, protect the environment, conserve resources, help feed hungry people, and pursue peace, and since animal-centered diets violate and contradict each of these responsibilities, committed Jews (and others) should sharply reduce or eliminate their consumption of animal products.

One could say "*dayenu*" (it would be enough) after any of the arguments above, because each one constitutes by itself a serious conflict between Jewish values and current practice that should impel Jews to seriously consider a plant-based diet. Combined, they make an urgently compelling case for the Jewish community to address these issues.

A Vegetarian View of the Torah

As the Torah verse at the beginning of this chapter (Genesis 1:29) indicates, God's initial intention was that people be vegetarians. The foremost Jewish Torah commentator, Rashi, states the following about God's first dietary plan: "God did not permit Adam and his wife to kill a creature to eat its flesh. Only every green herb were they to all eat together."[1]

Most Torah commentators, including Rabbi Abraham Ibn Ezra, Maimonides, Nachmanides, and Rabbi Joseph Albo, agree with Rashi. As Rabbi Moses Cassuto states in his commentary *From Adam to Noah*,

God told Adam: "You are permitted to use the animals and employ them for work, to have dominion over them in order to utilize their services for your subsistence, but you must not hold their life cheap nor slaughter them for food. Your natural diet is vegetarian...."[2]

These views are consistent with the statement in the Talmud that people were initially vegetarians: "Adam was not permitted meat for purposes of eating."[3]

The great thirteenth-century Jewish commentator Nachmanides indicates that one reason behind this initial human diet is the kinship between all sentient beings:

Living creatures possess a soul and a certain spiritual superiority [to non-human creation] which in this respect make them similar to the possessors of intellect [human beings] and they have the power of affecting their own welfare and their food and they flee from pain and death.[4]

God's original dietary plan represents a unique statement in humanity's spiritual history. It is a divine blueprint for a vegetarian world order. Yet how many millions of people have read this Torah verse (Genesis 1:29) and passed it by without considering its meaning?

After stating that the original humans were to consume a purely vegetarian diet, the Torah indicates that animals were not initially created to prey on one another but rather to subsist on purely vegetarian food:

And to every beast of the earth, and to every fowl of the air, and to every thing that creeps upon the earth, wherein there is a living soul, I have given every green herb for food. (Genesis 1:30)

Immediately after giving these dietary laws, God saw everything He had made and "behold, it was very good" (Genesis 1:31). Everything in the universe was as God wanted it, in complete harmony, with nothing superfluous or lacking.[5] The vegetarian diet was a central part of God's initial plan.

The strongest support for vegetarianism as a positive ideal in Torah literature is in the writing of Rabbi Abraham Isaac Ha-Kohen Kook (1865–1935). Rav Kook was the first Ashkenazic Chief Rabbi (Rav) of pre-state Israel and a highly respected and beloved Jewish spiritual leader and thinker. He was a writer on Jewish mysticism and an outstanding scholar of Jewish law. He spoke powerfully on vegetarianism, as recorded in A Vision of Vegetarianism and Peace (edited by Rav Kook's disciple Rabbi David Cohen, "The Nazir of Jerusalem").

Rav Kook believed that the permission to eat meat was only a temporary concession to the practices of the times, because a God who is merciful to His creatures would not institute an everlasting law permitting the killing of animals for food.[6]

People are not always ready to live up to God's will. By the time of Noah, humanity had morally degenerated. "And God saw the earth, and behold it was corrupt, for all flesh had corrupted their way upon the earth" (Genesis 6:12). People had morally degenerated to such an extent that they would eat a limb torn from a living animal. So, as a concession to people's weakness,[7] God granted permission for people to eat meat: "Every moving thing that lives shall be food for you; as the green herb have I given you all" (Genesis. 9:3).

According to Rav Kook, because people had descended to such an extremely low spiritual level, it was necessary that they be taught to value human life above that of animals, and that they concentrate their efforts on first working to improve relations between people. He writes that if people had been denied the right to eat meat some might have eaten the flesh of human beings instead, due to their inability to control their lust for flesh. Rav Kook regards the permission to slaughter animals for food as a "transitional tax," or temporary dispensation, until a "brighter era" can be reached, when people will return to vegetarian diets.[8]

Just prior to granting Noah and his family permission to eat meat, God states:

> And the fear of you and the dread of you shall be upon every beast of the earth, and upon every fowl of the air, and upon all where-with the ground teems, and upon all the fish of the sea; into your hands are they delivered. (Genesis 9:2)

Now that there is permission to eat animals, the previous harmony between people and animals no longer exists. Rabbi Samson Raphael Hirsch argues that the attachment between people and animals was broken after the flood, which led to a change in the relationship of people to the world.[9]

The permission given to Noah to eat meat is not unconditional. There is an immediate prohibition against eating blood: "Only flesh with the life thereof, which is the blood thereof, shall you not eat" (Genesis 9:4). Similar commands are given in Leviticus 19:26, 17:10, and 12 and Deuteronomy 12:16, 23, and 25, and 15:23. The Torah identifies blood with life: " ... for the blood is the life" (Deuteronomy 12:23). Life must be removed from the animal before it can be eaten, and the Talmud details an elaborate process for doing so.

When the Israelites were in the wilderness, animals could only be slaughtered and eaten as part of the sacrificial service in the sanctuary (Leviticus 17:3–5). The eating of "unconsecrated meat," meat from animals slaughtered for private consumption, was not permitted. All meat which was permitted to be eaten had to be an integral part of a sacrificial rite. Maimonides states that the Biblical sacrifices were a concession to the primitive practices of the nations at that time: people (including the Hebrews) were not then ready for forms of Divine service which did not include sacrifice and death (as did those of all the heathens); at least the Torah, as a major advance, prohibited *human* sacrifice.[10] God later permits people to eat meat even if not as part of a sacrificial offering:

> When the Lord your God shall enlarge your border as He has promised you, and you shall say: "I will eat flesh," because your soul desires to eat flesh; you may eat flesh, after all the desire of your soul. (Deuteronomy 12:20)

This newly-permitted meat was called *basar ta'avah*, "meat of lust," so named because rabbinic teachings indicate that meat is not considered a necessity for life.[11]

The above verse does not *command* people to eat meat. Rabbinic tradition understands the Torah as acknowledging people's desire to eat flesh and permitting it under proper circumstances, but not as requiring the consumption of meat. Even while arguing against vegetarianism as a moral cause, Rabbi Elijah Judah Schochet, author of *Animal Life in Jewish Tradition*, concedes that "Scripture does not command the Israelite to eat meat, but rather permits this diet as a concession to lust."[12] Similarly, another critic of vegetarian activism, Rabbi J. David Bleich, a noted contemporary Torah scholar and professor at Yeshiva University, states, "The implication is that meat may be consumed when there is desire and appetite for it as food, but it may be eschewed when there is not desire and, *a fortiori*, when it is found to be repugnant."[13] According to Rabbi Bleich, "Jewish tradition does not command carnivorous behavior...."[14]

Commenting on the above Torah verse (Deuteronomy 12:20), the respected Torah scholar and teacher Dr. Nehama Leibowitz (1905–1997) points out how odd this allowance is and how grudgingly the permission to eat meat is granted. She concludes that people have not been granted dominion over animals to do with them as they desire, but that we have been given a "barely tolerated dispensation" to slaughter animals for our consumption, if we cannot resist temptation and feel the need to eat meat.[15] Rav Kook also regards the Torah verse as clearly indicating that the Torah does not view the slaughter of animals for human consumption as an ideal state of affairs.[16]

The Talmud expresses this negative connotation associated with the consumption of meat:

> The Torah teaches a lesson in moral conduct, that man shall not eat meat unless he has a special craving for it ... and shall eat it only occasionally and sparingly.[17]

The sages also felt that eating meat was not for everyone:

Only a scholar of Torah may eat meat, but one who is ignorant of Torah is forbidden to eat meat.[18]

Some authorities explain this restriction in practical terms: only a Torah scholar can properly observe all the laws of animal slaughter and meat preparation. While there are few conditions on the consumption of vegetarian foods, only a diligent Torah scholar can fully comprehend the many regulations governing the preparation and consumption of meat. However, master kabbalist Rabbi Isaac Luria explains it in spiritual terms: only a Torah scholar can elevate the "holy sparks" trapped in the animal.[19]

How many Jews today can consider themselves sufficiently scholarly and spiritually advanced to be able to eat meat? Those who do diligently study the Torah and are aware of conditions related to the production and slaughter of meat today would, I believe, come to conclusions similar to those in this chapter.

Rav Kook writes that the permission to eat meat "after all the desire of your soul" is a concealed reproach and an implied reprimand.[20] He states that a day will come (the Messianic Period) when people will detest the eating of the flesh of animals because of a moral loathing, and then people will not eat meat because their soul will not have the urge to eat it.[21]

In contrast to the lust associated with flesh foods, the Torah looks favorably on vegetarian foods. In the Song of Songs, the divine bounty is poetically described in references to fruits, vegetables, nuts, and vines. There is no special *bracha* (blessing) recited before eating meat or fish, as there is for other foods such as bread, cake, wine, fruits, and vegetables. The blessing for meat is a general one, the same as that over water or any other undifferentiated food.

Typical of the Torah's positive depiction of many non-flesh foods is the following evocation of the produce of the Land of Israel:

For the Lord your God brings you into a good land, a land of brooks of water, of fountains and depths, springing forth in valleys and hills; a land of wheat and barley, of vines and fig trees and pomegranates; a land of olive oil and date honey; a land wherein you shall eat bread without scarceness, you shall not lack anything in

it... And you shall eat and be satisfied, and bless the Lord your God
for the good land that He has given you. (Deuteronomy 8:7–10)

Rav Kook believes that there is a reprimand implicit in the many laws and
restrictions over the preparing, combining, and eating of animal products
(the laws of *kashrut*), because they are meant to provide an elaborate appa-
ratus designed to keep alive a sense of reverence for life, with the aim of
eventually leading people away from meat eating.[22] He also believes that
the high moral level involved in the vegetarianism of the generations
before Noah was a virtue of such great value that it cannot be lost forever.[23]
In the future ideal time (the Messianic Age), people and animals will again
not eat each others' flesh.[24] People's lives will not be supported at the
expense of animals' lives. Rav Kook based these views on the prophecy of
Isaiah:

And the wolf shall dwell with the lamb,
And the leopard shall lie down with the kid;
And the calf and the young lion and the fatling together;
And a little child shall lead them
And the cow and the bear shall feed;
Their young ones shall lie down together,
And the lion shall eat straw like the ox....
They shall not hurt nor destroy in all My holy mountain...
(Isaiah 11:6–9)

In a booklet that summarizes many of Rav Kook's teachings, Joseph Green,
a twentieth-century South African Jewish vegetarian writer, concludes
that Jewish religious ethical vegetarians are pioneers of the messianic era;
they are leading lives that prepare for and potentially hasten the coming of
the Messiah.[25]

His view is based on the Jewish belief that one way to speed the arrival
of the Messiah is to start practicing the behaviors that will prevail in the
Messianic time. For example, the Talmud teaches that if all Jews properly
observed two consecutive Sabbaths, the Messiah would immediately

come.[26] Perhaps this means symbolically that when all Jews reach the level of fully observing the Sabbath in its emphasis on devotion to God and compassion for people and animals, the conditions for the messianic period will have arrived. Based on Rav Kook's teaching, if all people became vegetarian in the proper spirit, with compassion for all animals and human beings, and with a commitment to preserve and honor God's world, this might hasten the coming of the Messiah.

Although most Jews eat meat today, God's high ideal—the initial vegetarian dietary law—stands supreme in the Torah for Jews and the whole world to see. It is the ultimate goal toward which all people should strive.

How Vegetarianism Can Help Reduce Global Threats

A. Helping Hungry People

Can a shift to vegetarian diets make a difference with regard to world hunger? Consider these statistics:

1. It takes up to sixteen pounds of grain to produce one pound of feedlot beef for human consumption.[27]

2. While the average Asian consumes between three hundred and four hundred pounds of grain a year, the average middle-class American consumes over two thousand pounds of grain, eighty percent of which comes in the form of meat from grain-fed animals.[28]

3. Over seventy percent of the grain produced in the United States and over one-third of the world's grain is fed to animals destined for slaughter.[29]

4. If Americans reduced their beef consumption by ten percent, it would free up enough grain to feed all of the world's people who annually die of hunger and related diseases.[30]

5. U.S. livestock consume over six and a half times as much grain as the U.S. human population does. According to the Council for Agricultural Science and Technology, an Iowa-based non-profit research group, the grain fed to animals to produce meat, milk, and eggs could feed five times the number of people that it currently does if it were consumed directly by humans.[31]

6.   While fifty-six million acres of U.S. land produce hay for livestock, only four million acres of U.S. land are producing vegetables for human consumption.[32]

7.   While one hectare (about 2.5 acres) of land growing potatoes can feed twenty-two people, and one hectare growing rice can feed nineteen people, that same area producing beef can feed only one person.[33]

8.   Feeding grain to livestock wastes ninety percent of the protein, almost a hundred percent of the carbohydrates, and a hundred percent of the fiber of the grain. While grains are a rich source of fiber, animal products have no fiber at all.[34]

This evidence indicates that the food being fed to animals in the affluent nations could, if properly distributed, potentially end both hunger and malnutrition throughout the world. A switch from animal-centered diets would free up land and other resources, which could then be used to grow nutritious crops for people. This new approach would also promote policies that would enable people in the underdeveloped countries to use their resources and skills to raise their own food.

With so much hunger in the world, explicit Jewish mandates to feed the hungry, help the poor, share resources, practice charity, show compassion, and pursue justice, as well as the lessons from many experiences of hunger in Jewish history, point to vegetarianism as the diet most consistent with Jewish teachings about hunger.

B. Destructive Use of Resources

Unfortunately, the wisdom of *bal tashchit* (the Torah mandate not to waste) is seldom applied today by our society. Instead we have planned obsolescence and bigger and more wasteful celebrations, homes, SUVs, and product packaging, resulting in ever-swelling landfills that leave a growing blot on the landscape and the planet. Our society's animal-centered diets are extremely wasteful:

1.   About eight hundred million acres (forty percent of U.S. land area) are devoted to livestock grazing, and an additional sixty million acres are used to grow grain to feed livestock.[35] Land that grows potatoes,

rice, and other vegetables can support about twenty times as many people as land that produces grain-fed beef.

2. As stated in the previous section, the average person in the United States eats over five times as much grain (mostly in the form of animal products) as a person in a less developed country; it takes up to sixteen-pounds of grain and soybeans to produce one pound of feedlot beef for our plates, and more than two-thirds of the grain grown in the United States is fed to farm animals, whom we then slaughter and eat.

3. The standard diet of a meat eater in the United States requires 4,200 gallons of water per day (for animals' drinking water, irrigation of crops, meat processing, washing, cooking, etc.).[36] A person on a purely vegetarian (vegan) diet requires only 300 gallons per day.[37]

4. Animal agriculture is the major consumer of water in the U.S. According to Norman Myers, author of *Gaia: An Atlas of Planet Management*, irrigation, primarily to grow crops for animals, uses over eighty percent of U.S. water.[38] Almost ninety percent of the fresh water consumed annually in the U.S. goes to agriculture, according to agriculture expert David Pimentel.[39] The production of only one pound of edible beef in a semi-arid area such as California requires as much as 5,200 gallons of water, as contrasted with only twenty-five gallons or less to produce an edible pound of tomatoes, lettuce, potatoes, or wheat.[40] *Newsweek* reported in 1988 that "the water that goes into a 1,000 pound steer would float a (naval) destroyer."[41]

5. An animal-based diet also wastes energy. In the United States, an average of ten calories of fuel energy is required for every calorie of food energy produced; many other countries obtain twenty or more calories of food energy per calorie of fuel energy.[42] To produce one pound of steak (five hundred calories of food energy) requires 20,000 calories of fossil fuels, most of which is expended in producing and providing feed crops.[43] Seventy-eight calories of fossil fuel are required for each calorie of protein obtained from feedlot-produced beef, but only two calories of fossil fuel are needed to produce a calorie of protein from soybeans.[44] Grains and beans require only two to five percent as much fossil fuel as beef.[45] The energy needed to produce a pound of grain-fed beef is equivalent to one gallon of gasoline.[46]

6. According to a comprehensive study sponsored by the U.S. Departments of Interior and Commerce, the value of all raw materials used to produce food from livestock is greater than the value of all oil, gas, and coal produced in this country.[47] The production of livestock foods accounts for a third of the value of all raw materials consumed for all purposes in the U.S.[48]

As these facts indicate, vegetarianism is the diet most consistent with the principle of *bal tashchit*.

C. Ecological Damage from Current Animal Agriculture

Modern agricultural methods used in meat production are a prime cause of the environmental crises facing the United States and much of the rest of the world today.

1. According to mathematician Robin Hur, nearly six billion of the seven billion tons of eroded soil in the United States has been lost because of cattle and feed lot production.[49] Agronomist David Pimentel writes that about ninety percent of U.S. cropland is losing soil at a rate at least thirteen times faster than the sustainable rate.[50] William Brune, a former Iowa State conservation official, warned that two bushels of topsoil are being lost for every bushel of corn (most of which is fed to animals) harvested in Iowa's sloping soils.[51] Lower yields are occurring in many areas due to erosion and the reduction in fertility that it causes.[52]

2. Grazing animals have destroyed large areas of land throughout the world, with overgrazing having long been a prime cause of erosion. Over sixty percent of all U.S. rangelands are overgrazed, with billions of tons of soil lost each year.[53] Cattle production is a prime contributor to every one of the causes of desertification: overgrazing of livestock, over-cultivation of land, improper irrigation techniques, deforestation, and prevention of reforestation.

3. In the United States, more plant species have been eliminated due to overgrazing by livestock than by any other cause.[54]

4. Mountains of manure produced by cattle raised in feedlots wash into and pollute streams, rivers, and underground water sources. U.S. livestock produce an astounding 1.4 billion tons of manure per year (this amount works out to almost 90,000 pounds per second!), or about 130 times the amount excreted by the U.S. human population.[55] Food geographer Georg Borgstrom has estimated that American livestock contribute five times more organic waste to the pollution of our water than do people, and twice as much as does industry.[56]

5. The tremendous amount of grain grown to feed animals requires extensive use of chemical fertilizer and pesticides, which cause air and water pollution. Various constituents of fertilizer, particularly nitrogen, are washed into surface waters. High levels of nitrates in drinking water cause illnesses in people and animals. According to Norman Myers' *Gaia*, fertilizers and pesticides are responsible for over half of U.S. water pollution.[57]

6. The quantity of pesticides and other synthetic poisons used has increased by four hundred percent since 1962, when Rachel Carson wrote *Silent Spring*, the book that so eloquently sounded the alarm about the dangers of pesticides to human health, rivers, and wildlife.[58] Also, in a "circle of poison," pesticides banned or heavily restricted in the U.S. are legally exported to poor countries, where they are then used on foods imported back into the United States. Because of accumulation of pesticides in the body fat of animals, people who eat meat and other animal products ingest large amounts of pesticides, which then build up in *their* body fat.

7. Demand for meat in wealthy countries leads to environmental damage in poor countries. Largely to turn beef into fast-food hamburgers for export to the U.S., the earth's tropical rain forests are being bulldozed at a rate of a football field per second.[59] Each imported quarter-pound fast-food hamburger patty requires the destruction of fifty-five square feet of tropical forest for grazing.[60] Half of the rain forests are already gone forever, and at current rates of destruction the rest will be gone by the middle of this century. What makes this especially ominous is that half of the world's fast-disappearing species of plants and animals reside in tropical rain forests. We are risking the loss of species that

might hold secrets for cures of deadly diseases. Other plant species might turn out to be good sources of nutrition. Also, the destruction of rain forests is altering the climate and reducing rainfall, with potentially devastating effects on the world's agriculture and habitability.

D. How Animal-Based Agriculture Contributes to Global Warming

While recent concern about global warming is necessrary (and overdue), the many connections between typical American (and other Western) diets and global warming have generally been overlooked. Modern intensive livestock agriculture and the consumption of meat greatly contribute to the four major gases associated with the greenhouse effect: carbon dioxide, methane, nitrous oxides, and chlorofluorocarbons.[61]

The burning of tropical forests releases tons of carbon dioxide into the atmosphere—carbon dioxide that the trees are no longer there to absorb. Also, the highly mechanized agricultural sector uses enormous amounts of fossil fuel to produce pesticides, chemical fertilizer, and other agricultural resources, and this also contributes to carbon dioxide emissions. Cattle emit methane as part of their digestive process, as do the termites who feast on the charred remains of trees that were burned to create grazing land and land to grow feed crops for farmed animals. The large amounts of petrochemical fertilizers used to produce feed crops create significant quantities of nitrous oxides. Likewise, the increased refrigeration necessary to prevent animal products from spoiling adds chlorofluorocarbons to the atmosphere.

Conclusion

When we consider all of these negative environmental and climate-change effects, and then add the harmful effects of animal-based diets on human health and global hunger, it is clear that animal-centered diets and the livestock agriculture needed to sustain them pose tremendous threats to global survival. It is not surprising that the Union of Concerned Scientists (UCS) ranks the consumption of meat and poultry as the second most harmful consumer activity (surpassed only by the use of cars and light trucks).[62] It is clear that a shift toward vegetarianism is imperative if we are to turn our planet from its present catastrophic path. Jeremy Rifkin summarizes well the negative effects of animal-based agriculture:

> The ever-increasing cattle population is wreaking havoc on the earth's ecosystems, destroying habitats on six continents. Cattle raising is a primary factor in the destruction of the world's remaining tropical rain forests. Millions of acres of ancient forests in Central and South America are being felled and cleared to make room for pastureland to graze cattle. Cattle herding is responsible for much of the spreading desertification in the sub-Sahara of Africa and the western rangeland of the United States and Australia. The overgrazing of semiarid and arid lands has left parched and barren deserts on four continents. Organic runoff from feedlots is now a major source of organic pollution in our nation's ground water. Cattle are also a major cause of global warming....The devastating environmental, economic, and human toll of maintaining a worldwide cattle complex is little discussed in public policy circles....Yet, cattle production and beef consumption now rank among the gravest threats to the future well being of the earth and its human population.[63]

The aims of vegetarians and environmental activists are similar: simplify our lifestyles, have regard for the earth and all forms of life, and apply the knowledge that the earth is not ours to do with as we wish. In view of the many negative effects of animal-based agriculture on the earth's environment, resources, and climate, it is becoming increasingly clear that a shift toward vegetarian diets is a planetary imperative.

13: CONCLUSION

I am a Jew because the faith of Israel [the Jewish people] demands no abdication of my mind.

I am a Jew because the faith of Israel asks every possible sacrifice of my soul.

I am a Jew because in all places where there are tears and suffering the Jew weeps.

I am a Jew because in every age when the cry of despair is heard the Jew hopes.

I am a Jew because the message of Israel is the most ancient and the most modern.

I am a Jew because Israel's promise is a universal promise.

I am a Jew because for Israel the world is not finished; men will complete it.

I am a Jew because for Israel man is not yet fully created; men are creating him.

I am a Jew because Israel places man and his unity above nations and above Israel itself.

I am a Jew because above man, image of the divine unity, Israel places the unity that is divine. (Edmond Fleg, "Why I Am a Jew")[1]

WHAT A WONDERFUL PATH JUDAISM IS! JUDAISM proclaims a God who is the Creator of all life, whose attributes of kindness, mercy, compassion, and justice are to serve as examples for all our actions. Judaism teaches that every person is created in God's image, and therefore is of supreme value.

Judaism asserts that people are to be co-workers with God in preserving and improving the earth. We are to be stewards of the world's resources to see that God's bounties are used for the benefit of all. Nothing that has value may be wasted or destroyed unnecessarily.

Judaism stresses that we are to love other people as ourselves, to be kind to strangers, "for we were strangers in the land of Egypt," and to act with compassion toward the homeless, the poor, the orphan, the widow, even to enemies, and to all of God's creatures.

Judaism places great value on reducing hunger. A Jew who helps to feed a hungry person is considered, in effect, to have "fed" God.

Judaism mandates that we seek peace. Great is peace, for it is one of God's names, all God's blessings are contained in it, it must be sought even in times of war, and it will be the first blessing brought by the Messiah.

Judaism exhorts us to pursue justice, to work for a society where each person has the ability to obtain, through creative labor, the means to lead a dignified life for himself and his family.

Judaism stresses involvement, nonconformity, resistance to oppression and injustice, and a constant struggle against idolatry.

This book discusses how this ancient, marvelous Jewish outlook speaks to the earth's gravest problems. It suggests four main themes:

1. The world faces many critical problems today: vast poverty, threatened ecosystems, widespread hunger, global climate change, dwindling resources (including water and fossil energy), war and violence, and rapid population growth.

2. The application of Jewish values such as pursuing justice, sharing resources, acting with kindness and compassion, loving our fellow human beings, working as partners with God in protecting the earth, and seeking and pursuing peace will contribute to finding solutions to these problems.

3. There has been too little effort to apply the Jewish tradition to the many critical problems that threaten the world today. In fact, there has generally been a shift away from these basic Jewish values at the very time when the world needs them perhaps more than ever before.

4. In the face of today's urgent problems, Jews must return to our universal Jewish values and our mission: to be "a light unto the nations," a

kingdom of priests and a holy people, descendants of prophets, champions of social justice, eternal protesters against the corrupt, unredeemed world, dissenters against destructive and unjust systems. We must work for radical changes that will lead to a society where there is an end to oppression, violence, hunger, poverty, and alienation. Jews must become actively involved in the missions of global survival and Jewish renewal.

The afternoon service for Yom Kippur includes the book of Jonah, who was sent by God to Nineveh to urge the people to repent and change their evil ways in order to avoid their destruction. Today the whole world is Nineveh, in danger of annihilation and in need of repentance and redemption, and each one of us must be a Jonah, with a mission to warn the world that it must turn from greed, injustice, and idolatry, so that we can all avoid global oblivion.

AFTERWORD

ON SEPTEMBER 11, 2001 THOUSAND OF INNOCENTS WERE killed in terrorist attacks that brought down the World Trade Center and a part of the Pentagon. Only days earlier, a U.N.-sponsored gathering of Non-Governmental Organizations in Durban, South Africa, endorsed a slanderous resolution accusing the state of Israel of practicing apartheid and comparing the Jewish state to Nazi Germany.

These are not easy days to advocate worldwide cooperation and amity or to promote concern for the globe's neediest people and for the planet's ecosystems. Some self-proclaimed representatives of these causes are even declaring that the United States and Israel deserve to be assaulted by fiendish suicidal terrorism because of our moral failings and misdeeds.

Judaism and Global Survival purposely focuses on problems that confront the entire world and all of its human (and animal) inhabitants. This book has avoided intensive treatment of the crises of peace, security, and coexistence that hover over our beloved Israel, because these are best engaged at length and in depth in other publications and forums. But the current moment requires that something be said about these questions.

Just as the Torah and Jewish tradition command us (as has been repeatedly documented in this book) to love our neighbor and the stranger in our midst, work to preserve God's creation, and extend ourselves to fellow human beings who are suffering, they also clearly outline the unbreakable tie between the Jewish people and our eternal homeland. The same religious Zionist tradition taught by the late masters Chief Rabbi Abraham Isaac Ha-Kohen Kook, Chief Rabbi Yitzhak HaLevi Herzog, and Rabbi Joseph B. Soloveitchik, which incorporates their compelling exhortations to promote justice and understanding among all peoples, to care for the vulnerable, and to act as stewards of God's earth, also expresses their sense of the centrality of the Jewish State as an intended model of right-eousness, fellowship, and social responsibility. Jewish history teaches us to act on behalf of those who are enslaved as we have been, and it demon-strates that fair and open societies are the healthiest and most productive ones for Jews to live in. It also reminds us that, because of the Crusades and pogroms and jihads, the Jews need a safe and well-defended country to live in and flee to.

So, while this book is presented in the spirit of encouraging alliances and partnerships among all people of good heart and idealistic faith, it is also based on the premises—it is astonishing they even need to be uttered!—that the Jewish people have the same right to be in our histor-ical homeland and to practice self-determination that every nation should enjoy; that Israel has gone vastly further toward democracy and human dignity and protecting the rights of all its citizens than has any other country in the region (though, of course, there is much further yet to go); and that Jews have the same entitlement as any religious and ethnic group to defend our own and to pursue our particular path. There are those who declare that they are allies of peace and justice but who question or attack Israel's right to exist, defame Israel's social accomplishments and the civic freedoms achieved by her citizens, scoff at America's sympathy for Israel (based as it is on her status as a fellow successful nation of immigrants—though Jews have lived continuously in the land since before King David ruled it three thousand years ago), and claim that everything would be fine in the Middle East and the world if Israel would just close up shop or if America would leave Israel to her fate. They are no friends at all of equity and harmony. They are enemies, who single out Israel, the United States, and the Jews for special and invidious treatment, just as Osama bin Laden, Saddam Hussein, Ayatollah Khomeini, and Goebbels and his close ally the Mufti did, and before them Torquemada, Antiochus, Haman, and Pharaoh.

It is, of course, necessary to make a distinction between sincere critics and malicious or falsely innocent foes. It is entirely legitimate to disagree with specific policies of any particular Israeli government (there have, after all, been seven different Prime Ministers in the past decade). And if peace is ever to be achieved Israel will have to make extensive compromises and sacrifices. But this should never be allowed to serve as a cover for those who want Israel not only to be cooperative and forthcoming but, either explicitly or for all practical purposes, to commit suicide.

Those of us who advance Judaism and its teachings as blueprints for global comity and conscience should not be ashamed of demanding that our tradition, people, and historic patrimony receive the same respect and deference that all heritages and nationalities merit. The principles of equality and human rights, of the divine importance of every individual and the preciousness of our shared earth, which animated Eleanor Roosevelt and Dr. Martin Luther King, Jr, and Rachel Carson (as well as Rabbi Abraham Joshua Heschel and Albert Einstein) emanate from our Torah. Every person is a universe, every murder destroys an entire world, each human being is created in the image of God. Jews, too!

We must march under the banner of our community and of the historic wisdom of our holy texts. The world needs to be repaired and redeemed. Jews have an indispensable role in that redemption, and our continuity and the acceptance of our valid claims are necessary if we are to go on contributing as our teachers have eternally instructed. We will aid and contribute, and live and die, as members of the Jewish people, and as emblems of the sweet message and majesty of Judaism.

APPENDIX A: ACTION IDEAS

It is not the study that is the chief thing, but the doing. (Kiddushin 40b)

THIS BOOK ATTEMPTS TO DEMONSTRATE THAT JEWISH values can help solve many of the world's critical problems. As the above quotation indicates, it is crucial to *apply* these values, to put Jewish teachings into practice and help shift the world from its present direction, heading toward potential disaster.

In attempting to change the world, sometimes we have to begin by changing ourselves. Rabbi Israel Salanter, the founder of the *mussar* (ethics) movement in Lithuania, taught: "First a person should put his house together, then his town, then his world."

If you feel that global crises are so great that your efforts will have little effect, consider the following. The Jewish tradition teaches: "You are not obligated to complete the task, but neither are you free to desist from it."[1] Each of us must make a start and do whatever he or she can to help improve the world. As stated in Chapter 1, Judaism teaches that a person is obligated to protest when there is evil and, if necessary, to proceed from protest to action. Each person is to imagine that the world is evenly balanced between good and evil, and that her or his actions can determine the destiny of the entire world.[2]

Even if little is accomplished, trying to make improvements will prevent the hardening of *your* heart and will affirm your acceptance of moral responsibility. Even the act of consciousness-raising is important, because it may lead to future action for change. Here are some things that each person can do:

1. Become well informed. Learn the facts about global problems and the applicable Jewish values from this and other books (see Bibliography).

2. Inform others. Wear a button. Put bumper stickers where many people will see them. Make and display posters. Write timely letters to editors of local publications. Set up programs and discussions. Become registered with community, library, or school speakers' bureaus.

3. Simplify your lifestyle. Conserve energy. Recycle materials. Bike or walk whenever possible, instead of driving. Share rides. Use mass transit when appropriate.

4. Become a vegetarian, or at least sharply reduce your consumption of animal products. As discussed in Chapter 12, vegetarianism is the diet most consistent with such Jewish values as showing compassion to animals, taking care of one's health, preserving the environment, sharing with hungry people, conserving resources, and pursuing peace.

5. Work with organizations and groups on some of the significant issues discussed in this book. For contact information, see Appendix C. If there are no local groups or if you differ with such groups on some important issue, set up a group in your synagogue, Jewish center, or Hillel.

In the summer of 2000, sixteen environmental groups banded together in Switzerland to unveil a new Climate Voice web site that lets visitors send messages to the world's political leaders calling for action to address climate change. The groups—which include the World Wildlife Fund, Greenpeace International, and Friends of the Earth—aimed to generate ten million public messages to heads of state and prime ministers before international climate change talks that were held in The Hague in November 2000, where crucial decisions on implementation of the Kyoto climate change treaty were made.[3]

6. Encourage your public and congregational libraries to order, stock, and circulate books on global issues and Jewish teachings related to them. Donate your duplicate copies, request that libraries regularly acquire such books and subscribe to relevant magazines, and, if you can afford it, buy some to donate.

7. Speak or organize events with guest speakers and/or audio-visual presentations on how Jewish values address global issues.

8. Ask rabbis and other religious leaders to give sermons and/or classes that discuss Judaism's teachings on current problems.

9. Ask principals of yeshivas and day schools to see that their curricula reflect traditional Jewish concerns with environmental, peace, and justice issues. Volunteer to speak to classes and to help plan curricula.

10. Contact editors of local newspapers and ask that more space be devoted to global issues. Write articles and letters using information from this book and other sources.

11. Try to influence public policy on the issues discussed in this book. Organize letter-writing campaigns and group visits to politicians to lobby for a safer, saner, more stable world.

12. Engage with rabbis and religious educators and leaders on how we should be applying to today's critical issues such Jewish mandates as "seek peace and pursue it," "*bal tashchit*," "justice, justice shall you pursue," and "love your neighbor as yourself."

13. As an outgrowth of Jewish teachings on helping hungry people and conserving resources, work to end the tremendous amount of waste associated with many Jewish organizational functions and celebrations. Encourage friends and institutions to simplify, reduce, and serve less lavish celebratory feasts (and put this into practice at your own celebrations). Request that meat not be served, since production of meat wastes grain, land, and other resources. Refraining from eating meat also expresses identification with the millions of people who lack an adequate diet, as well as the billions of farmed animals slaughtered each year. Reclaim leftover food from *simchas* to donate to shelters and food kitchens. Recommend to people hosting a celebration that they donate a portion of the cost of the event to Mazon or another group working to reduce hunger.

14. Help set up a committee to analyze and reduce energy consumption in the synagogue.[4] Apply steps taken to reduce synagogue energy use as a model for similar action on other buildings and homes in the community.

15. Set up a social action committee in your synagogue, temple, Jewish center, day or afternoon school, or campus to help people get more involved in educational and action-centered activities. Build coalitions with other social justice groups in the community.

16. Raise the consciousness of your synagogue and other local Jewish organizations and individuals. Ask questions such as:

What would the Jewish prophets say about our society today? about our Judaism? about our synagogue activities? Why are Jewish teachings about achieving a better world through *tikkun olam* so little known?

Have we forgotten amid our many important *shiurim* (classes) that it is not study that is the chief thing, but action? Are we segregating God inside our synagogues? Shouldn't Jewish commitment include sensitivity to ethical values and social idealism as well as ritual practice, Torah study, and charity—and a public application of these values?

Have we forgotten who we are, what we stand for, and Whom we represent? Have we forgotten our roles: to be a chosen people, a light unto the nations, a holy people, descendants of the prophets—the original champions of social justice?

If God is sanctified by justice and righteousness, why are we so complacent in the face of an unredeemed, immoral, unjust world?

Are we taking our ethical ideals and prophetic teachings seriously enough? If we are told "justice, justice, shall you pursue" and "let justice well up as waters and righteousness as a mighty stream," why is there so much complacency about poverty, exploitation, corruption at every level of government, and corporate connivance that affect our health and safety?

Considering the many threats to our (and God's) world, from global warming, destruction of tropical rain forests, depletion of the ozone layer, acid rain, rapid loss of biodiversity, soil erosion and depletion, and widespread air and water pollution, and in light of Judaism's strong environmental messages, shouldn't the preservation of the global environment be given greater priority on the Jewish agenda?

APPENDIX B: MISCELLANEOUS BACKGROUND MATERIAL

A. Jewish Values vs. Conventional Values Held by Many People

One of the primary factors behind many of the world's problems today is the sharp discrepancy between Jewish values and those believed and practiced by much of the world, including many Jews. Consider:

Jewish Values	Conventional Values
1. Prophets	1. Profits
2. Love your neighbor as yourself.	2. Suspect your neighbor as yourself.
3. Just weights; just measures	3. Let the buyer beware.
4. People created in God's image	4. People treated as consumers
5. God	5. Me
6. The Earth is the Lord's.	6. The earth exploited for convenience and profit
7. People are co-workers with God in efforts to improve the world.	7. Do your own thing. Seek personal advantage.
8. Sanctity of every life	8. Lives endangered to increase gain

9. *Tzedek, tzedek tirdof* (Justice, justice shall you pursue).

9. Society filled with injustice

10. *Tza'ar ba'alei chayim* (kindness to animals)

10. Animals treated cruelly to meet human desires

11. God provides food for all; share your bread with the hungry.

11. Millions die annually due to lack of food; "enough for the world's need, but not its greed."

12. Leave the corners of the field and the gleanings of the harvest for the poor.

12. Centralized help; let the government handle social problems.

13. I am my brother's keeper.

13. "What's in it for me?"

14. Sumptuary laws that limit expenditures on *simchas*

14. Lavish affairs; wastefulness

15. Sabbatical year; let the ground lie fallow.

15. Fertility of soil destroyed by planting single crops annually

16. Jubilee; redistribution of wealth

16. Growing rich–poor gaps

17. To be

17. To have; to consume; to appear

18. Dignity of labor

18. Little pride in work

19. Seek peace and pursue it.

19. My country right or wrong; excessive arms expenditures

20. Be kind to the stranger.

20. Discrimination and animosity between groups

In order to solve the many critical problems that the world now faces, it is essential that the values of the world be influenced by Jewish values!

B. Global Warming Resolution

Whereas Judaism teaches that "the earth is the Lord's and the fullness thereof" (Psalm 24:1), and that people are to be partners and co-workers with God in preserving the earth's environment, and

Whereas there is mounting evidence that we are already experiencing global warming, including the facts that all ten of the warmest years on record have occurred in the last fifteen years, and the hottest year in recorded history occurred in 1998, and

Whereas scientists with the Intergovernmental Panel on Climate Change, the authoritative international group charged with studying this issue, concluded in their *Assessment Reports* (which received contributions and peer review from over 2,500 of the world's leading climate scientists, economists, and risk-analysis experts) that the observed global temperature increase during the last century "is unlikely to be entirely natural in origin," that "the balance of evidence suggests that there is a discernible human influence on human climate," and the average global temperature will increase by between 2.5 and 10.4 degrees Fahrenheit in the next century, and

Whereas the main cause of this global warming has been the increase in atmospheric concentrations of heat-trapping gases, including carbon dioxide, methane, nitrous oxides, and chlorofluorocarbons, which act as a "greenhouse," trapping heat radiated out from the earth, and climate scientists have linked the increases of these heat-trapping gases in the atmosphere to human activities, especially the burning of fossil fuels (coal, oil, and natural gas), cattle ranching, deforestation, and rice farming, and

Whereas global warming has potentially very severe consequences, including damage to human health; the loss of ecologically important plant and animal species; severe stress on forests, wetlands, and other natural habitats; dislocation of agriculture and commerce; intensified food shortages; expansion of the earth's deserts; rise in sea levels due to the melting of polar ice caps; and increased numbers of hurricanes, floods, and other severe weather events,

This organization resolves to urge elected officials including President Bush and other decision makers to make the struggle against global warming a major priority; to press for legislation that will significantly reduce greenhouse gas emissions; to move to inform our community and our nation that we can make lifestyle changes that will reduce contributions to global warming; and to attempt to involve other (synagogues, groups, campuses) in programs and activities to educate their members about the risks of global warming and steps that can be taken to reduce it.

APPENDIX C: GUIDE TO JEWISH ACTIVIST GROUPS

Listed below are just a few of the many Jewish organizations working in a wide variety of areas to improve the world, to organize members of their communities to contribute and help, and to involve Jews in changing society. Some of these websites have links to numerous other groups; you can also contact other organizations near you to find opportunities to join in and help make a difference.

1. Jewish Environmental Organizations

The Coalition on the Environment and Jewish Life (COEJL)
Supported by a broad range of American Jewish organizations, COEJL is the central hub that mobilizes, informs, and represents the Jewish community of North America in environmental advocacy, education, coalition-building, and action campaigns. www.coejl.org

Endangered Spirit
Jewish outdoor adventure program for teens, adults, and families. Their day trips in the Midwest and West, and longer journeys to Argentina or Costa Rica, include Shabbat observance, kosher food, and study of Jewish writings about the natural world. www.endangeredspirit.com

Hazon
Organizes bike rides to raise awareness of ecological concerns in Judaism and funds for Jewish environmental organizations. www.hazon.org

Mosaic Outdoor Clubs of America
Network of twenty branches across North America that plan outdoor and environmental activities for Jewish adults, and an annual Labor Day national event. www.mosaics.org

2. Environmental Groups in Israel
Note: some of the listed websites are in Hebrew; click on the "English" icon.

Arava Institute for Environmental Studies
Academic research and teaching center and regional base for conservation activity, located at Kibbutz Ketura. www.arava.org

Committee for Public Transportation
Leading the fight against the disastrous Trans-Israel Highway and for rational transportation policy in Israel. c/o Henry Gold, 58 Katzenelenbogen St., Suite #11, Jerusalem 93871. (E-mail messages to *American Friends of the Committee for Public Transportation* can be sent care of arachel@netvision.net.il. *The Committee for Quality of Life-Har Nof*, which is battling to save the Jerusalem Forest—the last major green area in Israel's capital—can also be reached at the Katzenelenbogen St. address.

Heschel Center for Environmental Learning and Leadership
Works to strengthen the Israeli environmental movement through training leaders, producing publications (including reports on Israel's condition in partnership with the Worldwatch Institute), creating a library, and advising foundations to help build a sustainable society. www.heschelcenter.org

Israel Union for Environmental Defense (IUED)
Known in Hebrew as *Adam Teva v'Din*, this is Israel's leading environmental advocacy organization, working to save the air, water, open spaces, and public health through litigation, legislative and regulatory reform, and active cooperation with local citizens groups. www.iued.org.il

Ministry of Environment (Israeli government). www.environment.gov.il

Neot Kedumim
The Biblical Landscape Reserve in the Judean foothills, featuring a panorama of ecosystems and flora from the Bible and the history of Israel, as well as research and numerous publications on ecology in Jewish tradition. www.neot-kedumim.org.il

Society for the Protection of Nature in Israel (SPNI)
More Israelis participate in SPNI's programs than in those of any other non-profit organization in the country: hikes, field study centers, natural history materials, and public campaigns. www.spni.org

There are numerous other environmental groups in Israel, including Green Action, the student organization Green Course, the coordinating umbrella of NGO's Haim U'Sviva, the Institute for Sustainability Studies at Kibbutz Gezer, and others, as well as local activists in several cities. The organizations listed above can assist you in locating additional groups.

3. Jewish Organizations Combating Hunger and Poverty
Note: Again, hundreds of groups are working to prevent poverty and to help poor people achieve self-reliance. These are just a few.

American Jewish World Service
Provides humanitarian aid, emergency relief, volunteers, and support to local programs in the developing world that are working for economic progress, sustainable agriculture, health, and education. www.ajws.org

Beyond Shelter Coalition
An alliance of more than thirty Jewish congregations, schools, and organizations in Manhattan educating, campaigning, and raising funds for permanent housing for the homeless. www.beyondsheltercoalition.org

Jewish Council on Urban Affairs
Works with Chicago communities and neighborhoods to promote cooperation between groups and policies that create jobs, housing, and community investment; develops educational resources to teach Jews about social justice. www.jcua.org

Jewish Fund for Justice
Through grantmaking, technical assistance, and education, JFJ provides aid to grass-roots organizations that are seeking social justice and trying to help people and communities in poverty to achieve self-sufficiency and lasting advancement. www.jfjustice.org

Mazon: A Jewish Response to Hunger
Collects and allocates donations to hunger relief organizations in the U.S., Israel, and around the world, and encourages Jews to set aside three percent of the cost of festive occasions for feeding the hungry. www.mazon.org

North American Conference on Ethiopian Jewry (NACOEJ)
In Israel, provides educational opportunities, training, social support, and needed meals; in Ethiopia, brings jobs, food, and life support; works for the immigration to Israel of all those in Ethiopia who are eligible, to rescue them from oppression, disease, and starvation. www.circus.org/nacoej

National Jewish Coalition for Literacy
Recruits and organizes thousands of American Jews, in over forty local affiliates, to help children learn to read. www.njcl.net

Yachad
The Washington, D.C. area's Jewish housing and development corporation mobilizes synagogues, churches, non-profit organizations, Jewish volunteers (both professional and physically hands-on) and financial resources to help rebuild urban neighborhoods and build partnerships between communities. www.yachad-dc.org

4. Other Activist Jewish Organizations

A selected list of both local and national, alternative and mainline, American and Israeli groups. Over the last twenty-five years, many of the established Jewish organizations have become more involved in supporting social change and promoting activism, in part because some of the current leaders spring out of the Jewish counterculture of the 1960s and 1970s. Also, since the early 1980s, a whole set of new Jewish groups has emerged, addressing many different aspects of human needs and community involvement.

Amos: the National Jewish Partnership for Social Justice
Acts as a catalyst and consultant to Jewish organizations to renew and expand the Jewish community's dedication to social justice. Amos' website has links to national and local Jewish institutions addressing these issues. www.amospartnership.org

AVODAH: the Jewish Service Corps
A one-year program in New York City for young adults, working at a social-justice-connected job, living communally, and studying issues and Jewish values together. www.avodah.net

Center for Business Ethics and Social Responsibility
A project of the Jerusalem College of Technology, the Center seeks to promote integrity in business and economic honesty through the study and transmission of Jewish ethical teachings. Its programs include an excellent website containing an online library of dozens of articles analyzing the Torah's outlook on a variety of economic questions; conferences and forums in Israel; and the weekly Jewish Ethicist, sent out via e-mail. The College is also starting a Center for Judaism and the Environment, which will engage in research, teaching, publishing, and participation in Israel visits and tours. www.besr.org

The Coalition for the Advancement of Jewish Education (CAJE)
Brings together thousands of Jewish educators at annual national summer conferences and in other forums and projects; CAJE's national task forces, sessions at conferences, and publications take on many important issues and discuss how to address them in an educatoinal context. www.caje.org

Edah
Promoting the invigoration of modern Orthodoxy and the ways Jewish tradition speaks to the contemporary world; Edah's conferences, online journal, and other programs treat many specific social and political topics. www.edah.org

Jewish Labor Committee
Represents the Jewish community within the trade union movement, and keeps workers' rights and labor's ability to organize on the agendas of Jewish organizations and the larger Jewish world. JLC is at 25 East 21st St., New York, NY 10010.

Jewish Social Justice Network
Housed at the Jewish Fund for Justice, JSJN is a consortium of twelve local activist Jewish groups from Los Angeles to Boston to Minneapolis-St. Paul cooperating on information, training, leadership development, and coordinated issue campaigns, to promote Jews' involvement in their projects and build the visibility of Jewish social change efforts. www.jfjustice.org/jsjnhome.htm

Lishma
This six-week summer study program for young adults at Camp Ramah in California incorporates full-day community service projects and regular exploration of texts about the sources and values behind social involvement. www.lishma.org

National Council of Jewish Women (NJCW)
For over a century, the national NCJW and its more than a hundred local sections have tried to improve the lives of women, children, and families through research, education, advocacy, and community service. The website has links to information on domestic violence, gun control, the federal judiciary, and other issues. www.ncjw.org

Religious Action Center of Reform Judaism (RAC)
The largest, most active, best informed national headquarters for advocacy of Jewish principles is also the hub for Reform Jewish social action all around North America. RAC provides leadership, research, publications, models for local programming, participation in broad coalitions on numerous issues, and influential ongoing contacts with government. You can sign up on RAC's website to receive action alerts via e-mail about legislation and issues needing immediate attention. www.rac.org

Pardes Institute
Energetic, inspiring coed yeshiva in Jerusalem for younger adults from all Jewish orientations includes in its intensive program both study of sources on communal responsibility and ongoing projects of service and self-investment. www.pardes.org.il

Shefa Fund
A public foundation that encourages Jews to use their *tzedakah* activities to create a more just society and to transform American Jewish life, Shefa's work includes grantmaking, investing, and education. A major initiative is the TZEDEC community investment project, which organizes Jewish institutions and individuals to invest in low-income community development to help create housing, small businesses, financial services, and credit in impoverished communities. www.shefafund.org

Shalom Center
This Philadelphia-based activist group is a division of Aleph: Alliance for Jewish Renewal. The website's sections on Seeking Peace, Healing the Earth, and Pursuing Justice include topical articles, Words of Torah, and links to organizations. www.shalomctr.org

SocialAction.com
Online Jewish magazine of involvement and convictions packed with opinion pieces, Torah discussion (including new pieces for each weekly portion), and action ideas on a variety of hot issues; with numerous links to all sorts of groups and sites. www.SocialAction.com

Washington Institute for Jewish Leadership and Values
Dedicated to renewing American Jewish life by integrating Jewish learning, values, and social responsibility; sponsors such programs as Jewish Policy Leaders Study Groups; the Jewish Civics Initiative community service program for high school students around the U.S.; and *Panim el Panim* seminars in Washington, D.C., for high school students. www.epu.org

Yakar Center for Tradition and Creativity
In addition to active schedules of Torah study, prayer, meditation, and the arts, this popular Jerusalem gathering place sponsors the Yakar Center for Social Concern—programs and panels on a variety of issues. www.yakar.org

Ziv Tzedakah Fund
An organization dedicated to *mitzvahs*—how to give money, what the Jewish sources ask of us, how *mitzvah* heroes improve the world and how each of us can do so as well. Based on the teachings and connections of Danny Siegel, the Ziv website provides ideas, texts, motivation, and links to many groups doing wonderful good deeds. www.ziv.org

5. Another Form of Activism
A much-expanded listing of activist Jewish organizations and contacts is scheduled to be available later in 2002 on the website of the Institute for Jewish Activism, www.jewishactivism.net.

American Jewish World Service's Jewish Volunteer Corps
Sends Jewish adults of all ages to participate in projects throughout the world and International Jewish College Corps (seven-week summer program of study and service). www.ajws.org.

The Jewish Agency for Israel's Amitim Program
Sends North American and Israeli Jews in their twenties for eight months of service to underdeveloped Jewish communities in the former Soviet Union, and soon in other countries. www.amitim.org

The Joint Distribution Committee's Jewish Service Corps
Adults of all ages serve overseas for a year in Europe or India to strengthen Jewish communal life. www.jdc.org.

The World Jewish Peace Corps
Beginning in July, 2002, volunteers will train in Israel for a year of service in India or South Africa. www.wjpc.org. You can get more information about and find out how to contact these and other volunteer programs through the *Jewish Coalition for Service*. jewishservice.org

APPENDIX D: GENERAL GROUPS INVOLVED WITH GLOBAL ISSUES

Once again, only a small sampling of groups is given, but many more groups can be located through links on the websites indicated below.

Food First: www.foodfirst.org
International Food Policy Research Institute: www.cgiar.org/ifpri
International Rescue Committee: www.theirc.org
Jubilee USA: www.jubileeusa.org
National Audubon Society Population and Habitat Program:
      www.audubonpopulation.org
National Labor Committee: www.nlcnet.org
Natural Resources Defense Council: www.nrdc.org
Population Reference Bureau: www.prb.org
Sierra Club: www.sierraclub.org
Union of Concerned Scientists (UCS): www.ucsusa.org
U.S. Environmental Protection Agency (EPA): www.epa.gov
Vegetarian Resource Group: www.vrg.org
Vegsource: www.vegsource.com
Worker Rights Consortium: www.workersrights.org
Worldwatch Institute: www.worldwatch.org

APPENDIX E:
JEWISH PUBLICATIONS

This is a brief list of important Jewish publications. A more complete list (and updates) can be found in the American Jewish Yearbook, published by the American Jewish Committee.

The American Rabbi: David Epstein; david@inpubco.com; (818) 225-9631

Amit: Rita Schwalb; amitmag@aol.com; www.amitchildren.org; (212) 447-4720

Azure (Shalem Center in Israel): www.shalem.org.il

Baltimore Jewish Times: Phil Jacobs; editorial @jewishtimes.com; www. jewishtimes.com; (410) 752-3504

B'Nai B'rith International Jewish Monthly: Jason Silberberg erozenman@bnaibrith.org

The Call (The Workman's Circle): Erica Sigmon; ericas@circle.org; (212) 889-6800 (extension 225)

CCAR Journal: Elliot Stevens; estevens@ccarnet.com, (212) 972-3636

Commentary (American Jewish Committee): Neal Kozodoy; commentary@compuserve.com; (212) 751-1174

Congress Monthly (American Jewish Congress): Jack Fischel; (212) 879-4500; 15 East 84 Street, New York, NY 10028

Conservative Judaism (Rabbinical Assembly): Martin Cohen; rapubs@jtsa.edu; www.rabassembly.org; (212) 280-6065

Farbrengen (Chabad of California): Chaim Cunin; editor@farbrengen. com; (310) 208-7511

Emunah: Faith Reichwald; info@emunah.org; www.emunah.org; (212)564-9045

Forward: Andrew Silow-Carroll; newsdesk@forward.com; www.forward.com; (212) 889-8200, ex. 417

Haaretz daily (English language version): www.Haaretzdaily.com

Hadassah Magazine: Alan M. Tigay; www.hadassah.org; (212) 355-7900;

The Jerusalem Post: Amotz Asa-El; ijp@jpost.co.il; www.jpost.com; (02)531-5450

The Jerusalem Report: David Horovitz; jrep@jreport.co.il; www.jrep.com; (02) 531-5440

Jewish Action (Orthodox Union): Charlotte Friedland; ja@ou.org; www.ou.org, .(212) 613-0646

Jewish Currents: Editorial committee; (212) 924-5740

Jewish Observer (Agudath Israel of America): Rabbi Nissin Wolpin; aiamail@aol.com; (212) 269-2843

Jewish Week (New York): Gary Rosenblatt; editor@jewishweek.org; www.thejewishweek.com; (212) 921-7822

The Jewish Press: Irene Klass; jpeditor@aol.com; www.thejewishpress.com; (718) 330-1100

Journal of Halacha and Contemporary Society: Rabbi Alfred Cohen: Rabbi Jacob Joseph School, 3495 Richmond Road, Staten Island, New York 10306; (718) 982-8745

Jewish Theological Magazine (Jewish Theological Seminary (JTS)) : Esther Kustanowitz; ekustanowitz@jtsa.edu; www.jtsa.edu. (212) 678-8950

Lilith: Susan Weidman Schneider; lilithmag@aol.com; www.lilithmag.com; (212) 757-0818

Midstream (World Zionist Organization): Leo Haber; (212) 339-6020; info@midstream.org; www.midstream.org

Moment: Hershel Shanks; editor@momentmag.com; www.momentmag.com;

The Reporter (Women's American ORT): Roberta Zulawski; rzulawski@waort.org; (212) 505-7700

Shalom The Jewish Peace Letter (Jewish Peace Fellowship (JPF)) Murray Polner; jpf@forusa.org; www.jewishpeacefellowship.org; (845) 358-4601, ex.35

Sh'ma Susan Berrin: susanb@jflmedia.com; (781) 449-9894

Social Action.com (Jewish Resources for Social change): An on-line Jewish magazine; Rabbi Susan P. Fendrick; www.SocialAction.com

Tikkun: Michael Lerner; magazine@tikkun.org; www.tikkun.org

Tradition (Rabbinical Council of America): Michael Shmidman; patturn27@aol.com; (212) 807-7888

Tzaddik (Breslov of Tzefat, Israel): Talya Lipshutz; nnmc@nnmc.org.il; 011-972-4-682-7132

Wellsprings (Chabad Lubavitch): Baila Olidort; editor@e-wellsprings.org; www.e-wellsprings.org; (718) 953-1000;

Yated Ne'eman (Agudath Israel of America): Rabbi Pinchus Lipschutz; editor@yated.com; (845) 369-1600

NOTES

Preface
1. Union of Concerned Scientists (www.ucsusa.org).
2. Abraham Joshua Heschel, *The Insecurity of Freedom*, New York: Farrar, Strauss, and Giroux, 1967, 218.

Chapter 1: Involvement and Protest
1. *Tanchuma* to *Mishpatim*.
2. Babylonian Talmud: *Shabbat* 99b.
3. Midrash *Genesis Rabbah* 54:3.
4. *Shabbat* 55a, *Tanchuma Tazria* 9.
5. R. Judah Loew, *Netivot Olam*, *Shaar Hatochaha*, end of chapter 2. The result of failing to speak out against injustice is well expressed by the following state-ment by the German theologian Martin Niemoller:

> In Germany, the Nazis first came for the Jews, and I didn't speak up because I was not a Jew. Then they came for the communists, and I didn't speak up because I was not a communist. Then they came for the trade unionists, and I didn't speak up because I wasn't a trade unionist. Then they came for the gypsies, and I didn't speak up because I was not a gypsy. Then they came for the Catholics, and I didn't speak up because I was not a Catholic. Then they came for me ... and by that time, there was no one to speak up for me.

> Quoted in Jack Doueck, *The Chesed Boomerang: How Acts of Kindness Enrich Our Lives*, Deal, New Jersey: Yagdiyl Torah Publications, 1999, 83.

6. *Orchot Zaddikim* 24, Jerusalem: Eshkol 1967, 160; see also Rabbeinu Yonah, *Sharei Teshuvah, Shaar Sh'lishi,* No. 5, 187, and 195.

7. American Jewish Congress, *Congress Bi-Weekly* 31/8, May 11, 1964: 6.

8. Abraham Joshua Heschel, *The Insecurity of Freedom*, New York: Farrar, Straus and Giroux, 1967, 92.

9. *Shabbat* 55a.

10. *Pirke Avot* 2:21.

11. *Judaism* 19 (1970): 38–58.

12. *Pirke Avot* 5:20.

13. Abraham Joshua Heschel, *The Prophets*, Philadelphia: Jewish Publication Society, 1962, and *The Insecurity of Freedom*, 9–13 and 92–93.

14. Midrash *Genesis Rabbah.*

15. Quoted in Norman Lamm, *The Royal Reach*, New York: Phillip Feldheim Inc., 1970, 131.

16. David Shatz, Chaim I. Waxman, and Nathan J. Diament, eds., *Tikkun Olam: Social Responsibility in Jewish Thought and Law*, Northvale, New Jersey: Jason Aronson, 1997, 3.

17. Ibid, 4; also see Joseph B. Soloveitchik, "Confrontation," *Tradition* 6:2, 1964: 5–29.

18. Jonathan Sacks, *The Persistence of Faith*, London: Jews' College, 1990, 27.

19. "Why We Went" (paper of the Social Action Commission, Union of American Hebrew Congregations, New York); quoted in Rabbi Henry Cohen, *Justice, Justice: A Jewish View of the Black Revolution*, New York: Union of American Hebrew Congregations, 1968, 18.

20. Many Jewish groups that are actively working on environmental and social justice issues are discussed in Appendix C. This section focuses on components of the Jewish community that are not sufficiently involved.

21. Heschel, *Prophets*, 10–11.

22. Heschel, *Insecurity of Freedom*, 3, 4.

23. Quoted in Samuel Chiel, *Spectators or Participants*, New York: Jonathan David, 1969, 57.

24. Quoted in Albert Vorspan and Eugene Lipman, *Justice and Judaism: The Work of Social Action*, New York: Union of American Hebrew Congregations, 1969, 231.

25. *Pesachim* 66b.

Chapter 2: Human Rights and Obligations

1. *Yalkut Shimoni* 1:13.
2. Cited in Rabbi J. H. Hertz, *The Pentateuch and Haftorahs*, London: Soncino Press, 1958, 17.
3. *Pirke Avot* 3:18, citing Genesis 1:27.
4. *Sifre* to Deuteronomy 11:22.
5. *Sotah* 14a.
6. Maimonides, Guide to the Perplexed, part 2, chapter 54.
7. "The Last Days of Maimonides," in Abraham Joshua Heschel, *The Insecurity of Freedom*, New York: Farrar, Straus, and Giroux, 1967, 291.
8. Hertz, *The Pentateuch and Haftorahs*, 563.
9. Martin Buber, *Tales of the Hasidim, The Early Masters*, New York: Schocken Books, 1947, 227.
10. Cited in J. H. Hertz, *The Pentateuch and Haftorahs*, 563.
11. Rabbi Pinchas Eliyahu of Vilna, *Sefer HaBris*, section II, discourse 13, quoted in Dovid Sears, *Compassion for Humanity in the Jewish Tradition*, Northvale, New Jersey/Jerusalem: Jason Aronson, 1998, 6.
12. Ibid, 13:31, cited in Sears, *Compassion*, 8.
13. Ibid, 13:5, citing II Samuel, 15:19, cited in Sears, *Compassion*, 7.
14. Mishnah *Pe'ah* I.
15. Quoted in Samuel Dresner, *Prayer, Humility, and Compassion*, Philadelphia: The Jewish Publication Society, 1957, 196.
16. *Pirke Avot* 1:12.
17. *Shabbat* 31a.
18. Quoted in Hertz, *The Pentateuch and Haftorahs*, p. 504. In Jewish numerology, the number thirty-six is associated with righteousness, and the Talmud states that there are thirty-six *tzaddikim* (righteous individuals) in the world at any time (*Sukkot* 45b).
19. Ibid.
20. Ibid.
21. There were several privileges that the stranger did not share. The cancellation of debts every Sabbatical year applied only to natives. While the Israelite was prohibited from charging a fellow Israelite interest on loans, this was not applicable when the loan was to a non-Israelite. Also, a foreigner, if captured, did not enjoy the benefits of the laws requiring the periodic freeing of all slaves.
22. *Yalkut* to Judges 4:4 from *Tanna de Vei Eliyahu*.
23. *Tosefta Sanhedrin* 13:2.
24. *Gittin* 61a.

25. *Yerushalmi Demai* 4:6 (24a).

26. Henry Cohen, *Justice, Justice: A Jewish View of the Black Revolution*, New York: Union of American Hebrew Congregations, 1968, 51–52.

27. Many other statements by Jews of the Middle Ages indicated concern for the treatment of non-Jews by Jews. Levi b. Isaac ha-Hasid, a French Jew of the tenth century, stated:

> Treat with equal honesty the Christian as your brother in faith. If a Christian make a mistake to his loss, call his attention to it. If a Jew be a tax gatherer, he should demand no more from a Christian than from a Jew. A Jew shall not be untruthful in business with Jew or gentile.

Rabbi Yehudah ben Samuel of Regensburg wrote in his *Sefer Hasidim*:

> Mislead no one through thy actions designedly, be he Jew or non-Jew....Injustice must not be done to anyone whether he belongs to our religion or another.

In his *Sefer Mitzvot Gadol*, Moses ben Coucy wrote in 1245:

> Those who lie to non-Jews and steal from them belong to the category of blasphemers, for it is due to their guilt that many say the Jews have no binding law.

These quotations are found in "Jew and Non Jew," Tract No. 3, Popular Studies in Judaism, Union of American Hebrew Congregations, Cincinnati.

28. *Tradition*, no. 2, Summer 1966, 8.

29. Midrash *Deuteronomy Rabbah* 3:3.

30. Rabbi Ahron Soloveichik, *Logic of the Heart, Logic of the Mind: Civil Rights and the Dignity of Man*, Jerusalem: Genesis Press, 1991, quoted in Dovid Sears, *Compassion for Humanity in the Jewish Tradition*, Northvale, New Jersey/Jerusalem: Jason Aronson, 1998, 53.

31. *Kiddushin* 20a.

32. Soloveichik, *Logic of the Heart*, quoted in Sears, *Compassion*, 19.

33. Ibid.

34. Heschel, *Insecurity*, 86.

35. Ibid, 87.

36. Ibid, 93.
37. Ibid, 95.

Chapter 3: Social Justice

1. Quoted in J. H. Hertz, *The Pentateuch and Haftorahs*, London: Soncino, 1957, 820. Rabbi Hertz also offers a Chassidic rebbe's interpretation of this Biblical verse: "Do not use unjust means to secure the victory of justice" (p. 820).
2. Rabbi Emanuel Rackman, "Torah Concept of Empathic Justice Can Bring Peace," *The Jewish Week*, April 3, 1977, 19.
3. Rabbi Levi Yitzchak Horowitz, the Bostoner Rebbe, "And You Shall Tell Your Son," *Young Israel Viewpoint*, Spring 1997. Quoted in Dovid Sears, *Compassion for Humanity in the Jewish Tradition*. Northvale, New Jersey/Jerusalem: Jason Aronson, 1998, 22.
4. *Ketubot* 68a.
5. Maimonides, *Mishneh Torah*, *Zeraim*, Gifts to the Poor, 10:7.
6. Maimonides, *Mishneh Torah*, Gifts to the Poor: 10:7.
7. *Shabbat* 63a.
8. *Baba Batra* 88b.
9. Maimonides, *Mishneh Torah*, *Hilchot Avadim* 9:8.
10. *Sotah* 14a.
11. Midrash *Exodus Rabbah*, *Mishpatim* 31:14.
12. *Pirke Avot* 3:21.
13. *Betza* 32a.
14. *Eruvin* 41.
15. Genesis 18:2; *Abot de Rabbi Nathan* 7:17a, b.
16. *Betzah* 32b.
17. *Yebamot* 79a.
18. Samson R. Hirsch, *Horeb*, trans. Dayan Dr. I Grunfeld, London: Soncino, 1962, vol. 1, 54–55.
19. Samuel Dresner, *Prayer, Humility, Compassion*, Philadelphia: Jewish Publication Society, 1953, 183.
20. In Judaism, there are only two limits to compassion. The first is that a judge must apply the law equally, without regard to whether a person is rich or poor. Second, one need not show compassion to those who lack compassion and practice cruelty. A Talmudic sage taught: "He who is compassionate to the cruel will, in the end, be cruel to the compassionate" (*Yalkut*, Samuel 121).
21. *Gittin* 62a; *Berachot* 40a.

22. For a detailed study of the Jewish tradition on compassion for animals, see Noah J. Cohen, *Tsaar Ba'alei Chayim: The Prevention of Cruelty to Animals, Its Basis, Development, and Legislation in Hebrew Literature*, New York: Feldheim, 1976. Also see *The Vision of Eden*, an unpublished manuscript by Rabbi Dovid Sears.

23. Rabbi Moshe Cordovero, *Tomer Devorah*, Chapter 2, quoted in Dovid Sears, *Compassion for Humanity in the Jewish Tradition*, Northvale, New Jersey/Jerusalem: Jason Aronson, 1998, 3.

24. *Shabbat* 151b.

25. *Shabbat* 31a.

26. *Baba Metzia* 4:2.

27. *Baba Kamma*, 113b.

28. *Sanhedrin* 81a.

29. *She'iltot, Parshat VaYechi*.

Chapter 4: Ecology

1. Paul Flucke, "For the Sin of Terricide," in *New Prayers for the High Holy Days*, Rabbi Jack Riemer, ed., New York: Media Judaica, Inc., 1970, 44.

2. *Shabbat* 10a; *Sanhedrin* 7.

3. Mishnah *Kiddushin* 4:12; Jerusalem Talmud: *Kiddushin* 66d.

4. Mishnah *Baba Batra* 2:8.

5. Mishnah *Baba Batra* 2:8–9.

6. Mishnah *Berachot* 30:5

7. Story told by Rabbi Shlomo Riskin in "Biblical Ecology, A Jewish View," a television documentary, directed by Mitchell Chalek and Jonathan Rosen.

8. *Shabbat* 10a; *Sanhedrin* 7.

9. Kook, *A Vision of Vegetarianism and Peace*, Section 2; Also see J. Green, "Chalutzim of the Messiah—The Religious Vegetarian Concept as Expounded by Rabbi Kook" (lecture given in Johannesburg, South Africa), 2.

10. Ibid.

11. *Kiddushin* 32a.

12. *Sefer Hachinuch*, 530.

13. *Hullin* 7b.

14. *Shabbat* 140b.

15. *Baba Kamma* 91b.

16. *Berachot* 52b.

17. *Shabbat* 67b.

18. Maimonides, *Mishneh Torah*, Laws of Kings and Wars 6:8, 10.

19. *Sefer Ha-Hinukh*, 529.

20. Rabbi Samson Raphael Hirsch, *Horeb*, Sections 397, 398.

21. Ibid, Section 400.

22. Midrash *Ecclesiastes Rabbah* 1:18.

23. Quoted in David Miller, *The Secret of Happiness*, New York: Rabbi David Miller Foundation, 1937, 9.

24. World Scientists' Warning to Humanity, Union of Concerned Scientists, 1992, www.ucsusa.org.

25. Ed Ayres, *God's Last Offer: Negotiating for a Sustainable Future*, New York/London: Four Walls Four Windows, 1999, 27.

26. Ibid.

27. Paul G. Irwin, *Losing Paradise: The Growing Threat To Our Animals, Our Environment, and Ourselves*, Garden City Park, New York: Square One Publishers, 2000, 38.

28. World Scientists' Warning to Humanity.

29. CNN.com, Reuters, August 24, 2000.

30. Ibid.

31. Ibid.

32. *Washington Post*, Ted Plafker, September 7, 2000.

33. *Baltimore Sun*, Heather Dewar, Tom Horton, and Frank Langfitt, September 9, 2000.

34. MSNBC.com, Miguel Llanos, May 1, 2001.

35. Francis Moore Lappé, et al., *World Hunger: Twelve Myths*. New York: Grove Press, 1998, 41.

36. Ibid.

37. Ibid.

38. Ibid.

39. *Portland Oregonian*, Richard L. Hill, January 19, 2001.

40. *Los Angeles Times*, Gary Polakovic, January 14, 2001.

41. For a detailed analysis of how the misapplication of technology has been a prime cause of pollution problems, see Barry Commoner, *The Closing Circle*, New York: Bantam Books, 1974.

42. Irwin, *Losing Paradise*, 38.

43. Wisconsin Department of Public Instruction, "Pollution: Problems, Projects, and Mathematics Exercises," Bulletin No. 1082, 50.

44. *Salt Lake Desert News*, Associated Press, October 22, 2000.

45. A national Jewish organization that is applying Jewish values to the solution of current environmental threats is the Coalition on the Environment and

Jewish Life (COEJL), a collaboration of twenty-nine national Jewish organizations spanning the spectrum of Jewish religious and communal life, which serves as the voice of the organized Jewish community on a wide array of environmental issues. COEJL is the Jewish member of the National Religious Partnership for the Environment.

46. S. R. Hirsch, "The Sabbath," in *Judaism Eternal*, edited and translated by I. Grunfeld, London: Soncino, 1956, 22, 23.

Chapter 5: Environmental Issues in Israel

1. Sam Kiley, "Israel is being Poisoned," *Times of London*, July 4, 2000.
2. Statistical Yearbook, 2000, the Israeli Central Bureau of Statistics.
3. Ibid.
4. Ibid.
5. Ibid.
6. Ibid.
7. Zafrir Rinat, "Mekorot: Drinking water shortage is expected next year," *Ha'aretz*, December 11, 2000.
8. Ibid.
9. The Jewish National Fund advertisements can be found at www.jnf.org.
10. "Israel could run out of water by 2010," *Jerusalem Post* International Edition, September 1, 2000, 5.
11. Ibid.
12. Ibid.
13. Herb Keinon, "Touching Bottom," *Jerusalem Post* International Edition, 32.
14. Ibid.
15. Ibid.
16. "Rivers of Darkness," *Jerusalem Post* International Edition, August 9, 1997.
17. Ibid.
18. Ibid.
19. Planet Ark, Reuters, Danielle Haas, June 22, 2000.
20. Ibid.
21. "Bay Watch," *Jerusalem Report*, October 4, 2000, 19.
22. "Israel is being Poisoned," *Times of London*, July 4, 2000.
23. Ibid.
24. Ibid.
25. Ibid.
26. Ibid.

27. Zafrir Rinat, "Water pollution alarm bells in TA area," *Ha'aretz*, November 24, 2000.

28. Ibid.

29. Liat Collins, "Tel Aviv's air among worst in country," *Jerusalem Post* International Edition, November 8, 1997, 5.

30. Ibid.

31. Israel Union for Environmental Defense Report, www.iued.org.

32. Ibid.

33. D'vora Ben Shaul, "Solutions That Go to Waste," *Jerusalem Post*, January 2, 1998, 15.

34. Liat Collins, "Green and Fighting Fit," *Jerusalem Post*, April 21, 2000, 17.

35. D'vora Ben Shaul, "O Galilee, my Galilee," *Jerusalem Post* International Edition, February 1, 1997, 20.

36. Liat Collins, "Jerusalem of Green?" *Jerusalem Post*, January 17, 1997, 14; also see Philip Warburg, "The Ungreening of Jerusalem," *Jerusalem Report*, June 8, 1998, 54.

37. Veronique Bouquelle, "Transportation in Israel," Public Information Pamphlet #1, The Israel Union for Environmental Defense, 1.

38. Ibid.

39. Bouquelle, "Transportation," provides an extensive analysis of Israel's transportation problems and potential solutions.

40. *Jerusalem Post*, November 9, 2001, 16.

41. Ibid.

Chapter 6: Hunger

1. *Baba Batra* 9a.

2. Midrash *Tannaim*.

3. Passover Haggadah.

4. *Avot de Rabbi Nathan*, chapter 23.

5. Gary Gardner and Brian Halweil, "Underfed and Overfed—The Global Epidemic of Malnutrition," Worldwatch Paper #150, March 2000, 11.

6. Ibid, 12.

7. Ibid, 13.

8. Frances Moore Lappé, et al., *World Hunger: Twelve Myths*, New York: Grove Press, 1998, 2.

9. Based on calculations using data from the "2000 World Population Data Sheet," Population Reference Bureau, 1875 Connecticut Avenue, NW, Washington, D.C. 20009-5728, www.prb.org.

10. Rifkin, Jeremy, *Beyond Beef*, New York: Dutton, 1992, 177.

11. *Philadelphia Inquirer*, October 13, 1974, 9B.

12. Lester R. Brown, *In the Human Interest*, New York: Norton, 1974, 21.

13. Lester R. Brown, *Tough Choices: Facing the Challenge of Food Scarcity*, New York: W.W. Norton, 1996. For another perspective on future world food prospects: The International Food Policy Research Institute (a project of the Consultative Group on International Agricultural Research) held a major international conference, the Sustainable Food Security Forum, in Bonn, Germany in September, 2001. The focus of the conference was to assess trends in hunger, population, and food production over the next twenty years. The report issued at the conference concluded that it is possible to reduce hunger and increase food production between now and 2020, but only if proper policies and investments are adopted. IFPRI stated that 800 million people in the world are currently food-insecure (i.e., are either on their way to starvation or don't know where their next meal is coming from). The United Nations World Food Summit in 1996 set the goal of reducing hunger by fifty percent by 2025. The UN's world Food and Agriculture Association (FAO) now acknowledges that this goal is not likely to be met. IFPRI's report states that hunger could be reduced by half or more, if developed and developing nations agreed on the necessary principles. These would include the investment of about $10 billion per year (equal to what governments currently spend on weaponry each week); in rural infrastructure (such as roads) and in irrigation, primary education, basic health care, and agricultural research to increase yields per acre. A move away from the consumption of meat would also make a significant difference: IFPRI says that eighty percent of the increased demand for grain in the less-developed world will be for grain used as feed for livestock. Without adopting policies such as these, we will see the hunger crisis (especially in sub-Saharan Africa) worsen. Detailed studies and articles on many aspects of these projections toward the year 2020 can be found at the IFPRI website.

14. A detailed analysis of root causes of world hunger is in Lappé, *World Hunger*. The group behind the book and the research is Food First/Institute for Food and Development Policy, 398 60th Street, Oakland, CA 94618; Phone (510) 654-4400; email foodfirst@igc.org; www.foodfirst.org.

15. World Population Data Sheet.

16. Food First analysis at www.foodfirst.org.

17. Ibid.

18. Calculated from Food and Agriculture Organization, *1992 FAO Production Yearbook*, Vol. 46, Rome: FAO, 1993, cited in Lappé, *World Hunger*, 8.

19. Food and Agriculture Organization, *1995 FAO Production Yearbook*, Vol. 49, Rome: FAO, 1996, cited in Lappé, *World Hunger*, 8.

20. Food First analysis at www.foodfirst.org.

21. China's progress in greatly reducing hunger is discussed by Frances Moore Lappé and Joseph Collins, *Food First: Beyond the Myth of Scarcity* (Boston, Houghton, Mifflin, 1977), 95–96, 166–167, 400–401.

22. See Lappé, *World Hunger*, 16.

23. The analysis in this paragraph is based on material from the Institute for Food and Development Policy, www.foodfirst.org.

24. Ibid.

25. See Lappé, *World Hunger*.

26. www.foodfirst.org.

27. Lappé, *Food First: Beyond the Myth of Scarcity*, 77.

28. For a documented, comprehensive discussion of the effects of colonialism and neocolonialism in creating and spreading hunger, see Lappé, *Food First*, 75–92.

29. "The Farm Report," Farm Animal Reform Movement, Box 30654, Bethesda, MD 20824, www.farmusa.org.

30. www.globalhunger.net.

31. *Pirke Avot* 1:14.

32. *Berachot* 55a.

33. Paper on world hunger from Mazon, the ad hoc Jewish committee on hunger, New York, 1975.

34. Class before Passover given at Young Israel of Staten Island, attended by author.

35. Jay Dinshah, *The Vegetarian Way*, *Proceedings of the 24th World Vegetarian Conference*, Madras, India, 1977, 34.

36. "The Energy-Food Crisis: A Challenge to Peace—A Call to Faith" statement from the Inter-religious Peace Colloquium, held in Bellagio, Italy, May 1975. As this book was going to press, the December 7, 2001 issue of the *Jewish Week* reported that twenty-seven fervently Orthodox rabbis, under the leadership of the Agudath Israel of America, will issue formal guidelines to sharply reduce waste and extravagence at Jewish weddings.

Chapter 7: Peace

1. Midrash *Leviticus Rabbah* 9:9.
2. *Pirke Avot* 1:12.
3. *Yalkut Shimoni*, Yithro 273.
4. Midrash *Leviticus Rabbah* 9:9.
5. Midrash *Deuteronomy Rabbah* 5:15.
6. Ibid.
7. *Gittin* 59b.
8. Midrash *Genesis Rabbah* 38:6.
9. *Shabbat* 6:4
10. *Avoda Zarah* 17b.
11. *Avot de Rabbi Nathan* 51:27.
12. *Pirke Avot* 4:1.
13. *Sifra Kedoshim* 11:8.
14. I Chronicles 22:8–9.
15. *Pirke Avot* 5:11.
16. Rabbi Maurice Eisendrath, "Sanctions in Judaism for Peace," in *World Religions and World Peace*, Homer A. Jack, ed., Boston: Beacon, 1968.
17. Quoted in "World Hunger," World Vision 19, February 1975, p. 5.
18. *Staten Island Advance* article by Susan Fong, July 1, 1980, 1.
19. *Ta'anit* 4:2; *Megilla* 3:5.
20. *Sanhedrin* 39b.
21. *Avot de Rabbi Nathan*, chapter 23.
22. Rabbi J. H. Hertz, *The Pentateuch and Haftorahs*, London: Soncino, 1957, 501, 502.
23. *Tanchuma Mishpatim* I.
24. Quoted in Rabbi Samuel Belkin, *In His Image*, New York: Abelard Schuman Limited, 1960, 227.
25. *Baba Metzia* 32b.
26. *Sanhedrin* 74a.
27. Ibid.
28. Maimonides, *Mishneh Torah*, *Hilchot Melachim*, 7:7.
29. *Nedarim* 32a.
30. Quoted in Richard G. Hirsch, *Thy Most Precious Gift, Peace in Jewish Tradition*, New York: Union of American Hebrew Congregations, 1974, 8.
31. *Shabbat* 23b.
32. *Baba Kamma* 93a.
33. *Yoma* 23a; *Shabbat* 88b; *Gittin* 36b.

34. J. C. Herold, *The Mind of Napoleon*, New York: Columbia University Press, 1955, 76.
35. *Chayei Moharan* 546, Quoted in Dovid Sears, *Compassion for Humanity in the Jewish Tradition*, Northvale, New Jersey/Jerusalem: Jason Aronson, 1998, 34.
36. See "Judaism and Peacemaking," *Fellowship*, Jan–Feb. 1976, 14, 15.
37. Maimonides, *Mishneh Torah, Hilchot Melakim*, 3:9
38. Action Memo, Synagogue Council of America, January 1970, 1.
39. Shawn Perry, ed., "Words of Conscience, Religious Statements on Conscientious Objection," National Interreligious Service Board for Conscientious Objectors, Washington, D.C. Also see Allen Solomonow, ed. *Roots of Jewish Nonviolence*, Nyack, NY: Jewish Peace Fellowship, 1981.
40. Ibid.
41. Ibid.

Chapter 8: International Concerns

1. Lester Brown, *World Without Borders*, New York: Vintage, 1973, 41.
2. Calculation based on data in the "2001 World Population Data Sheet," Population Reference Bureau, 1875 Connecticut Avenue, NW, Washington, D.C. 20009-5728.
3. Much attention and organizing energy has been devoted in recent years to the problem of sweatshop working conditions in developing countries. Universities, celebrities, and shoe manufacturers have been surprised by revelations that their apparel is made by underage workers toiling long hours for little pay in unhealthful and dangerous conditions. The U.S. labor movement grew in part out of unions formed by immigrant workers (many of them Jewish) employed in garment sweatshops in the early twentieth century. Jewish experience and values should lead us to join in the movement to eliminate sweatshops everywhere. Contact the Worker Rights Consortium (founded by United Students Against Sweatshops, supportive university administrations, and UNITE, the garment workers union) at www.workersrights.org, the National Labor Committee (which has uncovered and publicized some of the worst violators) at www.nlcnet.org, or Co-op America's site, www.sweatshops.org.

    Dozens of the poorest countries in the world are crushed by huge amounts of debt owed to wealthier countries, international agencies, and foreign banks. Much of this debt came about because of improvident lending policies in previous decades, and because many of these countries have been ruled by oppressive and corrupt governments that squandered or stole most of the money as it came in. Energy costs have soared; prices of raw materials produced by developing countries have plunged; wealthier countries have held onto protectionist trade policies to limit imports of agricultural produce, textiles, and other products. International organizations such as the International Monetary Fund have required draconian fiscal policies and budgets from poorer nations, squeezing their ability to provide for the neediest citizens and increasing the anger and poverty of their people.

When wealthy countries face recession and debt, as the U.S. does currently, they engage in deficit spending and widen the social safety net. The IMF doesn't allow poor countries in the same fix to do so; it insists on "Herbert Hoover style" economic policies. Now that some of these countries have chosen democratic governments that are trying to improve their nations' circumstances, they are trapped by the huge debts accrued long before. As the debt has deepened and misery has spread, a coalition of concerned groups around the world (including major churches, rock stars, and advocates for children, health care, and the environment) has gradually come together to propose a debt jubilee. Based on the principle in the Torah that all debts in the Land of Israel were forgiven every seven years and that all land returned to its original owners every fifty years (Leviticus 25:8–13), the international jubilee movement has proposed that all of the debts of poor countries be cancelled (in exchange for greater spending on public health and education and responsible, responsive government). The target date was the civil year 2000, divisible by the Biblical 50, but only some of the countries achieved partial debt relief. The effort continues; for more information, contact www.jubileeusa.org.

Polls show that most Americans believe that the United States spends far too much on foreign aid to needy nations around the world. That's because Americans think that perhaps one-tenth of the federal budget, rather than a fraction of one percent, is invested to assist poor countries' development and to promote sustainable agriculture, environmental protection, health, nutrition, and infrastructure. In fact, foreign aid now costs the U.S. less than one-tenth of one percent of its Gross Domestic Product. In contrast, the Marshall Plan in the 1940s cost over two percent of the country's GDP. Professor Jeffrey Sachs of Harvard has proposed that the United States, Japan, and Europe each increase their foreign assistance by a fraction of a percent of Gross Domestic Product, which would produce tens of billions of additional dollars. Writes Sachs: "This country [and its partners in Europe in Asia are] so rich that we wouldn't have to do much, relative to our income, to accomplish an enormous amount of good [in areas such as] disease control, primary education, clean water, and other vital needs of impoverished places with strategic significance....[A] few added tenths of one percent of GDP...could do what was never before possible in human history: ensure that the basic needs...of all impoverished children in this world [are met]" (*Washington Post*, November 21, 2001). The events of September 11 have reminded many Americans who believed they could remove themselves from the rest of the world that poverty, instability, tyranny in any corner of the globe can affect us all. And there is also a compelling moral argument. The World Health Organization reports that less than one-tenth of one percent of the income of wealthier countries (an American expense equal to ten cents a day from each U.S. citizen) could save at least eight million lives each year by providing basic health expenses that poor countries can't afford, to combat tuberculosis, malaria, AIDS, and other widespread illnesses. The same WHO report compared the share of income spent by each advanced country on foreign aid: the U.S. is dead last, behind Greece and Portugal. If the U.S. donated a small portion of what Americans think we do, diseases that cripple the societies and economies of poor countries (and threaten everyone, in this era of international travel) could be beaten back. (*New York Times*, December 25, 2001). Properly managed and supervised, international assistance from governments and agencies can make an incalculable difference in the lives of our fellow human beings who live in the shadows of want and pain.

4. Ibid.
5. Ibid.
6. Ronald J. Sider, *Rich Christians in an Age of Hunger*, Downers Grove, IL: Intervarsity Press, 1979, 33.
7. "World Population: More Than Just Numbers," Population Reference Bureau booklet. Washington, D.C., 2000.
8. Sider, 34.
9. Lester Brown, *In the Human Interest*, New York: Norton, 1974, 165.
10. "2000 World Population Data Sheet," Population Reference Bureau, 1875 Connecticut Avenue, NW, Washington, D.C. 20009-5728, www.prb.org.
11. Frances Moore Lappé, et al., *World Hunger*, 2.
12. Robert L. Heilbroner, *The Great Assent: The Struggle for Economic Development in Our Time*, New York: Harper and Row, 1963, 33–36. Also see Lappé et al., *World Hunger*, 3 for a discussion of these factors.
13. The biblical Jubilee year is discussed in Leviticus 25:8–55.
14. Much of the background information in this section came from Hilary French, *Vanishing Borders: Protecting the Planet in the Age of Globalization*, New

York/London: W.W. Norton, 2000; Lappé, *World Hunger*; and Walden Bello, *The Future in the Balance: Essays on Globalization and Resistance*, Oakland, California: Food First Books, 2001.

15. Hilary French, *Vanishing Borders*, 6.
16. Ibid.
17. Ibid.
18. Ibid, 7.
19. Ibid.
20. Ibid, 6.
21. Jerry Mander, "Economic Globalization: The Era of Corporate Rule," Nineteenth Annual E. F. Schumacher Lectures, October 1999, Salisbury Congregational Church, Salisbury, Connecticut, www.schumachersociety.org.
22. Ibid.
23. Ibid.
24. Jean-Bertrand Aristide, *Eyes of the Heart: Seeking a Path for the Poor in the Age of Globalization*, Monroe, Maine: Common Courage Press, 2000, 5.
25. Ibid.
26. Mander, "Economic Globalization."
27. Ibid.
28. Ibid.
29. Aristide, *Eyes of the Heart*, 11–12.
30. Ibid.
31. Quoted in Maude Barlow, "Water as Commodity—the Wrong Prescription," Food First Backgrounder, Summer 2001.
32. Ed Ayres, "The Global and the Local," *WorldWatch*, September/October, 2001, 3.
33. Bello, *The Future in the Balance*, 60.
34. Information on the Statement and Call can be obtained from The Shalom Center, 6711 Lincoln Drive, Philadelphia, PA 19119, www.shalomctr.org, or the Religious Working Group on the World Bank and IMF, P.O. Box 29132, Washington, D.C. 20017.
35. Ibid.
36. Ibid.
37. Ibid.
38. Ibid.
39. *Shavuot* 39a.
40. *Pirke Avot* 1:14.

41. *Sanhedrin* 105a; also see *Yalkut*, II Kings, 296; Jerusalem Talmud: *Pe'ah* 1:1; and Dovid Sears, *Compassion for Humanity in the Jewish Tradition*, Northvale, NJ/Jerusalem: Jason Aronson, 1998, 53–56.

42. Philip Goodman, ed., *The Sukkot and Simchat Torah Anthology*, Philadelphia: The Jewish Publication Society, 1973, 114.

43. Mechilta D'Rabbi Ishmael.

44. Quoted in Martin Buber, *Ten Rungs: Hasidic Sayings*, New York: Schocken Books, Inc. 1961, 81.

45. *Sanhedrin* 37a.

46. Rabbi Nachman of Breslov, *Likkutei Moharan* I, 5:1; quoted in Dovid Sears, *Compassion for Humanity*, Northvale, NJ/Jerusalem: Jason Aronson, 1998, 93, 94.

47. *Ta'anit* 4:2; *Megilla* 3:5.

48. Robert Gordis, "The Vision of Micah," in *Judaism and Human Rights*, R. Konvitz, ed., New York: W.W. Norton, 1972, 287.

49. Ibid.

Chapter 9: Energy

1. H. Josef Haber, "Bush Plan Focuses on Boosting Energy Supply," *The Associated Press*, Washington, D.C., May 17, 2001.

2. Ibid.

3. Ibid.

4. The classic discussion of these two energy paths is in *Soft Energy Paths: Toward a Durable Peace* by Amory B. Lovins, Washington, D.C.: Friends of the Earth International, 1977.

5. Soft energy path fuels and methods are discussed in *Renewable Energy: Sources for Fuels and Electricity*, edited by Thomas B. Johansson and Henry Kelly, Washington D.C.: Island Press, 1993 and *Renewing Our Energy Future*, Office of Technology Assessment of the U.S. Congress, Washington, D.C.: U.S. Government Printing Office, 1995.

6. Philip Shenon, "Battle Lines in Congress Are Quickly Drawn by Republicans and Democrats," *New York Times*, May 18, 2001.

7. Ibid.

8. Ibid.

9. Ibid.

10. Ibid.

11. Ibid.

12. Ibid.

13. Jim Motovelli, "Balancing Act," *E Magazine*, November/December 2000, 30.
14. Denis Hayes, *The Official Earth Day Guide*, 25.
15. Ibid, 7.
16. Ibid.
17. Denis Hayes, "Energy: The Case for Conservation," Worldwatch Paper #4, Washington, D.C.: Worldwatch Institute, 1976, 20–25.
18. Planet Ark, Reuters, September 20, 2000, www.planetark.org.
19. Ibid.
20. *Los Angeles Times*, Dan Morain, April 19, 2000.
21. Ibid.
22. Ibid.
23. Donella Meadows, "Deregulation in California didn't help consumers, or the environment," *Grist Magazine*, www.gristmagazine.com.
24. Planet Ark, Reuters September 29, 2000, www.planetark.org.
25. Ibid.
26. Ibid.
27. www.epa.gov or call 1-888-782-7937.
28. Ibid.
29. The EPA report is available at www.epa.gov.otaq.fetrends.htm and www.sierraclub.org.
30. Daniel B. Wood, *Christian Science Monitor*, May 14, 2001.
31. "Bush-Cheney Oil and Coal Plan Turns Back the Clock," May 7, 2001, www.ucsusa.org.
32. Ibid.
33. Mike Allen and Eric Pianin, *Washington Post*, May 9, 2001; Joseph Kahn, *New York Times*, May 9, 2001.
34. "Bush-Cheney Oil and Coal Plan Turns Back the Clock," May 7, 2001, www.ucsusa.org.
35. Ibid.
36. Pollution effects from energy are discussed in *Energy for a Technological Society* by Joseph Priest, Reading, Massachusetts: Addison-Wesley, 1979, 51–93; also see www.100toppollutionsites.com.
37. Anna Gyorgy, ed., *No Nukes*, Boston: South End Press, 1979, 243; also see www.ucsusa.org.
38. Ibid.
39. Denis Hayes, *The Official Earth Day Guide*, 127.

40. V. E. Archer, J. D. Gillam, and J. K. Wagoner, "Respiratory Disease Mortality Among Uranium Miners" *Ann NY Acad Sci*, 271:280–93. NRC Contract No. AT (49-24-0190), October 31, 1975.

41. *Tamid* 32a.

42. *Ta'anit* 23a; *Midrash Leviticus Rabbah* 25:5.

43. Quoted in Hayes, *Official Earth Day Guide*, 34–35.

44. *Toronto Globe and Mail*, Martin Mittelstaedt, September 13, 2001. Environmental news from *Grist Magazine*, September 13, 2001; www.grist magazine.com.

45. Ibid.

46. Ibid.

47. John H. Barton, "Intensified Nuclear Safeguards and Civil Liberties," NRC Contract No. AT (49-24-0190), October 31, 1975.

48. Jewish statements about the importance and dignity of labor include:

> When you eat from the labor of your hands, you shall be happy and it shall be well with you. (Psalms 128:2)

> Great is labor, for it honors him who performs it. (*Nedarim* 49b)

> Artisans are not required to stand up from their labor when a sage passes by. (*Kiddushin* 33a)

> A man is obliged to teach his son a trade, and whoever does not teach his son a trade teaches him (in effect) to become a robber. (*Tosefta Kiddushin* 1:11)

> Rabban Gamaliel, the son of Rabbi Judah the Prince said: "Excellent is the study of Torah when combined with a worldly occupation, for the effort demanded by both makes sin to be forgotten." (*Pirke Avot* 2:2)

> Sweet is the sleep of a laboring man, whether he eat little or much, but the satiety of the rich will not suffer him to sleep. (Ecclesiastes 5:11)

The dignity of labor is raised to the highest level in a rabbinic dictum. It concerns the Holy of Holies, the repository for the Ark of the Covenant, the most sacred part of the Holy Temple in Jerusalem. Only the high priest was permitted to enter, once a year on the Day of Atonement. The rabbinic statement reads:

> Great is work! Even the High Priest, if he were to enter the Holy of Holies on the Day of Atonement other than during the *Avodah* (worship service), is punished by death; yet for labor in it (for repair or mending), even those ritually unclean or blemished were permitted to enter. (*Mechilta*)

Judaism considers all types of work to be dignified and ennobling, if through them an individual is participating in the creative process God intended for people: to improve the world. Consistent with this, the sages of Yavneh, the most famous academy of Talmudic times, stated:

> I am a creature, and my fellowman is a creature. I work in the city. He works in the fields. I rise early to go to my work. He rises early to go to his work. Just as he does not feel superior in his work, so I do not feel superior in mine. And if you should say that I do more for Heaven than he does, we have learned that it makes no difference. One may give more and one may give less, providing that his intention is toward Heaven. (*Berachot* 17a)

49. *Avot de Rabbi Nathan* 11:23a.
50. *Avot de Rabbi Nathan* 31.
51. Fact Sheet from Solar Lobby, 1001 Connecticut Ave., NW, Washington, D.C. 20014. Also see the paper "Jobs and Energy," Environmentalists for a Full Economy, Washington, D. C.
52. Denis Hayes, *The Official Earth Day Guide*, 14, 16.
53. "Bush-Cheney Oil and Coal Plan Turns Back the Clock," May 7, 2001, www.ucsusa.org.
54. Ibid.
55. Contact: COEJL, the environmental arm of JCPA, (212) 684-6950, ext. 210, fax: (212) 686-1353, www.coejl.org.
56. Ibid.
57. Ibid.
58. The complete statement can be obtained from www.coejl.org or www.webofcreation.org.

59. CARE (Conservation and Renewable Energy) is discussed in *The Community Energy CARE-ing Handbook*, by Leonard Rodberg and Arthur Waskow, Washington, D.C.: Public Resource Center, 1980.

Chapter 10: Global Climate Change

1. Extensive coverage of global warming is found at www.heatisonline.org, and in Ross Gelbspan, *The Heat is On: The Climate Crisis, the Cover Up, the Prescription*, Reading, Massachusetts: Perseus Books, 1998.
2. www.heatisonline.org.
3. *New York Times*, Andrew C. Revkin, October 26, 2000; also see Ed Ayres, "Leaked report says climate scientists now see higher projected temperatures," Worldwatch, January/February 2001, 11.
4. Ibid.
5. Tiffany Wu, "Earth warming faster than expected, humans to blame," January 22, 2001, www.enn.com.
6. Clare Nullis, "Report Shows Global Warming Risks," Associated Press Report, February 19, 2001.
7. www.climatehotmap.org; also see Leonie Haimson, "Taking the Earth's temperature for a March checkup," *Grist Magazine*, April 20, 2000, www.gristmagazine.com.
8. Unless otherwise indicated, the examples are all from the "Global Warming Early Warning Signs" notes (www.climatehotmap.org).
9. www.heatisonline.org.
10. *Salt Lake Desert News*, Associated Press, October 24, 2000, www.deseretnews.com.
11. Ibid.
12. Fox News, Associated Press, November 3, 2000; *London Telegraph*, George Jones, David Graves, and Charles Clover, November 1, 2000; *London Independent*, Michael McCarthy, November 2, 2000.
13. Ibid.
14. Ibid.
15. Information about COEJL can be found at www.coejl.org.
16. Ibid.
17. The complete statement can be obtained from www.coejl.org or www.webofcreation.org.
18. *Los Angeles Times*, Reuters, Tiffany Wu, January 22, 2001.
19. Tom Cohen, *Seattle Post-Intelligencer*, Associated Press, November 26, 2001.

20. An extensive analysis of steps to reverse global warming and the benefits of such a reversal are at www.heatisonline.org.

Chapter 11: Population Growth

1. Judith Zimmerman and Barbara Trainin, ed., *Jewish Population: Renascence or Oblivion*, New York: Federation of Jewish Philanthropies of New York, 1979, xiii.
2. Ibid.
3. A good source for current, reliable statistics on population is the Population Reference Bureau, 1875 Connecticut Avenue, NW, Washington, D.C. 20037, (202) 483-1100, www.prb.org. Their annual "World Population Data Sheet" is especially valuable. They also produce modules and other background material on various aspects of population. A source for many valuable population-related articles is *Beyond the Numbers: A Reader on Population, Consumption, and the Environment*, Laurie Ann Mazur, ed., Washington, D.C.: Island Press, 1994.
4. "2001 World Population Data Sheet," Population Reference Bureau, Washington, D.C.
5. Calculation based on the "2001 World Population Data Sheet."
6. Ibid.
7. Ibid.
8. Ed Ayres, *God's Last Offer: Negotiating for a Sustainable Future*, New York/London: Four Walls Eight Windows, 1999, 43, 44.
9. Calculation based on the "2001 World Population Data Sheet."
10. "World Population: More Than Just Numbers," Population Reference Bureau booklet, 1999.
11. Jim Motovelli, "Balancing Act," *E Magazine*, November/December 2000, 29. The article's 2000 population estimate of 275 million was changed to 281 million to be consistent with the 2000 census, as reported on the front page of the December 29, 2000 *New York Times*.
12. Ibid, 31.
13. Calculation based on the "2000 World Population Data Sheet."
14. The "World Scientists' Warning" can be found at www.ucsusa.org.
15. 2000 World Population Data Sheet. An example is that the population doubling time for Africa was only 29 years, while it was 653 years for Northern Europe, where many countries have stabilized or decreasing populations. The 2001 Data Sheet did not include doubling times.
16. Calculation based on the "2001 World Population Data Sheet."

17. The group Zero Population Growth is located at 1346 Connecticut Avenue, NW, Washington, D.C. 20036; www.zpg.org.

18. Negative Population Growth can be contacted at P.O. Box 53249, Washington, D.C. 20009, 1-800-764-7393, www.npg.org, e-mail: npg@npg.org.

19. David S. Shapiro, "Be Fruitful and Multiply," in *Jewish Bioethics*, Fred Rosner and J. Bleich, ed., New York: Sanhedrin Press, 1979, 71, 72.

20. Maimonides, *Sefer Hamitzvot*, 212.

21. *Yebamot* 61b.

22. Ibid.

23. Other statements in the Jewish tradition which show the great importance placed on raising a family include:

> To refrain from having children is to impair the divine image. (Midrash *Genesis Rabbah* 34:14)

> One who brings no children into the world is like a murderer. (*Yevamot* 63b)

> A childless person is like one who is dead. (*Nedarim* 64b)

> Was not the world created only for propagation? (*Hagiga* 2b)

In his *Sefer Hamitzvot*, Maimonides comments on the purpose of the first *mitzvah*:

> God has commanded us to be fruitful and multiply with the intention of preserving the human species.... (Commandment 212)

The *Sefer HaChinuch* (Book of Education) also cites having children as a fundamental positive commandment, because without it, none of the other mitzvot could be fulfilled. The Talmud teaches that when one is brought to judgment, one of the first questions asked is "Did you undertake to fulfill the duty of procreation?" (*Shabbat* 31a). The importance of reproduction in order to populate the earth is also indicated by the prophet Isaiah:

> For thus says the Lord, the Creator of the heavens: He is God,
> He fashioned the earth and He made it, He has established it;

> He did not create it to be waste; He has fashioned it so that it
> will be inhabited. (Isaiah 45:18)

24. Maimonides, *Mishnah Torah, Hilchot Ishut*, 15:16.
25. *Sanhedrin* 19b.
26. *Sanhedrin* 99b.
27. "Prospecting the Jewish Future: Population Projections, 2000–2080," *American Jewish Year Book*, 2000, American Jewish Committee, 103–146.
28. Ibid, 104.
29. Ibid, 104, 105.
30. Ibid, 105.
31. Ibid, 110.
32. Dr. Seymour P. Lachman, "Jewish Population in Accelerating Decline," *Young Israel Viewpoint,* Chanukah, 1992 issue, 14.
33. "Prospecting the Jewish Future," 105.
34. Ibid.
35. Ibid, 110.
36. Ibid, 118, 119.
37. Ibid, 119.
38. Ibid.
39. Ibid.
40. "Jewish Population in Accelerating Decline," viii.
41. *The Jewish Week*, November 26, 1982, 5.
42. Frank, "Population Panic," 13.
43. Ibid.
44. David M. Feldman, "Jewish Population: The Halachic Perspective," in *Jewish Population*, 42.
45. See Trude Weiss Rosmarin, "The Editor's Corner," *Jewish Spectator*, Fall 1978, 2–4.
46. Cohen, "Coming Shrinkage," 21.
47. Lisa Keys, "Jewish Education Nears Crossroads," *Jewish World*, September 8–14, 2000, 2.
48. Ibid.
49. Ibid.
50. Chaim Waxman, "How Many Are We? Where Are We Going?" *Jewish Life*, Spring/Summer 1982, 44.
51. Rashi's commentary on Genesis 41:50, based on *Ta'anit* 11a.

52. This might be even more appealing to Jews when it is considered that this can be read as Z-PIG, or "Zero Pig," and the dietary laws forbid the eating of pig flesh.

53. 2000 U. S. Census, as indicated on the front page of the December 29, 2000 *New York Times.*

54. 2000 World Population Data Sheet.

55. A challenging analysis of the true causes of world hunger is in *World Hunger: Twelve Myths,* by Frances Moore Lappé, et al., New York: Grove Press, 1998. Also see Chapter 6 of this book.

56. I am indebted to my friend Yosef Ben Shlomo Hakohen for the analysis in this and the next two paragraphs.

57. *Jewish Population,* x.

Chapter 12: Vegetarianism—A Global Imperative?

1. Rashi's commentary on Genesis 1:29.

2. Quoted in Nehama Leibowitz, *Studies in Bereshit* (Genesis), 3rd ed., Jerusalem: World Zionist Organization, 1976, 77.

3. *Sanhedrin* 59b.

4. Nachmanides, commentary on Genesis 1:29.

5. Rabbi J. H. Hertz, *The Pentateuch and Haftorahs,* London: Soncino Press, 1958, 5; also see Nehama Leibowitz, *Studies in Deuteronomy,* 3rd ed., Jerusalem: World Zionist Organization, 137.

6. Rabbi Abraham Isaac Ha-Kohen Kook, *A Vision of Vegetarianism and Peace,* Sections 1 and 4; also see Leibowitz, *Studies in Deuteronomy,* 138.

7. Kook, *A Vision,* Sections 7, 12; Rabbi Samuel H. Dresner, *The Jewish Dietary Laws, Their Meaning for Our Time,* New York: Burning Bush Press, 1959, 21–25; Cassuto, commentary on Genesis 1:29.

8. Kook, *A Vision,* Sections 1–7; also see Leibowitz, *Studies in Genesis,* 77.

9. Samson Raphael Hirsch's commentary on Genesis 9:2.

10. Reverend A. Cohen, *The Teaching of Maimonides,* New York: Bloch Publishing Co., 1927, 180.

11. See Leibowitz, *Studies in Deuteronomy,* 135.

12. Elijah J. Schochet, *Animal Life in Jewish Tradition,* New York: Ktav, 1984, 300.

13. Rabbi J. David Bleich, "Vegetarianism and Judaism," *Tradition,* Vol. 23, No. 1 (Summer, 1987), 86. This article can also be found in Rabbi J. David Bleich, *Contemporary Halakhic Problems,* Volume III, New York: Ktav, 1989, 237–250b.

14. Ibid, 87.

15. Leibowitz, *Studies in Deuteronomy*, 136.
16. Ibid. Also see Kook, *A Vision*, Sections 1, 2, and 4.
17. *Chulin* 84a.
18. *Pesachim* 49b.
19. This issue is discussed in detail in Richard H. Schwartz, *Judaism and Vegetarianism*, New York: Lantern Books, 2001, 124–127.
20. Kook, *A Vision*, Section 4; also see the discussion in J. Green, "Chalutzim of the Messiah: The Religious Vegetarian Concept as Expounded by Rabbi Kook," (lecture given in Johannesburg, South Africa), 2.
21. Ibid, 2, 3.
22. Rabbi Abraham Isaac Kook, "Fragments of Light," in *Abraham Isaac Kook*, ed. and trans. Ben Zion Bokser, New York: Paulist Press, 1978, 316–21.
23. Kook, *A Vision*, Sections 1, 2, 4, 6, and 32; also see Rabbi Alfred Cohen, "Vegetarianism from a Jewish Perspective," *Journal of Halacha and Contemporary Society*, Vol. 1, No. II (Fall, 1981), 45. This article can also be found in Roberta Kalechofsky, *Judaism and Animal Rights: Classical and Contemporary Responses*, Marblehead, Massachusetts: Micah Publications, 1992, 176–194.
24. Hertz, *Pentateuch and Haftorahs*, 5; also see Kook, *A Vision*, Sections 6, 32.
25. Green, "Chalutzim of the Messiah," 1.
26. *Shabbat* 118b.
27. John Robbins, *The Food Revolution: How Your Diet Can Help Save Your Life and the World*, Berkeley, Calif: Conari Press, 2001, 293; Frances Moore Lappé, *Diet for a Small Planet*, New York: Ballantine, 1991, 445, 446.
28. Robbins, *Food Revolution*, 163.
29. Ibid, 160, 163.
30. Ibid.
31. Joanne Stepaniak, *The Vegan Sourcebook*, Los Angeles: Lowell House, 1998, 59.
32. 1992 Census of Agriculture, Table OA, U.S. Department of Commerce, Bureau of the Census.
33. Robbins, *Food Revolution*, 105.
34. Robbins, John, *Diet for a New America*, 352.
35. Michael Brower and Warren Leon, *The Consumers Guide to Effective Environmental Choices: Practical Advice from the Union of Concerned Scientists*, New York: Three Rivers Press, 1999, 59.
36. Frances Moore Lappé, *Diet for a Small Planet*, 20th anniversary edition, New York: Ballantine, 1991, 76, based on presentation of agronomist Georg

Borgstrom to the Annual meeting of the American Association for the Advancement of Science (AAAS), 1981.

37. "Facts of Vegetarianism," Booklet of the North American Vegetarian, Society, P.O. Box 72, Dolgeville, NY 13329, p. 3.

38. Joanne Stepaniak, *The Vegan Sourcebook*, Los Angeles: Lowell House, 1998, 63.

39. Ibid.

40. Tom Aldridge and Herb Schlubach, "Water Requirements for Food Production," *Soil and Water*, No. 38 (Fall, 1978), University of California Cooperative Extension, 13–17; Paul and Anne Ehrlich, *Population, Resources, Environment*, San Francisco: Freeman, 1972, 75–76.

41. "The Browning of America," *Newsweek*, Feb. 22, 1981, 26ff, cited in Lappé, *Diet*, 76.

42. John S. and Carol E. Steinhardt, "Energy Use in the U.S. Food System," *Science*, April 19, 1974.

43. Lappé, *Diet*, 10.

44. Ibid, pp. 74, 75, based on work of Drs. Marcia and David Pimentel at Cornell University.

45. Ibid, 74.

46. Alan B. Durning, "Cost of Beef for Health and Habitat," *Los Angeles Times*, September 21, 1986, 3.

47. "Raw Material in the United States Economy: 1900–1977," Technical Paper 47, U.S. Department of Commerce, U. S. Department of Interior, Bureau of Mines, p. 3, cited in Lappé, *Diet*, 66.

48. Ibid, Table 2, 86.

49. Rifkin, *Beyond Beef*, 203.

50. Stepaniak, *The Vegan Sourcebook*, 61.

51. Lappé, *Diet*, 80.

52. Ibid, 81.

53. Keith Akers, *A Vegetarian Sourcebook*, New York: Putnam, 1983, 87; 120–124.

54. Stepaniak, *Vegan Sourcebook*, 62.

55. Ibid, 65. This same source indicates that one agricultural textbook, *Modern Livestock and Poultry Production*, estimates that at least two billion tons of manure are produced annually on U.S. farms.

56. Georg Borgstrom, *The Food and People Dilemma*, Duxbury Press, 1973, p. 103, cited in Lappé, *Diet*, 84.

57. Stepaniak, *Vegan Sourcebook*, 64.

58. Albert Gore, introduction to new edition of *Silent Spring* by Rachel Carson, Boston: Houghton Mifflin, 1994, xix.
59. Pamphlet of Rain Forest Action Network, 300 Broadway, San Francisco, CA 94133.
60. *Newsweek*, Sept. 14, 1987, p.74; Julie Enslow and Christine Padoch, *People of the Tropical Rainforest*, Berkeley: University of California Press, 1988, 169.
61. Jeremy Rifkin, *Beyond Beef*, 123.
62. Michael Brower and Warren Leon, *The Consumer's Guide*, 50.
63. Rifkin, *Beyond Beef*, 1–2.

Chapter 13: Conclusion
1. Edmond Fleg (1874–1963) was a French essayist, playwright, and poet, whose main writings deal with Judaism and the Jewish people. Fleg's use of "Israel" in this poem is in the Talmudic sense of "the Jewish people," not specifically the historical or modern state.

Appendices
1. *Pirke Avot* 2:21.
2. *Tosefta Kiddushin* 1:13
3. *Business Week*, Reuters, August 22, 2000, www.businessweek.com.
4. An excellent resource for this is *The Community Energy CARE-ing Handbook: An Activist's Guide for Energizing Your Community toward Conservation and Renewable Energy*, by Leonard Rodberg and Arthur Waskow (see Bibliography). ENERGY STAR for Congregations, a free technical support and information service of the U.S. Environmental Protection Agency, has a one-hundred-page guide, "Putting Energy into Stewardship," at www.epa.gov.

ANNOTATED BIBLIOGRAPHY

A. Books Relating Judaism to Current Issues

Amsel, Nachum. *The Jewish Encyclopedia of Moral and Ethical Issues*. Northvale, New Jersey: Jason Aronson, 1996. Short essays summarizing Jewish teachings on many issues.

Artson, Bradley Shavit. *Love Peace and Pursue Peace: A Jewish Response to War and Nuclear Annihilation*. New York: United Synagogue of America, 1988. A survey of peace and war issues, based on Jewish sources from all periods.

Belkin, Samuel. *In His Image: The Jewish Philosophy of Man as Expressed in Rabbinic Tradition*. New York: Abelard-Schuman Limited, 1960. The many ramifications in Jewish law of the concept that man is created in the image of God.

Bernstein, Ellen, ed. *Ecology and the Jewish Spirit: Where Nature and the Spirit Meet*. Woodstock, Vermont: Jewish Lights Publishing, 1998. A wide variety of Jewish perspectives on environmental issues.

Bernstein, Ellen and Dan Fink. *Let the Earth Teach You Torah: A Guide to Teaching Ecological Wisdom*. Wyncote, Pennsylvania: Shomrei Adamah, 1992. Guidebook for teaching Jewish perspectives on the human relationship with nature.

Broyde, Michael and John Witte, eds. *Human Rights in Judaism: Cultural, Religious, and Political Perspectives*. Northvale, New Jersey: Jason Aronson, 1998. A wide variety of Jewish perspectives on human rights issues.

Bush, Lawrence and Jeffrey Dekro. *Jews, Money, and Social Responsibility: Developing a "Torah of Money" for Contemporary Life*. Philadelphia, Pennsylvania: The Shefa Fund, 1993. Insights on Torah teachings related to obtaining and donating money.

Cohen, Jeremy. *"Be Fertile and Increase, Fill the Earth and Master It": The Ancient and Medieval Career of a Biblical Text*. Ithaca, New York: Cornell University Press, 1989. An interpretation that indicates that the above Torah verse

(Genesis 1:28) was rarely, if ever, read as a warrant for unrestrained exploitation of the world.

Carmell, Aryeh. *Masterplan: Judaism—Its Program, Meanings, Goals*. Jerusalem: Feldheim, 1991. Applies Judaism's *mitzvah* system to many aspects of life, including science, society, government, and the environment.

Doueck, Jack. *The Chesed Boomerang: How Acts of Kindness Enrich Our Lives*. Deal, New Jersey: Yagdiyl Torah Publications, 1999. Heartwarming and inspiring stories about how acts of kindness help both the giver and the receiver.

Dresner, Samuel H. *God, Man, and Atomic War*. New York: Little Books, Inc., 1966. The relationship of the Jewish tradition to one of the world's most critical problems: the threat of atomic war.

Fackenheim, Emil. *To Mend the World: Foundations of Post-Holocaust Jewish Thought*. Bloomington: Indiana University Press, 1994.

Fisher, Rabbi Adam D. *To Deal Thy Bread to the Hungry*. New York: Union of American Hebrew Congregations, 1975. Analysis of Jewish views related to hunger, and modern *mitzvot* to help reduce it.

Gordis, Robert. *The Root and the Branch: Judaism and the Free Society*. Chicago: University of Chicago Press, 1962. Shows relevance of the Jewish tradition to many moral issues of today.

Hakohen, Yosef Ben Shlomo, *The Universal Jew: Letters to My Progressive Father*. Jerusalem/New York: Feldheim, 1995. Judaism's universal messages, including a discussion of people's obligations to the earth and its creatures.

Hartman, David. *A Living Covenant: The Innovative Spirit in Traditional Judaism*. Woodstock, Vermont: Jewish Lights, 1998.

Heschel, Abraham J. *The Insecurity of Freedom*. New York: Farrar, Straus and Giroux, 1967. Wide-ranging set of essays on such issues as Jewish education, Judaism and civil rights, Soviet Jewry, and Judaism in the Diaspora.

———. *The Prophets*. Philadelphia: Jewish Publication Society, 1962. Comprehensive analysis of history's greatest protesters against injustice.

Hirsch, Richard G. *The Way of the Upright: A Jewish View of Economic Justice*. New York: Union of American Hebrew Congregations, 1973. Summary of Jewish ethical teachings related to economic behavior.

———. *There Shall Be No Poor*. New York: Union of American Hebrew Congregations, 1965. The application of the Jewish concern for economic justice to the problem of poverty.

———. *Thy Most Precious Gift, Peace in Jewish Tradition*. New York: Union of American Hebrew Congregations, 1974. Provides many sources for traditional Jewish views on war and peace issues.

Hirsch, Rabbi Samson Raphael. *Horeb,* translated by Dayan I. Grunfeld, New York/London/Jerusalem: Soncino Press, 1962. Analyzes a wide variety of *mitzvot,* including those that teach us how to relate to the earth and its creatures.

————. *The Nineteen Letters.* Jerusalem/New York: Feldheim, 1969. Fiery defense of traditional Judaism through eloquent letters to a critic.

Ingall, Martin, ed. *Choose Life: Judaism and Nuclear Weapons.* Wyncote, Pennsylvania: The Shalom Center, 1983. An anthology of articles, interviews, speeches, and sermons concerning Judaism and nuclear weapons.

Kellner, Menachem Marc, ed. *Contemporary Jewish Ethics.* New York: Sanhedrin Press, 1978. Has sections on political ethics, civil disobedience, pacifism, capital punishment, and business ethics.

Konvitz, R., ed. *Judaism and Human Rights.* New York: W.W. Norton, 1972. A collection of essays, mainly by contemporary Jewish scholars, relating the Jewish tradition to such issues as human rights, ecology, peace, and freedom.

Lamm, Norman, ed. *The Good Society.* New York: Viking, 1974. A survey of Jewish teachings on such issues and concepts as compassion, charity, ethics, and peace.

Landau Yehezkel. *Violence and the Value of Life in Jewish Tradition.* Jerusalem: Oz V'Shalom, 1984. Essays from rabbis of various backgrounds on Jewish responses to nuclear threats.

Landes, Daniel. *Confronting Omnicide: Jewish Reflections on Weapons of Mass Destruction.* Northvale, New Jersey: Jason Aronson, 1991. Fifteen essays by prominent Jews on the nuclear threat.

Lerner, Michael. *Jewish Renewal: A Path to Healing and Transformation.* New York: G. P. Putnam's Sons, 1994. A rethinking of Judaism by a Jewish Renewal leader with the aim of building spiritually rich Jewish lives and a more just society.

Levine, Aaron. *Free Enterprise and Jewish Law: Aspects of Jewish Business Ethics.* New York: Ktav, 1980.

Polner, Murray, ed. *The Disarmament Catalogue.* New York: Pilgrim Press, 1982. Collection of articles, stories, and cartoons related to the arms race.

Rackman, Emanuel. *One Man's Judaism: Renewing the Old and Sanctifying the New.* Gefen Books, 2000. Thoughtful essays by a renowned rabbi and former president of Bar Ilan University.

Regenstein, Lewis. *Replenish the Earth: The Teachings of the World's Religions on Protecting Animals and the Environment.* New York: Crossroads, 1991.

Rose, Aubrey, ed. *Judaism and Ecology*. New York/London: Cassell, 1992. Collection of very readable essays on ecology from Jewish perspectives.

Saperstein, Rabbi David, ed. *Preventing the Nuclear Holocaust: A Jewish Response*. New York: Union of American Hebrew Congregations, 1983. Considers Jewish responses to the nuclear arms race.

Schwartz, Richard H. *Judaism and Vegetarianism*. New York: Lantern Books, 2001. Argues that Jewish mandates to show compassion to animals, preserve health, help feed the hungry, preserve the earth, and pursue peace point to vegetarianism as the ideal diet.

Sears, Dovid. *Compassion for Humanity in the Jewish Tradition*. Northvale, New Jersey: Jason Aronson, 1998. Statements from classical Jewish sources on universal issues.

———. *The Vision of Eden: Animal Welfare and Vegetarianism in Jewish Law and Mysticism*. Unpublished manuscript. Sources and essays on Jewish teachings related to animals and vegetarianism.

Shatz, H., Chaim I. Waxman, and Nathan J. Diament, eds. *Tikkun Olam: Social Responsibility in Jewish Thought and Law*. Northvale, New Jersey: Jason Aronson, 1997.

Siegel, Danny. *Family Reunion: Making Peace in the Jewish Community: Sources and Resources from Tanach, Halachah, and Midrash*. Spring Valley, New York, 1989. Compelling argument, based on Jewish teachings, for nonviolent resolutions of conflicts at all levels.

Soloveitchik, Joseph Dov. *The Lonely Man of Faith*. Northvale, New Jersey: Jason Aronson, 1996. Thoughts of one of the most respected Orthodox Jewish leaders of the twentieth century.

Strassfeld, Sharon and Michael. *The Third Jewish Catalog: Creating Community*. Philadelphia: Jewish Publication Society, 1980. Has sections on social justice, ecology, and compassion for animals.

Tamari, Meir. *With All Your Possessions: Jewish Ethics and Economic Life*. Northvale, New Jersey: Jason Aronson, 1998. Torah teachings on many economic issues.

Vorspan, Albert and David Saperstein. *Jewish Dimensions of Social Justice: Tough Moral Choices of Our Time*. New York: UAHC Press, 1998. Jewish views on current social justice dilemmas.

Vorspan, Albert. *Great Jewish Debates and Dilemmas: Jewish Perspectives on Moral Issues in Conflict in the Eighties*. New York: Union of American Hebrew Congregations, 1980. Fine discussion of controversial issues facing the Jewish community and the world, such as energy, ecology, economic justice, zero population growth, and race relations.

Waskow, Arthur I. *Godwrestling, Round 2: Ancient Wisdom, Future Paths.* Woodstock, Vermont: Jewish Lights, 1996. Excellent application of Jewish tradition to "wrestle" with current problems such as injustice and violence.

Waskow, Arthur I., ed. *Torah of the Earth: Exploring 4,000 Years of Ecology in Jewish Thought.* Woodstock, Vermont: Jewish Lights, 2000. Wide variety of essays on various environmental issues.

Wurzburger, Walter S. *Living Jewish Ethics.* Pitspopany Press, 1999. Insights on applying Jewish values in the contemporary world.

B. Books Relating Other Religious Values to Current Global Issues

Ahmann, Mathew, ed. *Race: Challenge to Religion.* Chicago: Henry Regnery, 1963.

Leguire, Stan L., ed. *The Best Preaching On Earth: Sermons on Caring for Creations.* Valley Forge, Pennsylvania: Judson Press, 1996. Eloquent Christian sermons on environmental issues.

C. General Books on Issues on Global Survival

Brower, Michael and Warren Leon, eds. *The Consumer's Guide to Effective Environmental Choices: Practical Advice from the Union of Concerned Scientists.* New York: Three Rivers Press, 1999. Discusses contributions of various human activities to environmental threats.

Brown, Lester R. *Tough Choices: Facing the Challenge of Food Scarcity.* New York, London: Norton, 1996. Predictions of major food scarcities if current trends continue.

Brown, Lester R., et al., *State of the World 2001.* New York/London: W.W. Norton, 2001. Annual analysis of critical global issues.

———. *Vital Signs 2001: The Environmental Trends That Are Shaping Our Future.* Washington, D.C.: Worldwatch Institute, 2001. Annual update of important trends shaping the world.

Hayes, Denis. *The Official Earth Day Guide to Planet Repair.* Washington, D.C.: Island Press, 2000.

Lappé, Frances Moore. *Diet For a Small Planet.* New York: Ballantine, 1991.

Lappé, Frances Moore, et al. *World Hunger: Twelve Myths.* New York: Grove Press, 1998.

Lerner, Michael. *The Politics of Meaning: Restoring Hope and Possibility in an Age of Cynicism.* Reading, Massachusetts: Addison-Wesley, 1996. An attempt to reshape our economic and political lives based on love, caring, and compassion.

Tansey, Geoff and Joyce D'Silva, eds. *The Meat Business: Devouring a Hungry Planet*. New York: St. Martin's Press, 1999. Challenging essays on the negative impacts of animal-based agriculture on hunger, the environment, resources, animals, and human health.

SUBJECT INDEX

A

Aaron, 16, 81, 150
Abimelech, 75
Abraham, 4, 6, 27, 32, 46, 75, 92, 148, 150, 155
acid rain, 50, 124
Adam, 11, 149, 155, 163
Adam, Teva, v'Din (Humans, Nature, and Justice), *see* Israeli Union for Environmental Defense
Adelie penguin populations, 136
Adirondack Mountains, 124
Africa, 69, 71, 98, 103, 175
African-Americans, 24
Ahab, King, 75
air pollution, 60, 124
Akiva, Rabbi, 11, 12, 14
Alaska, 118, 137
Albo, Rabbi Joseph, 162
Alexandri, Rabbi, 88
Alexandria, 89
Alfven, Hannes, 126
Allied resistance, 94
Amazon, 106
American Council for an Energy-Efficient Economy, 121
American Jewish Committee, 150
American Jewish Congress, 3
American Samoa, 136

American Vegan Society, 78
Amidah, 82
Amos, 6, 8, 22, 26, 112
Andes mountains, 135
Angola, 98
animal agriculture, 105, 161–75
Animal Life in Jewish Tradition, 166
animals, 34, 43
    compassion for, 34
    treatment of, 34
Antarctic warming, 137
Antarctica, 136, 137
Antiochus, 182
Anti-Defamation League, 22
anti-Semitism, 22
Arab citizens of Israel, 63
Arab countries, 94
Arctic National Wildlife Refuge, 118
Arctic Ocean, 137
Arctic warming, 137
Ashdod, 56, 60
Ashkenazic Chief Rabbi, 42, 164
Asia, 71
Asian financial crisis, 105
Assessment Reports, 191
Australia, 107, 137, 138, 151, 175
Axelrad, Rabbi Albert, 94
Ayres, Ed, 106
Azzai, Ben, 11

INDEX OF BIBLICAL PASSAGES

251